WITHDRAWN

Coming in Contemporary

Coming of Age in Contemporary American Fiction

Kenneth Millard

Edinburgh University Press

© Kenneth Millard, 2007

Edinburgh University Press Ltd
22 George Square, Edinburgh

Typeset in 10.5/13 Adobe Sabon
by Servis Filmsetting Ltd, Manchester, and
printed and bound in Great Britain by
Biddles Ltd, King's Lynn, Norfolk

A CIP record for this book is available from the British Library

ISBN 978 0 7486 2173 6 (hardback)
ISBN 978 0 7486 2174 3 (paperback)

The right of Kenneth Millard
to be identified as author of this work
has been asserted in accordance with
the Copyright, Designs and Patents Act 1988.

York St John University
Check-Out Receipt

Customer name: ELLIE-LOUISE KIDGER

Title: Coming of age in contemporary American fic
ID: 38025005684587
Due: 03/02/2017 23:59

Total items: 1
27/01/2017 15:15
Checked out: 1
Overdue: 0
Hold requests: 0
Ready for pickup: 0

Tel: 01904 876700

Contents

Acknowledgements

I would like to thank Sarah Carpenter of The University of Edinburgh, Bert Bender of Arizona State University, Tony Hilfer of The University of Texas at Austin, Jocelyn Siler of the University of Montana, and Ethan and Rebecca for the long-word games ('What is this/Metamorphosis?'). I owe special thanks to Audrey and Jim ('What becomes of little boys, who run away from home/The world just keeps getting bigger, once you get out on your own'), to Caroline ('Don't tell me not to fly/ I simply must/ Don't bring around a cloud/To rain on my parade'), and to Simon: 'Bite on a bullet/And spit out a limousine'.

K. Millard
Edinburgh, Scotland

Introduction: Contemporary Coming of Age – Subject to Change

'The youth of America is their oldest tradition' – Oscar Wilde

This book is a critical study of coming of age as it is represented in the contemporary fiction of the United States. It is a work of advocacy on behalf of the individual novels that are included for detailed interpretation, and simultaneously, an extended argument about the significance of coming of age to our understanding of contemporary America. Adolescents are important because of the ways in which they are at the forefront of social change, even while they are simultaneously the products of an adult social culture that shapes their development. This is a dynamic relationship between the individual and society, and it has some parallels in the study of literature. The individual novel is conditioned by those traditions and conventions that it draws upon to constitute itself as a novel in the first place. But, at the same time, our understanding of those conventions is changed, however subtly, by each individual novel that interprets them for is own unique creative purposes. This brings us immediately to the issue of genre, which is particularly germane to the study of adolescence. Some knowledge of genre theory is invaluable as a guide to how adolescence in the novel might be approached. Recognising an individual work's relation to its proper genre is often fundamentally important to the act of interpretation, because it is a means to approach a text that enables us to identify important aspects of its meaning: 'The function of genre conventions is essentially to establish a contract between writer and reader so as to make certain relevant expectations operative, and thus to permit both compliance with and deviation from accepted modes of intelligibility' (Culler 1975: 147). It is necessary to interpret a text in terms of its genre in order to be a competent reader, and so that a text might be intelligible in the first place. Some texts, however, establish their individuality by transgressing or subverting the conventions of their genre. This is especially true of those texts designated 'literary', or of works that are not simply 'genre fiction', or of works that are innovative and experimental in the ways that they negotiate that contract with their genre. These works problematise the issue of genre, often by subtly transforming our idea of what constitutes the genre in the first place, or by changing our understanding of what is possible or permissible within the genre. In this respect, the works that are termed 'literary' can change an understanding of genre; their value lies in the ways that they transform the systems of signification that we understand them to be working within. This is a dynamic process in which the rules of the game are interrogated and disputed by innovative texts that challenge their generic affiliations. This is also an issue of value: by what interpretive paradigm or methodology might some texts be valued over others? If value is always contingent or relational, then what particular efficacy does genre theory have as a means to evaluate a novel? Susan Fraiman argues that it is crucial, that

> genre criticism plays a key role in canon formation both by policing individual categories and by maintaining hierarchical relationships among categories; that it regulates not only which texts we read but also, by alerting us to some elements over others, how we are able to read them. (Fraiman 1993: 2)

This relationship of value is especially relevant to adolescents because they have the potential to reconfigure the existing social structures and institutions to which they find themselves heir, and thereby in some senses change society. The word 'genre' comes from the Latin 'genus', meaning family; it might be argued that each adolescent grows up to constitute his or her own family in the future, and thereby changes the genre that one might term 'family'.

But what is the proper literary genre to which depictions of adolescence belong? The difficulties of genre, and their particular relevance to adolescence, are revealed in the very language of critical discussion of adolescence. For example, the word 'bildungsroman' was coined in Germany in 1819, and it means a novel recounting the early emotional development and moral education of its protagonist ('bildung': formation; 'roman': novel). It is a word that was used retrospectively to characterise a particular kind of narrative that had been identified in Wieland's *Agathon*, 1767, and Goethe's *Wilhelm Meister*, 1795, the latter was translated by Thomas Carlyle in 1824 as *Wilhelm Meister's Apprenticeship* and 'has established itself in literary history as the prototype of the Bildungsroman' (Buckley 1974: 12). 'Bildungsroman' has been widely adopted as a term in literary criticism to characterise the generic conventions of any novel of youthful development. Jerome Buckley, for example, uses it to interpret Stendhal's *Vie de Henry Brulard*, and he describes its protagonist in these terms: 'He must insist on his loneliness as a child, his distance from other boys, his greater sensitivity to suffering, and his awareness of social hypocrisies'

(Buckley 1974: 15). For Buckley these conventions also enable us to recognise works such as James Joyce's *A Portrait of the Artist as a Young Man* and D. H. Lawrence's *Sons and Lovers* as modern examples of the bildungsroman. For scholars of the original German novels, however, this provenance is less certain. James Hardin argues that 'there is no consensus on the meaning of the term Bildungsroman' (1991: x), and he supports Witte's belief that 'Any generalisation about the bildungsroman as a genre is apt to be bedevilled by the variant meanings of the word "Bildung" in German' (Hardin 1991: xii). Hardin's impatience with Buckley stems from disagreement over interpretations of the specifically Enlightenment context of 'bildung' and a tendency for critics to use the word ahistorically in ways that change its meaning. What value, then, does a technical term for a particular kind of late eighteenth-century novel have for the study of recent American texts that are removed both historically and culturally from the term's origin? This question haunts every study of fiction about coming of age; criticism attempts to situate the individual novel in relation to a term from which it derives its meaning, but the precise interpretation of that term, like the conventions of a genre, is endlessly disputed and contested. This is especially true of those novels that attract critical interest in the first place precisely because of the way that they function at the limit of generic convention.

Similar questions about genre inhabit the study of those works that are closely affiliated to the bildungsroman and to ideas about coming of age but which are designated 'autobiography' or 'memoir'. An autobiography is a story of the self that is closely related to the bildungsroman in many important formal and thematic ways. The protagonist of an autobiography commonly starts out as a novice, encounters and overcomes the challenges of adversity, and ends his or her story as a more mature adult character as a result of their experience. Is the depiction of that initial immaturity in an autobiography fundamentally different from its depiction in a coming-of-age novel? Only in the claim to veracity that it makes. Paul de Man defines the genre of autobiography as any 'text in which the author declares himself the subject of his own understanding' (De Man 1979: 922). This is an argument that undermines the autobiography's claim to be a work of 'non-fiction', or as Paul Jay interprets it, 'de Man rejects the idea that the subject in an autobiographical work represents a privileged form of referentiality' (Jay 1984: 18). The autobiography is a form of bildungsroman, but one that claims a value that is predicated on its supposed truthfulness. This is an often spurious distinction. These arguments about autobiography are attempts to circumscribe and delimit the field of those works that can be usefully considered together, to keep it in the family. To some extent these issues are insoluble, or as de Man tersely expressed it 'pointless and unanswerable' (De Man 1979: 919), but they require some consideration. In this respect, the current book might have included American memoirs such as Joan Didion's *Where I Was From* (2003), Dale Peck's *What We Lost: A Story of My Father's Childhood* (2003), Mary Karr's *The Liars' Club* (1994), J. T. Leroy's *Sarah* (2000) and *The Heart is Deceitful Above All Things* (2001), and Rick Moody's *The Black Veil* (2002). These works' representations of subjectivity, or narratives of the self's youthful development, are the inheritors of a rich legacy of American writing about personal development that goes back at least as far as *The Education of Henry Adams*, a work that Jerome Buckley argues is 'written in the third person and carefully shaped in contrived patterns, [and] has much of the irony and detachment we commonly associate with fiction' (Buckley 1974: 25).

Semantic difficulties with the word 'bildungsroman' are compounded by other problems of terminology. For example, the expression 'coming of age' is used to mean 'to reach full legal adult status', and it is commonly seen in studies of the bildungsroman. This is a term which is widely used in anthropology, for example in Margaret Mead's *Coming of Age in Samoa* (1928), and which had acquired a currency in literary studies by the time of Marjorie Garber's *Coming of Age in Shakespeare* (1981). The term also carries an imprecision and a cultural relativity that needs to be taken into account. When exactly does a character come of age and what specific experiences are deemed to be integral to it? Is it possible for fictional characters to come of age at any point, for example in their twenties? Douglas Coupland's *Generation X* (1991) is some form of contemporary bildungsroman, but of characters who are certainly older than adolescents. The same might be said of Coupland's *Microserfs*, Jonathan Franzen's *The Corrections*, or Jonathan Safran Foer's *Everything is Illuminated*. These are depictions of significant coming-of-age experiences, but none of their principal characters is adolescent. Formative experiences can occur at any age, but in terms of literary genre the expression 'coming of age' is conventionally used of adolescence: Huck is fourteen, Holden is sixteen. Barbara White, for example, defines her study of what she terms the female 'novel of adolescence' in terms of the parameters of age; this is a genre which

> although it shares some characteristics with developmental forms like the *Bildungsroman* and the initiation story, has to be defined in terms of the age of the protagonist. Accordingly, I have as a general rule restricted my discussion to fiction with major characters between twelve and nineteen. (White 1985: xii)

This is not an arbitrary distinction because twelve to nineteen is a commonly accepted understanding of the age of adolescence, but it does inevitably exclude the depiction of the experiences of characters beyond its parameters, some of which might be vitally concerned with coming of age. Perhaps, in fact, there is a trend in the bildungsroman of the early twenty-first century for characters to come of age in their twenties, where previously those experiences would have occurred during childhood and adolescence? Even for twelve- and nineteen-year-olds there is a considerable variation in depictions of that moment when coming of age is deemed to have occurred, and full legal adult status varies between cultures, especially in relation to such cultural markers as alcohol, sexual consent, driving license, and marriage. Moreover, neither Huck nor Holden attains full adult status at the end of their respective stories, and in this respect the genre might be said to give an account of a process that is necessarily incomplete. The specific age of a fictional character is therefore perhaps not the best guide to that teleological process which is the proper focus of the coming-of-age narrative.

One way to address these issues of genre is to maintain a close critical focus on the dramatisation of that 'innocence' which childhood and adolescence are often believed to exemplify. How is such innocence conceptualised and configured by these novels, what forms of social experience does it encounter, and what kind of maturity might it be said to achieve? These questions are especially important because innocence has a particular resonance in the context of American national mythology. For example, one particularly prevalent conception of the United States is that it originated as a nation by means of a decisive break with an Old World that had grown corrupt and moribund. This departure to the New World was widely understood in terms of a fresh start for mankind, both economically and spiritually, by which new opportunities would lead to a different future and a dynamic society that was innovative, forward-looking, and based on egalitarian principles of personal freedom. This utopian vision often used the figurative language of adolescence to describe the New World's emergent autonomy as a colony as it struggled to establish its own individual social identity independent of Old World habits and practices. America is the rebellious teenager, impatient with the authority of its European parents and eager to create its own character founded on a different set of values and priorities. So there is a confluence of the genre of the coming-of-age novel and a particularly, or even uniquely, American narrative of national identity; the individual new citizen's drive towards new forms of independence is coterminous with that of the burgeoning nation.

One of the most eminent modern formulations of this myth is found in R. W. B. Lewis's *The American Adam* (1955). For Lewis, in his study of nineteenth-century American literature, the quintessentially American protagonist is a version of Adam, caught momentarily in a state of prelapsarian innocence and then expelled forever into the unforgiving world of modern experience. This hero comes of age by coming to terms with that world's uniquely American strictures and challenges. Lewis identifies the emergence of this dominant mythology especially in early nineteenth-century American writing:

> The American myth saw life and history as just beginning. It described the world as starting up again under fresh initiative, in a divinely granted second chance for the human race, after the first chance had been so disastrously fumbled in the darkening Old World. (Lewis 1955: 5)

If it is accepted that Lewis's American-as-Adam thesis has been an influential or even dominant strain of the national mythology of the United States, then the genre of the coming-of-age novel has a unique position in terms of national identity because of the ways that it appropriates and refurbishes that mythology for its own contemporary purposes. In the genre of coming-of-age, the idea of the American Adam is perpetuated and revitalised in the context of late twentieth-century fictional conceptions of innocence. The protagonists of the contemporary American bildungsroman thus participate in their own individual creative interpretation of that original innocence which harks back to the story of the beginning of the nation. This is an invaluable lineage for the novel to align itself to, while still allowing for a contemporary inflexion, and it is a tradition that permits the individual novel to make claims of national significance.

The American as Adam is a seductive story, perhaps even 'the most fundamental narrative constituting America's national mythology' (Yanarella and Sigelman 1988: 4), but it is only one strain of American mythology and it carries with it a particular political ideology that subsequent critics have drawn attention to and taken issue with. One might argue that Lewis's methodology suffered from a debilitating ahistoricism in its interpretations of texts as portraying a point of origin before which there was little or no significant history, or one might point out that he put forward his arguments in the context of a historical period that he specifically designated the 'Age of Containment'. This is a significant debate for the coming-of-age novel; perhaps all works that attempt to define a point of origin might be accused of paying insufficient attention to the history that precedes them. Further, Leo Marx argued that the mythology of the American nation as a new beginning for mankind is a version of pastoral, and that 'The pastoral ideal has been used to define the meaning of America ever since the age of discovery, and it has not yet lost its hold on the native imagination' (Marx 1964: 3). This pastoralism, of which the American Adam is a significant manifestation, is itself the manifestation of a bogus nostalgia which encourages the veneration of an idealised past that probably never existed in the first place. Such nostalgia has a specific political ideology, a deeply conservative one, which fosters a sentimental retreat from contemporary challenges by evoking a lost historical utopia when the world was a better place: 'this ideal has appeared with increasing frequency in the service of a reactionary or false ideology, thereby helping to mask the real problems of an industrial civilisation' (Marx 1964: 7). The contemporary coming-of-age novel might be usefully understood as walking the line between presenting its protagonist as a newborn who is innocent of history and of depicting a protagonist whose coming of age consists principally of acquiring historical knowledge. The novels considered in the present work are particularly notable, among dozens of recent coming-of-age novels, for their ability to tread such a line with a tact and sophistication that distinguishes them as exceptional.

One might also historicise R. W. B. Lewis by arguing that *The American Adam* was one of a group of influential works produced in American studies in the early years of the Cold War that had a particular interest in the concept of innocence. These works included Leslie Fiedler's *An End to Innocence* (1955), Ihab Hassan's *Radical Innocence* (1961), and Henry Nash Smith's *Virgin Land* (1950). These studies of American national character were part of an attempt to identify and to characterise in detail particularly American qualities that could be institutionalised and defended; each of them devotes a great deal of attention to interpretations of the meaning of innocence and to its function as part of the national mythology:

> We may suppose that there has been a kind of resistance in America to the painful process of growing up, something mirrored and perhaps buttressed by our writers, expressing itself in repeated efforts to revert to a lost childhood and a vanished Eden . . . It has been said that America is always coming of age; but it might be more fairly maintained that America has come of age in sections, here and there – whenever its implicit myth of the American Adam has been a defining part of the writer's consciousness. (Lewis 1955: 129)

Hassan concurred with Lewis in his interpretation of the relationship between innocence and history, and, in a chapter called 'The Dialectic of Initiation in America', he argued that, 'But if American Innocence means anything, it must mean just this: that every generation, native or foreign-born, began its task anew despite the secret betrayals of history' (Hassan 1961: 36). Here Hassan argues that a continuing belief in American innocence is part of a wilful denial of history that is itself the expression of a political ideology that can only be debilitating. Fiedler, too, argued that the perpetual return to a faith in innocence is the expression of a retreat from history:

> In general our writers have no history, no development; their themes belong to a pre-adult world, and the experience of growing old tends to remain for them intractable. It is merely one aspect of that compulsive veneration of youth, that fear of all which is not simply strong and beautiful, so important in our total culture. (Fiedler 1955: 193)

For Fiedler, the constant return to beginnings is a part of a disproportionate faith in the new which is also debilitating, and he continues: 'The images of childhood and adolescence haunt our greatest works as an unintended symbolic confession of the inadequacy we sense but cannot remedy' (Fiedler 1955: 209–10). Fiedler's unhappiness is predicated on a strongly Freudian model of human personal development which, at the beginning of the twenty-first century, might not be the most appropriate paradigm by which to interpret American culture.

The novels included here might be seen as attempts to define an origin, to produce a compelling story of the American empire's beginnings, to construct an account of the birth of the nation. This is part of America's foundation myth. In whatever terms this point is defined it becomes the moment from which its independent identity began to take shape, and therefore it defines the terms and conditions of coming of age. To some extent this mythology has been abstracted and idealised independently of the historical circumstances that produced it, so that it is not recognised as a specific ideology that has been naturalised and universalised, or as Smith said of Frederick Jackson Turner's frontier thesis, 'worked into the very fabric of our conception of our history' (Smith 1950: 250) to the point where it is no longer understood as a belief system (such as Manifest Destiny) that was requisite to the needs of the time when it was most strongly expressed. If these works can now be seen as products of a particular period in American history then the question might be asked 'to what extent do their American mythologies survive beyond the historical circumstances of its production?' The novels of this book are part of a response to that question.

The novels included in this book also try to understand the contemporary moment (variously interpreted in each novel) in terms of a specific history that has shaped the late twentieth century to be the way that it is. In this way the novels historicise their protagonists even while they are presenting them as struggling with the urgent demands of contemporary society and culture. It might be argued that such an enquiry constitutes their own origin myth in seeking to contextualise themselves: historically, the fictional characters are looking for a sense of historical provenance or genealogy that defines their individual interpretation of 'contemporary'. Further, it might be argued that an interest in origins is as much a product of our early twenty-first-century academic culture as a mythology of innocent Adam in a western American Garden of Eden was a product of the early years of the Cold War. In this respect, any attempt to understand the historical circumstances of how the contemporary came to be the way that it is could be interpreted as an origin myth, because all such historical accounts are retrospective narratives of history that are open to dispute. This is an issue of the nature of historiography rather than of the coming-of-age novel, but it is important, nevertheless, to be alert to its implications because each novel here is involved in a process of defining for itself the contemporary in ways that are broadly historiographical.

In this respect, one very useful formal distinction for the novels included in this book is provided by Edward Said, who asked rhetorically 'Is the beginning of a given work its real beginning, or is there some other, secret point that more authentically starts the work off?' (Said 1975: 3). Of course the word 'authentically' is contentious, as Said knew, but for the purposes of the coming-of-age novel this is a particularly useful distinction. In many contemporary coming-of-age novels the narrative moves forward in time towards a point of maturity from which it can address that unspoken origin that began it, but which is antecedent to its beginning. The origin that such novels attempt to discover and to articulate is a story of history that offers an explanation for why and how they began as they did. This origin has a privileged (ontological) status as a form of historical 'explanation', but it is simultaneously a fabricated story that is often self-consciously recognised as a self-justifying fiction that is a necessary foundation to the constitution of subjectivity. Thus it might be the case that since structuralism 'the authority of a privileged origin that commands, guarantees, and perpetuates meaning has been removed' (Said 1975: 315), but such a myth of an origin is still a necessary and integral part of these fictional projects. The form and structure of these novels is often strongly expressive of a desire to create a myth of origins by which their protagonists can come to understand themselves, and this knowledge, despite a self-consciousness about its status as fiction, is a central component of coming of age. In this respect, these novels can be seen as part of a response to the common perception that America does not have a meaningful beginning, but was created *in vacuo*, a perception succinctly expressed by Baudrillard, who believed that 'America ducks the question of origins; it cultivates no origin, or mythical authenticity; it has no past and no founding truth' (Baudrillard 1988: 76). The novels included here refute that perception in their various attempts to locate the origin of the contemporary. The novels themselves are often very self-conscious about their protagonists' search for an origin, as the discussion of the egg and the embryo in *The Miracle Life of Edgar Mint* and *Middlesex* shows. It is worth comparing their anxieties about the status of their beginnings in fiction with that of seventeen-year-old Sam in Bobbie Ann Mason's novel *In Country*:

> During that month, she had originated. She didn't know why the moment of origin mattered. Scientists were trying to locate the moment of origin of the universe. They wanted to know exactly when it happened, and how, and whether it happened with a big bang or some other way. (Mason 1987: 192)

This is an explicit statement of the importance of origins that is shared not only by Udall and Eugenides, but by all of the novels that are included in the present study

The contemporary novel of adolescence is often characterised by a concerted attempt to situate the protagonist in relation to historical contexts or points of origin by which individuals come to understand themselves as having been conditioned. The individual novel often reveals a temporal structure in which the contemporary moment of coming-of-age is contextualised gradually by a consciousness of historical events that are antecedent to it and deeply inform it. In this respect contemporary coming-of-age novels are novels about knowledge of American history, and that knowledge itself becomes a significant part of the protagonist's coming of age. These contexts and origins become, in turn, the focus of the novel's social critique; they are the history with which the individual must come to terms, and it is here that the coming-of-age genre accomplishes more than the outline of the plight of a beleaguered individual innocent. The historical awareness that the adolescent acquires is at odds with the faith in the sovereign individual and the mythology of American self-determination that the genre of coming-of-age might appear to endorse. There is a struggle here between self-fashioning on the one hand, and historical determination on the other, and it is in the tension between the autonomy of the individual and the shaping pressure of history that the political ideology of each novel lies. How does the individual know and experience such contexts and origins? Are they understood in the contemporary period as merely the function of their modes of representation (as they are in Mason's novel)? What space is left for a belief in American personal freedom when those origins are discovered and experienced? Each novel addresses these questions differently. It is a tension that has a precedent in Huck Finn, whose freedom on the raft is temporary and illusory, and who has been described as the victim of 'environmental determinism' as he floats down the Mississippi River

(Stone 1961: 144). In these important ways, the protagonist of the bil-dungsroman is not simply an American Adam 'an individual emanci-pated from history, happily bereft of history, untouched and undefined by the usual inheritances of family and race' (Lewis 1955: 5), but a char-acter who comes of age specifically by understanding his or her place in history.

In an excellent article in *Critique*, Kirk Curnutt examines the contem-porary American coming-of-age novel (which he defines in terms of *Less than Zero*, *The Secret History*, and *Generation X*) to argue that the genre has lost its vital ethical dimension in the post-*Catcher* period. Unlike Evan Hunter's *The Blackboard Jungle* (1954) John Knowles' *A Separate Peace* (1961) or Sylvia Plath's *The Bell Jar* (1963), the contemporary coming-of-age novel is characterised by the absence of those ethical chal-lenges that gave earlier novels in the genre their subversive value. As a result, 'instead of confronting adult hypocrisy with unfettered idealism, these adolescents are emotionally and morally obtuse' (Curnutt 2001: 94). The politics of this obtuseness or insensitivity is, for Curnutt, a deeply conservative hopelessness by which young people express the belief that traditional narratives of self-determination have collapsed and that aspiration is futile:

> Lacking ethical discrimination, contemporary teens find little purpose in anti-social behaviour beyond fleeting titillation: previous generations of teens envi-sioned sex and drugs as forms of *gnosis* that transcended the sterile dictates of adult culture, whereas these young people desire only a reprieve from boredom. (Curnutt 2001: 98)

The contemporary adolescent (or at least the adolescent as presented to us by the contemporary adult novelist) has no moral agency and has suc-cumbed to what another critic designates 'the politics of despair' (Giroux 1997: 67). These arguments about the ethical consciousness or the moral conscience of contemporary adolescents are certainly useful for the novels that Curnutt interprets, but they are dependent upon a slight and specific selection of texts that makes no pretension to representing a wider range of fictional depictions of youth. Moreover, if we take *The Catcher in the Rye* as the definitive point of origin (Curnutt makes no reference to Huck Finn and his ethical challenges) and if we also assume that Holden is the unmediated voice of 1950s disaffected youth (rather than its imagined form as it was understood by the adult J. D. Salinger) then contemporary adolescents will perhaps inevitably appear less morally engaged than their predecessors. Nor do Curnutt's arguments take account of the ways in which the genre has been seized upon by women writers and authors from ethnic minorities for the opportunity it provides to write narratives of subjectivity that are full of ethical challenges in the context of the politics of the self in contemporary America. Curnutt turns, not to the kind of depictions of youth included in this book, but to the non-fiction work by William Finnegan, *Cold New World: Growing Up in a Harder Country* (1999), which argues that 'some fierce *constriction* has taken place, especially among young Americans, over the past twenty-five years' (Finnegan 1999: xvii).

There has been a considerable amount of commentary on the kind of anomie, ennui, or postmodern despair that Curnutt and Finnegan detect among contemporary adolescents. In particular, many commentators in cultural studies have asked why adolescents at the turn of the twenty-first century have adopted a style of nihilistic futility; is it simply another form of teenage affectation, or has teenaged affectation itself taken new and worrying forms of expression? There is a wealth of analysis of these questions from a variety of perspectives, among them James Milner's *Freaks, Geeks and Cool Kids*, Thomas Frank's *The Conquest of Cool*, Charles Acland's *Youth, Murder, Spectacle: The Cultural Politics of 'Youth in Crisis'*, Cohen and Krugman's *Generation Ecch!*, Marcel Danesi's *My Son is an Alien*, and the essays of Neil Campbell's *The Radiant Hour*. These works are invaluable interpretations of adolescence at the turn of the millennium as it is actually lived (rather than as it is imagined by adults in the form of the novel) and they constitute a genre of analysis that has a subtle and complex relation to the coming-of-age novel. This conjunction of two genres, the sociological and the literary, brings into sharp focus the relationship between politics and aesthetics, which is to some extent intractable, but which nevertheless warrants consideration because it is a relationship that haunts all of the novels included in the present study. For example, Franco Moretti has identified the emergence of the form as a prominent one in Western culture:

> Youth is 'chosen' as the new epoch's 'specific material sign', and it is chosen over the multitude of other possible signs, because of its ability to *accentuate* modernity's dynamism and instability. Youth is, so to speak, modernity's 'essence', the sign of a world that seeks its meaning in the *future* rather than in the past. (Moretti 1987: 5)

The investment in youth is a key part of the project of modernity, a 'sign' that is chosen by adults to epitomise those particular qualities of restlessness and disaffection that seem to them to be most urgent and problematical in contemporary society. Youth, here, is an exemplary opportunity for adult writers to express anxieties about their own social position, their perceptions of a dynamic and mutable society, and the predicament of young individuals who are in the process of being socialised by its challenges. In this respect 'innocence' is an idea that can be appropriated, imagined, and deployed as a means to dramatise in an urgent narrative form those challenges that adult novelists perceive to be the most pressing concerns of their day. This is especially true in the United States because of its historical investment in signs of the future. The use of the bildungsroman thus reveals how, 'prohibited from speaking as moral and political agents, youth becomes an empty category inhabited by the desires, fantasies, and interests of the adult world' (Giroux 1997: 35), and that, as a result, youth becomes 'an identity defined solely by and for the adults who, in a variety of ways, invest in it and use it to locate themselves' (Grossberg 1992: 176). The novels included in the present book, then, tell us less about the 'youth' that cultural studies investigates than they do about how the idea of youthful innocence is used by adults to address those issues deemed by them to be in most urgent need of expression in contemporary America. Adolescence, youth, innocence: they become an idealised fictional category which literary writers can use to give a particular urgency to representations of subjectivity and socialisation that highlight their own social and political anxieties. That (parasitical) process is necessarily different from the forms of analysis of youth that are provided by cultural studies, and yet it is easy to see why writers of fiction might turn to adolescence as a vehicle for a social critique. As Neil Campbell expresses it, 'central to the signification of youth has always been the search for empowerment from this position of subordination and alienation and from an adult-defined set of social norms which imposed a monologic authority' (Campbell 2000: 16). The situation of the adolescent as subaltern makes it ideal for the expression of that social disaffection which is often the creative impetus of the novel.

As the contemporary period changes, so too does its interpretation of the past. Successive generations of readers revalue the canon, and reassess what is most important about canonical works. This is an inevitable and inescapable process of reading in history. In this respect, two notable collections of essays on *The Catcher in the Rye* were published in the 1990s, both of which were attempts to recover what, if anything, still continues to be valuable about this canonical work. Jack Salzman conceded that 'Salinger's fiction no longer attracts the critical attention that it once did' (Salzman 1991: 8), and Joel Salzberg observed that we are now sufficiently distant from the novel's publication (in 1951) that recent criticism of it often has the tone of 'ceremonial rituals of remembrance' (Salzberg 1990: 2). This is partly because Salinger's novel is not as important to American literature as the idea of innocence that it is taken to exemplify, and which is long antecedent to it. For example, in another interpretation published in the 1990s, *The Catcher in The Rye: Innocence Under Pressure* (1993), Sanford Pinsker, in a chapter entitled 'Go West, My Son', draws attention to Holden's desire to run away to the frontier to work in a gas station pretending to be a deaf mute. This is an expression of Holden's need to escape the corruption of New York for a fresh start, free of the responsibilities of language, in that mythical American landscape, that virgin land, where he might recover the innocence he has already lost. In a further book, published in 2000, Pamela Steinle has an excellent chapter on 'The Question of Innocence' in which she argues that *The Catcher in The Rye* 'is written in the tradition of the American Adam yet conceived in a context of disillusionment and alienation from that very tradition' (Steinle 2000: 43). It is this Adamic tradition of Western movement, and the historical reinvention of innocence that accompanies it, rather than its 1950s teen idiom, that makes Salinger's novel valuable. *The Catcher in the Rye* was a novel that seemed to bring Huck's voice into the twentieth century, and to articulate a desire for a new beginning in the era immediately following the Holocaust and atomic weaponry; it is that urge to escape the challenges of growing up and of acquiring a history that marks Salinger's novel as a quintessential and enduring expression of American innocence.

One of the principal aims of this book is to explain the importance of the coming-of-age genre within the broader canon of American literature. This project is simultaneously one in which the contemporary participates in the reassessment of that which is most important in the past, and to show the value to the contemporary moment of literary paradigms that are antecedent to it. In these ways, this book hopes to promote contemporary American fiction which is not simply temporary American fiction, and to identify those works which are not simply great coming-of-age novels, but great American novels.

Chapter 1

In the Name of the Father

An important issue in the coming-of-age novel is the way in which finding a place in society is coterminous with finding a satisfactory relationship with the father. For the young male protagonist especially, the relation to the father is a vital means to socialisation, and he is often the principal figure through whom the codes of society are learned. Coming of age is thus a drama of coming to terms with the father, and with all the social and cultural governance for which he stands. With the frequency of divorce in contemporary American society this relation to the father is often problematised: how does the protagonist come to terms with a father who is absent, and what are the social implications of this challenge? In the novels explored in this chapter the father went missing before the narrative began. The search for the father is complicated in various ways, and therefore both novels are characterised not only by absent fathers, but also by various father-surrogates who are important potential role models. In this way, the efficacy of fathers is scrutinised, while simultaneously the desire for a relationship with the father dictates the shape of the protagonist's journey.

The father, of course, is also The Father, and in both of these novels the search for a literal or corporeal father is to some extent analogous to a search for a fulfilling spiritual belief. In this respect, the father here is not simply a symbol of acceptable social behaviour but also stands for a system of moral and ethical values for which the protagonist is in search. This value system is given an explicit religious dimension in the journeys of both novels: each is thus characterised by a search for a lost spirituality. This search is born out of a sense of sinfulness that the protagonists have inherited from their culture and from their initial predicament as fatherless children.

In this respect it is important to recognise the association between movement and reincarnation in both of these novels. The narratives are structured in terms of a sequence of resurrections whereby the central protagonist develops: in both novels, a shift in location is accompanied by an important shift in subjectivity. These shifts are often abrupt, sudden, and radical, so that a new place is coterminous with a significantly new sense of self; it is the structure of the 'born again'. Also, this structure of movement, of the journey, is paradoxically a means of getting back to the beginning. Edgar's journey is dedicated to returning to this story's point of origin, and Bone's narrative is a series of regressions in which he becomes increasingly empowered to address the trauma that initiated his story. In both cases, moving forward is a means of attaining a position from which the beginning can be fully understood and articulated. This cyclical structure is thus a means to achieve a knowledge of origins, and that search is given a characteristically American inflection by these novels' particular journeys.

Russell Banks, *Rule of the Bone*

Mark Twain's *Adventures of Huckleberry Finn* was published in 1885 and remains an important model for the contemporary first-person coming-of-age novel. Hemingway believed that 'All modern American literature comes from one book by Mark Twain called *Huckleberry Finn*' (Hemingway 1936: 29), Harold Beaver argued that it is 'the most consistently provocative bestseller, over a hundred years, that any American writer has ever produced' (Beaver 1987: Preface), and Peter Messent described it as 'the best-known novel in America's literary history' (Messent 1997: 86). Twain's accomplishment in sustaining the voice of fourteen-year-old Huck is the principal reason why the novel is both a children's classic and simultaneously the subject of a great deal of sophisticated academic criticism. That voice combines statements of the boy's inarticulacy and the necessary limits of his knowledge with a shrewd and discerning perception, especially of ethical issues. Huck's idiomatic language gives a strong sense of authenticity to his adolescent perspective, yet it does not disguise a perceptive awareness of the adult power relations of his southern society. Although Huck speaks to the reader like a boy, the predicament in which he finds himself and the nature of the journey he is committed to give his adventures an urgent adult dimension that goes to the heart of the structures of his culture. Huck's relationship with his father, the fact that he is technically 'dead' throughout the novel, his association with Judge Thatcher and the Widow Douglas, his perilous journey, the characters that he meets en route, and the fact that he is aiding a runaway slave: all of these aspects of his narrative give it a serious political resonance, even while they are recounted in a style that is faithful to the idiom of an adolescent. The voice of Huck Finn is still the model for the contemporary streetwise (male) adolescent, especially where a problematic relationship with the father is involved, or where the social structure of authority is challenged.

Russell Banks' *Rule of the Bone* was published in 1995, and any novel recounting the travelling adventures of a young white boy and an older black man is bound to invite comparisons with *Adventures of Huckleberry Finn*. Huck and Bone are both fourteen years old, and both of their journeys are characterised by a tight temporal compression: Bone's lasts for one year, and Huck's lasts for a few weeks. Bone flees his abusive stepfather in search of his biological father and finds the Afro-American known as I-Man. Huck escapes his alcoholic father and finds a surrogate, in some important respects, in the black slave Jim. Coming of age for Huck and Bone has a strongly ethical dimension, especially concerning the history and culture of American racism, the idea of people as property, and the proper conduct of fathers. Both of these white boys learn about freedom and responsibility, power and authority from their friendship with a black man, and this in turn has social consequences for the vision of the United States that their stories dramatise. The importance of the father to this quest is paramount:

> Drifting down the river toward a goal he can neither define nor scarcely imagine, Huck is in fact looking for another father to replace the one he has lost. And this quest is also a quest for himself, because once Huck has found his new father he will know at last who he himself really is. (Lynn 1959: 213)

Bone's search is more purposeful than Huck's; Bone has a specific sense of direction in his search for his father, one which makes explicit his need for a meaningful relationship with him, and which dramatises particular ideas about cultural value that coming of age is dedicated to discovering. For Bone, the father represents an idea of ethical and spiritual aspiration that acts as a focus for his episodic journey; his story is populated by bogus fathers, surrogate fathers, potential fathers: these are merely substitutes for the one true father that he seeks, and his coming of age is a story of learning to recognise authentic fatherly love, which is simultaneously a new form of self-respect.

Bone's story begins, in the summer that he turns fourteen, with a direct address to the reader which reveals his self-consciousness about the veracity of story-telling: 'You'll probably think I'm making a lot of this up just to make me sound better than I really am or smarter or even luckier but I'm not' (Banks 1996: 1). This strategy of demonstrating a reflexive awareness of the reader's credulity is seen in the opening paragraph of Huck Finn's story, where he reminds us of the earlier novel about Tom Sawyer: 'That book was made by Mr Mark Twain, and he told the truth, mainly. There was things which he stretched, but mainly he told the truth' (Twain 1994: 11). This emphasis on truthfulness is also an important part of Holden Caulfield's opening address to the reader, in which he disarms our expectations by disavowing 'all that David Copperfield kind of crap', and by insisting that conventions must be abandoned 'if you want to know the truth'. This is a particular form of appeal to the reader's engagement with the novel's voice, in which the speakers reveal an astute critical awareness that their stories, however spontaneously they are expressed, are nevertheless formally structured, and therefore run the risk of an artful contrivance which is contrary to the honesty that they hope their stories epitomise. Bone begins by claiming that his story is not a tall tale, that 'the truth is more interesting than anything I could make up', and this self-denigrating remark about his ability to fictionalise is a central part of his adolescent voice's claim to narrative authenticity (and a claim that he will subsequently contradict, both implicitly and explicitly, as his story becomes more complex and sophisticated).

This strategy at the beginning of the story-telling enterprise is augmented by the narrator's relationship with earlier texts; where Huck wants us to believe the account provided by *The Adventures of Tom Sawyer*, and Holden repudiates Dickens in favour of a high respect for his brother's book *The Secret Goldfish*, the first text that Bone engages with is the collection of his father's letters. Bone's father has absconded, and his letters provide Bone with a glimpse of family history: 'He said he wanted to come back. I almost felt sorry for him. Except I didn't believe him' (3). Bone, like Huck and Holden, is a shrewd and discerning critical reader, and he sees through the apparently heartfelt sentiments of his father's letters. These negotiations with antecedent texts, and texts which are in important senses progenitors, are part of the narrator's determination to establish a kind of honesty and sincerity that becomes integral to their moral vision of the United States. Learning to read critically is the first stage of their coming of age.

Bone's story also begins with the delineation of his family circumstances; his parents divorced ten years ago and his life is now dominated by his mother's drinking problem and his stepfather's hostility. Like Huck, Bone is an only child, and this is perhaps a significant contributory feature of that 'lonesomeness' which has an important bearing on crucial stages of his development. The indifference of Bone's parents, and their inability to cope with his occasionally feckless, teenage behaviour, is symptomatic of their own entrapment in a working-class culture that offers little prospect of a different future. Bone's parents pass on to him their own sense of powerlessness, and therefore, like them, he takes refuge in forms of escape. Bone suffers from low self-esteem; he is trapped in circumstances that make him feel 'I was no good and a failure at life', and his alienation is expressed in his feeling that he is 'kind of irritated at the world' (4). Bone's family circumstances are not unique, or even remarkable (certainly no worse that Huck's), but his ability to elucidate them in a voice that is persuasive and engaging is the novel's first achievement. Further, Bone has a dark family secret that he does not have the confidence or maturity to address at the novel's beginning. Twice Bone refers to his unwillingness to share this with the reader: 'I don't want to talk about that right now' (8), and, later, he tells us it is 'not something I want to go into right now' (42). Bone's coming of age consists partly of learning to come to terms with this secret (his sexual abuse by his stepfather) and learning to speak about it in the account of the formative experiences of his adolescence that he provides here. In this respect, his story is, like that of so many coming-of-age novels, one of returning to a traumatic beginning, and of resolving the violent and painful circumstances of his childhood. Bone's grandmother expresses his predicament bluntly, 'You don't *have* a father' (4).

The first significant crisis of Bone's coming of age concerns his expulsion from home. Bone steals a collection of antique coins that he finds in a briefcase under his stepfather's bed, and he sells them to buy dope. This theft is discovered by his parents and, after an angry confrontation, Bone moves out of the house to become a small-time dealer and thereby gain some respect among his peers. This incident is important because it removes him irrevocably from his family life and its intractable conditions but also for another specific reason: 'I knew I could never pay her back because it wasn't the money. Those coins of my grandmother's, they were like my inheritance' (15). There is an important moral dimension here that will become a major feature of Bone's development: he has a sensitivity to ethical issues, and to an idea of natural justice, that is consonant with his insistence on narrative honesty and fidelity. The theft of the coins might be usefully compared with his subsequent theft of a green silk nightgown from Victoria's Secret. There is no suggestion that Bone intends to sell this, and is it indicative of how badly awry his life becomes after he leaves home that he starts stealing merely for the sake of it. These early incidents are thus marked by Bone's ability to register important moral distinctions.

To some extent the novel's accomplishment consists of refraining from elucidating these incidents too fully. Bone does not interpret the events of his childhood with a retrospective, mature or adult consciousness, and this is fundamental to the integrity of his adolescent voice. Bone's language is punctuated with statements of his inarticulacy and with expressions of the (necessary) limits of his knowledge, but at the same time he reveals a native wit and an embryonic sense of aesthetic appreciation, and in these respects his voice gradually becomes a shrewd and discriminating one, even while it retains the demotic idiom of a fourteen-year-old. Where Huck remarks at an early stage 'You know what I mean – I don't know the words to put it in' (Twain 1994: 42), Bone uses expressions such as 'It was like my brain ran out of things to say to me' (226). The issue here, as Bone recognises, is that 'Basically people don't know how kids think' (29), an observation that has serious implications for the whole genre of coming-of-age that is devoted to the adult imagination's interpretation of how kids think.

Bone's emotional development retains a consistent focus on moral and ethical issues, and this is dramatised most strongly when he sees a young girl at his local mall who appears to be under the control of a man who is not her father. Bone experiences a visceral response to this girl's obvious vulnerability, and he feels a spontaneous desire to rescue her, and thereby exercise his sense of moral responsibility in the world. Despite the lack of affection in his upbringing, or perhaps because of it, Bone feels a duty of care towards this girl: 'I wanted to tell her something important about people but I didn't want her to have to know it yet, she was too young still' (29). This parental attitude is combined with a shrewd, critical perception of the man, Buster Brown, who has taken control of her. Bone is alert to the social signals of corrupt and duplicitous adults, and he recognises that they are a danger to children who are younger than himself. Bone can identify with her vulnerability, and he expresses it in a powerful image which also reveals his psychological acuity: 'I felt like I was baking in the sun with all the attention he was paying to me' (33). Bone recognises Brown's attention to the girl as manipulative, and he wants to save her from its consequences; the importance of Bone's moral conscience is further dramatised by the guilt that he feels when, following a chase through the mall, he is unable to rescue the girl: 'I felt guilty too because of losing my courage and deciding not to take her place' (40). The novel's emphasis on moral responsibility, and on the individual's freedom to make the right ethical decisions, is seen in Bone's desire to substitute himself for a stranger who is more powerless than himself. Bone's coming of age is consistently characterised by such moments of ethical choice, and his early expressions of guilt are symptomatic of a moral sense that will shape his future. The experiences of Bone's coming of age are structured around critical moments of ethical choice where his subjectivity is increasingly defined by a native sense of natural justice. As Bone expresses it himself, 'The more power you've got the more you're able to do the right thing' (73). Bone's coming of age is singularly dedicated to attempts to do the right thing, and in accordance with a system of ethical value that shapes his self-determination.

In some respects Bone's ethical development also reveals the valuable legacy of Huck Finn, who comments at one stage in his journey 'it hadn't come home to me before, what this thing was that I was doing' (Twain 1994: 91). Huck also has a strong sense of social justice, of right and wrong, and of the hypocrisy of adult social behaviour and power relations, and his journey is also one that only begins once he has escaped from his father. Pap Finn, 'the fond parent', imprisons Huck in a cabin in the woods so that he cannot be adopted by the Widow Douglas. Fearful of the violent attacks of his father, Huck escapes from the cabin by pretending to have been murdered, and thereby sets out on his journey down the Mississippi River which becomes the story of his coming of age. Huck's escape from the cabin is a violent erasure of the past, and a symbolic resurrection in which he is presumed dead and yet is re-born into a life of relative freedom and autonomy in which he must make his own moral choices independently of adults. Huck's rebirth is also attendant upon the symbolic murder of his father: the blood of the hog that Huck uses to fake his death recalls the description of Pap as a drunken pig. The symbolic treatment of the processes of coming of age is seen in two important early episodes of *Rule of the Bone* which have useful parallels with Huck's story. Bone escapes the perilous circumstances of his association with the biker gang, 'Adirondack Iron' in a fire in which he is assumed to have died. This chapter, entitled 'Presumed Dead', is also the culmination of the development of his moral conscience as regards crime. Bone is symbolically re-born at precisely that moment in his moral education when he realises 'it was wrong to be stealing stuff on this scale' (63). The fire is therefore a dramatic opportunity to abandon the criminal lifestyle he has fallen into, and, more importantly for Bone, to repudiate the values that it represents. The assumption that Bone has died in the fire gives him the chance to abandon his social predicament but also to reject its compromising ethical circumstances: 'There was a lot about right and wrong that my parents hadn't taught me, and now due to my situation I was having to work most of it out on my own' (68). This sense of having to make crucial decisions without parental guidance is an important aspect of the novel's politics. Although Bone comes from a 'broken home', and despite his drug-use and petty crime, he has a strong moral awareness and a determination to live his life in search of specific values that define what kind of adult he becomes. The absence of good parents does not make Bone less capable of subtle moral distinctions, and the absence of good parenting makes Bone only superficially delinquent; his coming of age reveals Bone's potential for moral transformation at every stage.

The fire facilitates Bone's escape from town and dramatises the annihilation of his past: ' "Check it out, you don't have a past, man! It's like being dead without having to die first" ' (98). This sloughing away of history prompts Bone to get the tattoo which is expressive of his fresh sense of identity. His new name, 'Bone', (until now he has been known as 'Chappie', the diminutive of his real name 'Chapman') is derived from the crossed bones of this tattoo, and helps him to feel a new sense of self-possession and control over his future, 'like I was a way new person with a new name and a new body even' (107). Bone grasps this cathartic opportunity for liberation and empowerment with great urgency, and his unequivocal commitment to a concept of subjectivity that is based on mutability might be interpreted as quintessentially American in its faith in personal freedom. Bone is well aware of the new access to power that his changed circumstances give:

> It's the kind of power as all those superheroes who have secret identities get from being able to change back and forth from one person into another. No matter who you think he is, man, the dude is always somebody else. (108)

The metamorphosis of the superhero is a comic-book fantasy of empowerment that is appropriate to a fourteen-year-old boy, and one that also expresses the rejection of a past that, at this stage, he cannot come to terms with. But Bone's choice of tattoo is also derived from a specific childhood memory of his grandmother reading to him J. M. Barrie's story of *Peter Pan* (the full title of which is *Peter Pan, or, The Boy Who Would Not Grow Up*), a story in which 'there's no adults and you get to stay a kid forever' (106). This Scottish text (recalling the Scottish text of Burns from which *The Catcher in the Rye* takes its name) becomes Bone's version of Never-Never-Land, a perpetual reminder of that moment of innocence before his parents separated: 'And whenever I looked at it myself I'd remember Peter Pan and my grandmother reading to me when I was a little kid' (106). Bone's most vivid and enduring memory of childhood innocence is one in which he listens to a story about the impossibility (and undesirability) of remaining a child forever; his skin is coloured by a nostalgia for this text and his new name comes from it. This is an important scene in which the skin becomes a crucial marker of identity, and this will later acquire a racial dimension.

Bone's coming of age is structured in terms of a series of cathartic resurrections; the fire facilitates a rejection of the past, and the tattoo gives fresh impetus to his new sense of the liberating potential of a different future. Bone's retreat to the summerhouse marks the final stage in this radical revision of his sense of identity. This episode is again characterised by a process of violent erasure that prepares the ground for a sense of the value of the new particular to the United States. The period at the summerhouse is a form of retreat or hibernation in which Bone does little other than eat and sleep but stores up the energy for the challenge of his new circumstances; it is a period of self-contemplation from which he emerges with a radically new sense of himself and his horizons. It is during the period at the summerhouse that Bone finds himself not only lost to his parents but presumed dead in the fire and then abandoned by his pal Russ who returns home to Au Sable. Here Bone is truly alone, and it is this existential isolation that precipitates a crisis in his sense of himself. After several weeks at the cabin and restless at 'the strain of being confined like that' (125), Bone finds a gun and shoots through the plate glass window to return to the world 'like a guy just released from jail' (130). The language of his self-expression is revealing:

'It was strange to stand there in front of the mirror and see myself like I was my own best friend, a kid I wanted to hang with forever . . . If I was going to be alone for the rest of my life this was the person I wanted to be alone with'. (130–1)

At this stage Bone conceptualises the process of self-realisation in solipsistic terms; he believes in a romantic myth of the sovereign individual which is yet to engage with the structures of society in a mature way. Not only does Bone look like Huck Finn here, wearing 'a lose pair of old jeans with paint stains that kind of fit me when I rolled up the bottoms practically to the knees' (130), but he has discovered in himself a talent for the tall tale, or what Huck called 'stretchers', when Bone tells a fellow passenger on the bus that he is 'an ancient type of wandering Jew' (113). But the form of Bone's metamorphoses, and the structure of his coming of age, is different from Huck's; where Huck learns to ventriloquise, or as one critic expresses it 'is reincarnated in a series of aliases' (Egan 1977: 20), Bone experiences new forms of self-identification that are not performances but which are epiphanies that jolt his story forward in a series of revelations of the self.

Once he leaves the summerhouse, Bone's coming of age is conducted in different terms; following the sudden and abrupt challenges of the early part of the story Bone's subsequent development becomes a journey towards adulthood which is simultaneously a journey back towards points of origin that need to be addressed and resolved (it is only in the novel's last chapter, for example, that Bone finally tells us he was born in 1979). In this respect Bone's meeting with the character called I-Man brings about a significant change in the form of Bone's story. I-Man is a surrogate father-figure, and Bone's journey is hereafter conducted under the specific cultural auspices of his guidance. I-Man is a Jamaican Rastafarian who finds himself in the United States partly because he has absconded from the poor conditions of seasonal labour. I-Man is thus an illegal alien, and Bone's relationship with him, like Huck's with Jim, is one in which they are both fugitive from the law. Both characters interrogate those social values that have made them outsiders. I-Man's racial difference becomes central to Bone's moral and spiritual coming of age because it provides a formal structure to his previous embryonic ethical sense. Like Bone, I-Man has changed his name as part of his escape from the oppressive conditions of migrant farm work, but 'he wouldn't tell me his slavery name' (156). Although he is rarely didactic, I-Man is an adult who is able to teach Bone valuable lessons about race, history, and spirituality. I-Man's Rastafarian philosophy in particular is attractive to Bone, partly because of its religious belief in the value of enlightenment offered by ganja, so that 'Getting high was like a religious experience for him' (157). Simultaneously, I-Man's philosophy concurs with Bone's sensitivity to ethical issues, which is already in search of an appropriate institutional structure. This chapter of the novel is called 'School Days' because it is the period of Bone's real education, and one with a strongly religious inflection. I-Man's different conception of God also appeals to Bone, because it is based on the principle of giving thanks, and when he meets I-Man, 'for the first time in my life I was actually happy' (154).

Many important aspects of Bone's coming of age come together when he meets I-Man: he finds a protective father-figure and prospers under his tutelage, he discovers a structure for his burgeoning sense of ethical value that gives new meaning to many aspects of his life, and he begins to learn new forms of knowledge that foster a sense of self-respect and a sense of his place in the world beyond solipsistic melancholy. Equally importantly, in terms of the narrative, at the same moment that Bone becomes a son to the older man, he becomes a father-figure himself, to the girl whom he has now successfully rescued from Buster Brown's abuse. This girl becomes '[his] personal responsibility now' (160), and Bone recognises that he has 'an obligation' to return her to her family (167). The use of the words 'responsibility' and 'obligation' are indicative of Bone's new maturity; he finds a valuable role as the girl's guardian at the same narrative moment that he falls under the guardianship of I-Man. This hierarchy of value gives Bone's moral sense an important structure of social responsibility.

Although I-Man is a mentor to Bone he refrains from telling Bone what to do; his signature phrase is 'Up to you, Bone', which he repeats at key moments. I-Man is a valuable surrogate because he permits Bone the freedom to make his own choices and decisions, and, by insisting on Bone's autonomy, I-Man encourages him to guide himself. This felicitous balance of education and autonomy in Bone's relationship with I-Man ideally allows for independent self-determination, in an emotional environment that Bone characterises as being 'like the Garden of Eden' (159). Bone quickly appreciates the value of this model of fatherhood: 'even though I-Man usually knew what I was going to do before I did a thing he never tried to make me do it' (270) and 'The good thing about I-Man was he never laid his agenda down on top of mine' (275). Moreover, Bone's increasing maturity is seen in his acknowledgement of the value of reciprocity in adult relationships: Bone feels strongly that he 'needed to feel useful to him once in a while in exchange' (178).

The invocation of Eden, the archetypal mythic home of innocence and site of its loss, is set against Bone's recognition that his circumstances are not ideal; his relationship with I-Man reminds him not of Huck Finn and Jim, but of another classic nineteenth-century novel about the racial politics of the United States, *Uncle Tom's Cabin*. Bone had studied this novel in seventh grade, and his astute perception of the circumstances of its production, 'it was pretty good considering a white woman wrote it' (160), is evidence of his critical understanding of the cultural implications of racial difference long before he meets I-Man. This novel, like *Peter Pan*, must to some extent shape Bone's coming of age because it introduces him to important social issues that subsequently become integral to his story. Something similar might be said about Bone's reading of *Evolution and Desire*, which he describes as 'a dog turd of a book' (123), and of his impatience with James Joyce's *Finnegans Wake*, of which he remarks, 'I don't know why people write books that normal people can't read' (124). These observations reveal that Bone has some aesthetic sense of how a properly engaging story should be told, and it is that tacit artistic sensibility that drives the imaginative form of his own narrative. These formal qualities are highly developed in Bone's narrative; there is rarely a wasted paragraph in the entire novel, and that particular economy and formal organisation shows Bone to have an artistic maturity in marshalling narrative structure that is, perhaps, unusual for an adolescent. Here one might usefully compare Blake Nelson's novel *Girl* (1994), the first-person narrative of Portland teenager Andrea Marr, described by the blurb of the Touchstone edition as 'a *Catcher in the Rye* for the "Grunge" generation'. Andrea's voice is often a breathless rush, and the novel's fidelity to her teenaged voice consists partly of refraining from structuring her immediate thoughts in accordance with the formal qualities of books she has studied. Bone's control over the shape and direction of his story is strong evidence of his literary education, or, as he puts it himself, 'I was always pretty good at reading' (124).

The thematic and structural control that Bone exercises in the organisation of his narrative is seen in the novel's dramatic interrogation of the idea of freedom. Both I-Man and Bone are in search of a sense of personal freedom, but, like Huck and Jim, that freedom is necessarily of different kinds. For example, when Bone first meets I-Man, the following exchange takes place:

> What're you doing here, man? I said keeping my light pointed down like he asked.
>   Same as you, mon.
>   What's that?
>   Tryin to get home, mon. Me jus' tryin to get home.
>   Yeah, well, I guess us too, I said. (150)

Although he does not yet conceptualise it in these terms, this metaphysical or spiritual concept of 'home' concurs closely with the implicit trajectory of Bone's coming of age. Following the false return home of chapters 10–14, in which Bone discovers that it is impossible for him to return to his parents after the changes he has experienced, the novel dramatises various interpretations of 'freedom' and 'home' in relation to coming of age. Bone sends the girl he has saved from abuse back to her mother in Milwaukee; this is a decision fraught with anxieties that problematise the value of 'home'. Simultaneously, Bone strikes out for the territory in the form of a flight to Jamaica with I-Man that turns out to be a homecoming for both of them: Jamaica is the home of Bone's real father. This is one important sense in which Bone's journey is a process of returning to a point of origin. This narrative and thematic structure also accords with I-Man's philosophy in ways that inform Bone's coming of age: 'He said, Jah knows you, Bone, but you don't know Jah. Not until you first know I-self. Him cyan be no daddy fe I-and-I. I-and-I mus' fin' him own daddy' (248). Only by internalising one's own sense of paternal authority can one achieve the kind of self-respect that permits knowledge of God.

Bone has always conceived of his absent father in idealised terms: 'Sort of a young Jack Kennedy, that was my real dad' (221). This image is parallel to Bone's ominous identification with Lee Harvey Oswald in chapter one. When Bone meets his father in Jamaica, the novel executes something of a subtle character assassination that dramatises Bone's gradual disillusionment. Bone's father is a drug-dealer, a phoney 'Doc' with two girlfriends in nearby towns. Even through Bone's delight at finally meeting him, which he describes as 'this incredible *relief*' (272), it is clear that Bone's father is duplicitous, corrupt, and feckless. His culpability in fleeing parental responsibility when Bone was four years old is matched by his indifference to Bone in Jamaica: 'All these years, he told me, he'd been like waiting for me to come to him on my own' (291). This passivity is a variation on the previous negligence by which he had refused child support or alimony when Bone was an infant; his mansion house is run like a nineteenth-century plantation with contemporary forms of enslavement, and by an unfortunate coincidence the name 'Papa Doc', by which he is often referred to, is the nickname of François Duvalier, the despotic president of neighbouring Haiti.

Bone's coming of age is partly a growing awareness of the fallibility of fathers, and this extends to his increasing scepticism about I-Man. When he arrives in Jamaica, Bone quickly realises that I-Man is a drug-dealer; that his posse is, like the Adirondack Iron gang of his hometown, an all-male group of immature adults and a poor substitute for a family; that I-Man does have a family, but one that he has abandoned to fend for themselves; that I-Man's Rasta magic is in fact a series of tricks rather than a supernatural phenomenon. Most of all, Bone recognises that both I-Man and his father are involved in an economic process of production and distribution that is uncomfortably close to the culture of slavery, of which this part of Jamaica is full of poignant echoes. This drug trade will ultimately cost I-Man his life in a shoot-out in which Bone's father is darkly implicated, at which point Bone confesses: 'It didn't make me feel any better to think of I-Man as flown off to Africa. Actually when it came right down to it, like now, I didn't believe any of that shit', (340).

Bone's ambivalence to both father figures reaches a crisis on his fifteenth birthday. Although his father throws a party, it is simply another party rather than any significant recognition of Bone; there is no specific celebration and no words from his father to mark the occasion. Disconsolate, Bone wanders the house alone and discovers I-Man having sex with his father's girlfriend. Bone reports this to his father, who immediately threatens to kill I-Man. This is a crucial moment in Bone's coming of age because it brings into direct conflict the two father-figures in ways that reveal sharply the inadequacy of both as role models. Bone's respect for I-Man is severely diminished, and the terms of his father's response also reveal his corrupt values:

> Because what's mine is mine. That's the rule I live by, Bone. And when some little nigger comes into my house and takes what's mine, he has to pay. He has to pay and pay, many times over. And the only thing that nigger owns is his worthless life, so that's what he'll have to pay with. (302)

The racism and reification of this speech are consonant with the values of the economic system that Bone's father lives by; possession, ownership, control, and commodification, are the hallmarks of the contemporary slavery in which both fathers are implicated. Although Bone's report to his father is a betrayal of I-Man, and one he later regrets, the ethical beliefs by which he has been trying to shape his identity are fundamentally challenged here, not only by fathers, but by his own involvement in an economic culture that he recognises as fundamentally corrupt and degrading. At his father's 'plantation' (304), Bone finds that his commitment to doing the right thing is impossible, and he expresses his disgust unequivocally: 'the whole thing made me want to puke sometimes' (286).

The fundamental importance of Bone's choice here is emphasised by both adults' use of the same language. At the critical juncture on his fifteenth birthday, Bone's father uses I-Man's signature expression, 'Up to you, Bone' (303), and when Bone asks I-Man if he should stay or go, I-Man replies again, 'Up to you, Bone' (304). Here the novel strategically compromises both men in order to emphasise Bone's free choice in his journey of self-determination, and to show that the very idea of wholly reliable fathers is one that he must now outgrow. The novel's use of the phrase 'up to you' succinctly illustrates its belief in American personal freedom, while, in this narrative context, its function is to show how freedom is circumscribed by social circumstances in which the authority of fathers cannot be trusted. The politics of freedom, for this adolescent, are shaped by ethical choices that interrogate the very idea of the father. This new knowledge precipitates Bone's final remove, from Montego Bay to backcountry Jamaica, where the novel's depiction of Bone's coming of age takes its final symbolic form.

Several critics have commented on the importance of the use of caves in Mark Twain's fiction. Harold Beaver, interpreting the symbolic drama of Tom Sawyer's descent into McDougal's Cave, argued that 'This Return-from-the-Dead and the Cave-as-Tomb were permanent fixtures of Twain's imagination' (Beaver 1987: 84). Kenneth Lynn draws attention to the 'extraordinary number of cemeteries, grottoes, caves, prisons' that characterise *The Innocents Abroad*, and he comments on that book's narrator:

> Of all these gruesome sights on his itinerary, prisons, particularly solitary confinement cells, attract him most powerfully. The fantasy of being locked up and forgotten seems to stir this tourist as deeply as the idea of being buried alive does the heroes of Poe. (Lynn 1959: 158)

Michael Egan argues that these places are all different figurative expressions of 'the eternal symbolic womb' that Twain describes in his autobiography: a cave in Hannibal, Missouri, which contained the corpse of a fourteen-year-old girl (Egan 1977: 21). Structurally situated immediately following the crisis in his relationship with his father and I-Man, Bone's retreat to the limestone caves dramatises the most urgent and fundamental revision of his subjectivity in the novel. This retreat to the symbolic landscape is a further removal from society, but one which brings Bone closer to an understanding of the forms of origin that his coming of age is devoted to recovering. The symbolic nature of this cavernous topography is revealed by Bone's unconscious recognition of it; although this region is completely unfamiliar to him, it 'turned out to be like I thought', and 'when we got there it was sort of the way I'd pictured' (307). These craters are the place of Bone's personal regression to face the demons of his childhood, and they are simultaneously the location of Africans' historical resistance to slavery. It is precisely in the conflation of these twin historical perspectives that the full significance of the experience at the caves consists. Bone's history lesson about the Ashanti rejection of British and American slavery is germane not only to the contemporary experience of violence and exploitation that he witnesses at his father's house but also seems to him 'like the Mohawks at home and other American Indians' (310). At this point in his coming of age, Bone discovers that national identity is founded on a history of violent racial conflict and subjugation, and that even his contemporary personal experience is, and always has been, conducted under the rubric of American ethnicity. This is why, following his experiences at the caves, Bone reaches a remarkable recognition: 'That was the other thing that had me all twisted up. Whiteness . . . I knew if I wasn't white, if I'd been a real Rasta-boy like I'd been pretending to be, I'd be dead now' (342). The privilege of race saves Bone, unlike I-Man, from death, and his personal understanding of how racial identity informs his fate as an individual is given national significance by its historical resonance with slavery. This is the novel's most ambitious chapter because it uses the coming-of-age genre as a means to dramatise the pressure of the legacy of slavery; it remains faithful to the mind and idiom of its fifteen-year-old narrator, while offering a social critique that has national significance, and in this respect also it is reminiscent of the achievement of *Huck Finn*.

Bone's drug-induced hallucinogenic vision of the experience of slavery at the limestone cave is a phantasmagorical allegory of the key aspects of his coming of age: the abuse by his stepfather, the exploitation of Africans as a commodity, the alienating power of a capitalist economy, the necessary betrayals of people born into that system, and the moral culpability of all white people associated with it. There is an audacious conflation here of Bone's personal history and the national history of the

United States, especially as regards origins. Bone's experience 'way down in the bottom of one of the cockpits' (315), reveals to him the extent to which his subjectivity is shaped by the specific material circumstances of national history. Following this experience, Bone's identity is fundamentally informed by his consciousness of race in ways that are more profound than his earlier adolescent preoccupation with image; Bone abandons his dreadlocks as he emerges from the underworld (in several senses of the word). Bone rejects another false image of himself here, as he moves towards new forms of self-knowledge that are historically engaged rather than purely solipsistic. After the scene at the caves, Bone's story accelerates towards a resolution in which he realises that even at fifteen 'I almost wasn't a kid anymore' (355). Bone rejects his father irrevocably, 'But Doc, my father, he looked evil' (372), and I-Man is killed in a gun battle because 'he tried to rip off some big-time American ganja dealer' (363). Bone discovers that the girl he rescued has died, and this is the literal realisation of the death of the younger self that Bone has undergone symbolically. This girl's death is part of the theme of infanticide that is common in the coming-of-age genre: Holden is deeply affected by the death of his younger brother Allie in *The Catcher in the Rye*, and this death also has its precedent in Twain; in fact, Harold Beaver argues of the death of Buck in chapter eighteen of *Adventures of Huckleberry Finn* 'the whole book, on this reading, thus turns into a long-drawn-out and puzzled requiem for Buck' (Beaver 1987: 119). Bone's story, like all coming-of-age novels, is a requiem for the younger person that he once was, a series of deaths and resurrections which is authorised by the voice of Huck Finn.

Bone is a white boy from upstate New York who is profoundly changed by his experience of racial difference. The scene at the novel's end, in which Bone blinds Jason as if by supernatural power, is evidence of the extent of his transformation. As Bone realises when he speaks to his former pal Russ, 'I'd changed in ways that even I didn't understand yet' (347). With a direct echo of Huck's famous valedictory, Bone says 'I'd decided to light out' (377), and he leaves behind another outmoded conception of himself, on a boat where his bunk is 'like a pointed coffin' (381). This final symbolic departure is concurrent with his abandonment of the textual conception of childhood innocence that he had previously found comfort in: 'No one in his right mind would want to stay a kid forever. Certainly not me' (387). Bone acknowledges the ethical value of facing the adult challenge of a duty of social responsibility, and he rejects the fantasy of *Peter Pan* and the memory of innocence that it once epitomised for him. Commenting on the conclusion of *Peter Pan* in chapter six, Bone had observed: 'The ending is actually sad. Although he does have his shadow' (106), and the conclusion of *Rule of the Bone* is similar, with Bone remembering those companions he has lost, especially the black Jamaican, I-Man, who has become his 'shadow'. This black adult, like Huck's companion Jim, is finally lost to the story, sacrificed to the development of the white protagonist in whom the reader is encouraged to make their principal investment.

One critic points out that for Huck 'the river is the moving representation of a universe so constructed that Huck's quest for freedom cannot succeed' (Stone 1961: 143). Huck ends up where he began, but Bone does not. The particular sequence of Bone's increasing removal from his hometown dramatises an irreconcilable separation from his origin; it is not suggested that Bone even intends to return to the United States. Bone's alienation is predicated on an experience of racial difference that becomes integral to his identity. I-Man disappears, only to be recuperated as a shadow presence in Bone's memory. As he sails away from Jamaica, Bone looks at the night sky: 'The stars were awesome, like zillions of tiny lights bobbing on a wide black ocean' (387). Bone's illuminating points of whiteness are configured in relation to a black background, and it is only by virtue of that blackness at night that Bone's constellations become visible. Bone's story ends with a creative synthesis of that ethical preoccupation and aesthetic impulse that compelled him to tell his story in the first place, looking at the stars and 'connecting the dots on my own' (388). In this respect, Bone's story is a subtle and imaginative interpretation of 'the racial disingenuousness and moral frailty' on which the history of the United States is founded (Morrison 1992: 6), and a testament to the creative and social value of the genre of coming of age.

Brady Udall, *The Miracle Life of Edgar Mint*

Brady Udall's first novel, *The Miracle Life of Edgar Mint* (2001) was published following the success of his short story collection *Letting Loose the Hounds* (1997) and it is the story of its eponymous protagonist's life in Arizona and Utah. Edgar is a young boy growing up on the San Carlos Indian Reservation in eastern Arizona; his father has abandoned him and his mother is an alcoholic. Playing alone outside one day, Edgar has an accident in which he is run over by a mailtruck driven by Nicolas Petenko, and, as a result of serious head injuries, Edgar spends three months in a coma. During his subsequent time in hospital, Edgar is befriended by a doctor, Barry Pinkley, and by a fellow patient, Art Crozier, who, in the absence of his parents, become major influences in

Edgar's life. Edgar eventually leaves hospital for a tough boarding school (occasionally reminiscent of the school in that classic bildungsroman, Charles Dickens's *David Copperfield*), from which he is later rescued by Mormon missionaries who grant him a new life in suburban Utah. But as Edgar grows up, he becomes increasingly preoccupied with the thought that the mailman must be suffering from terrible guilt in the mistaken belief that he has killed Edgar. Therefore, Edgar decides to devote his life to finding the mailman, in order that he can alleviate his guilt, and thereby remedy the painful circumstances with which the novel begins. This traumatic opening invites comparison with another novel included here, Geoffrey Wolff's *The Age of Consent*, in which Maisie Jenks spends three months in a coma following her dramatic suicide attempt. Both novels begin with the near-death experience of the protagonist, and both are subsequently dedicated to providing accounts of coming of age that consist principally of tracing back through history to a specific originatory moment with which the characters must come to terms. But although both novels have this special interest in origins, and in the narrative contrivances of historiography that identify points of origin, *The Miracle Life of Edgar Mint* associates the idea of beginnings with a specifically religious concept of original sin, and this gives Edgar's coming of age a distinctly spiritual inflection.

Edgar's story begins with the scene of his accident, but the beginning of the novel is also substantially devoted to providing an account of Edgar's parents' relationship, and in this respect the novel might be said to have two points of origin. Structurally, the novel alternates between an account of Edgar's near-death accident and the story of his parents' courtship. Edgar's accident occurred when he was seven years old, and he can remember nothing before that. This loss of memory has made Edgar a hoarder of historical artefacts and information; part of that information is the story of his parents' romance, the mixed ethnic nature of which has a crucial bearing on his identity and his fate. Edgar's father, Arnold Kessler Mint, is a would-be cowboy from Connecticut who has read too many Zane Gray novels, and Edgar's mother, Gloria, is a full-blood Apache from the San Carlos Indian Reservation just east of Globe, Arizona. Despite being a first-person narrative, the novel gives a full account of their courtship and romance prior to Edgar's birth, one that culminates in his father's abandonment of the family and his mother's subsequent descent into alcoholism. The narrative of Edgar's parents and of their beginnings is provided in the novel simultaneously with the story of Edgar's near-death experience and re-birth at the hospital called Saint Divine's. Edgar's origins are to some extent a contemporary interpretation of the cowboy and Indian story: his father was an easterner who foolishly aspired to the myth of the cowboy that he learned from western fiction; Arnold Mint was oblivious to the ethnic differences and cultural histories of Arizona, and he does not learn very much about the reality of life in the desert south west either. Arnold's courtship of an Apache girl is impetuous and unthinking, and it brings ruin to Edgar's mother. Gloria was flattered by Arnold's persistence and tempted by the escape from an economically deprived environment that he seemed to offer. A nineteenth-century western legacy is played out in late twentieth-century terms in the chapter called 'Cowboys and Indians', a chapter that emphasises that Arnold 'had no idea what he was getting into' (Udall 2001: 48). When Arnold discovers that Gloria is pregnant he abandons her in order to chase his ersatz cowboy dreams in another tough western town, Rock Springs, Wyoming because, 'Arnold was still hoping for his chance to ride a horse' (62). Gloria finds this abandonment inexplicable, except that 'Arnold was a white man' (62), and the Indian experience of white men has always been about duplicity and betrayal. As in many coming-of-age novels, the story of the protagonist's parents is integral to his identity, and as with other novels in the genre, the desire to reach back historically to a definitive point of origin is articulated partly by the image of the embryo: 'Once Arnold's sperm had penetrated one of her eggs to create a single cell that would eventually become little Edgar, everything went to hell' (61). Many contemporary coming-of-age novels find ways to accommodate accounts of the protagonist's parents prior to their conception as part of their full history, and the image of the sperm and the egg is seen also in Jeffrey Eugenides' *Middlesex*: 'Inside my mother a billion sperm swim upstream, males in the lead. They carry not only instructions about eye color, height, nose shape, enzyme production, microphage resistance, but a story, too' (Eugenides 2003: 210). That Udall's novel has two significant points of origin is typical of a desire to present a properly historicised account of the protagonist's coming of age; Edgar knows that he begins with a history that is antecedent to his birth, and he exhibits a characteristically American desire to understand that history. Simultaneously, Edgar's miraculous resurrection in hospital is another origin, and one that is as significant for him as his birth. This is also very similar to the beginning of Dorothy Allison's *Bastard out of Carolina*, which reveals a corresponding concern for the nature of origins, and which also begins with a near-death accident at the point of the protagonist's birth. The crucial antecedent here is Mark Twain's Huck Finn, who is symbolically reborn when he pretends to have died in order to escape the cabin in which his father has imprisoned him.

There are two conspicuous features of Edgar's self-presentation that call for particular interpretation: his consistent tendency to switch between the first and third person, and his use of the Hermes Jubilee type-writer. Initially the alternation between narrative positions 'I' and 'he' is a temporal or historical issue: the use of the first-person gives a dramatic immediacy to the voice that tells the story of a traumatic childhood, while the use of the third-person introduces a formal distance which is a consequence of the novel being necessarily a historical retrospective. The first chapter, for example, describing Edgar's accident, is told exclusively in the first-person; the fourth and fifth chapters speak of 'Edgar' in their titles with a dispassionate distance: 'Edgar lay in his bed completely still' (26). This shift occurs at the point where Edgar is recounting events about himself that have been told to him by others: 'So far, everything I've told you is second hand' (26). However, this alternation is a formal feature that the novel retains throughout, even to its final page: 'At eighteen Edgar got his driver's license' (417). The temporal interpretation of Edgar's use of this device is confirmed by this final retrospective use of the third person 'Edgar'; the novel's last few pages, written when Edgar is twenty-eight years old, are written wholly in the first person. Edgar's coming of age is signalled partly by the formal shift into an integrated present tense and first-person voice, one that no longer speaks of himself in the more distant third-person.

The question remains, however, why does the narrative perspective alternate throughout? It is perhaps the most conspicuous formal characteristic of the novel, sometimes even occurring in consecutive sentences: 'My stealing and spying and sneaking around had been found out and I was now being marched away to take my punishment. Edgar was so delirious with relief he almost collapsed into the snow at Principal Whipple's heels' (162). This is partly a psychological device to deal with painful and traumatic experiences; writing about some of Edgar's experiences in the third-person gives them a formal distance in which the personal pain is at one remove from 'I' and is therefore easier to manage and control. For example, the incident in which Edgar is forced to 'eat shit' by Rotten Teeth is recounted by the 'I' who 'kicked and thrashed and spit and gagged', but, immediately it is over, Edgar takes recourse to his typewriter 'and typed himself a little reminder: *don't tell anybody eat shit again*' (105). The third-person voice also permits Edgar a degree of creative licence; it is possible that the third-person is closer than the first-person to an element of fictionalisation, as if Edgar were writing about someone else who was not personally involved in the traumatic experiences he has to recount in writing. Most readers are seduced into a particular kind of relationship with the word 'I', and it is (sometimes mistakenly) associated with a sense of veracity that the third-person does not necessarily claim. The alternation of perspectives encourages sympathy with a 'he' who is fictional, but simultaneously insists upon the formal distance from the necessarily limited narrative perspective of any first-person position. This device addresses a central technical issue that all coming-of-age novels have struggled with: how does an adult writer depict with any degree of authenticity the consciousness of a child or adolescent while still retaining the freedom to accommodate some aspect of that inevitably mature adult perspective from which the novel is written? Udall's accomplishment here is to make that formal issue an integral dimension of Edgar's developing subjectivity, and it is therefore a key feature of the novel's innovative contribution to the history of the coming-of-age genre.

One significant consequence of Edgar's head injury is that he is unable to write. The doctors designate this condition '"Dysgraphia"' (54), and it is a serious impediment to Edgar's self-possession because it means that 'I could not perform the fundamental act of writing my own name' (55). It is Edgar's friend at the hospital, Art, who thinks of the solution of presenting him with a typewriter, the Hermes Jubilee, which Edgar carries with him throughout the whole novel. Once he overcomes its strange appearance, Edgar quickly discovers the pleasure that typing can give him 'like pulling the trigger of a pistol' (58), a suitably western image for the power that he finds in hitting the keys. The typewriter as pistol also emphasises its mechanisation, and Edgar often draws attention to the physicality of this method of self-composition in ways that distinguish it from speaking or writing. There is something institutional about a manual typewriter, even depersonalised or objective; for example, he depicts himself working on it 'like a courtroom stenographer' (77). The typewriter is cumbersome and industrial, and Edgar's possession of it in the novel often goes against the grain of naturalistic possibility. The transcript of Edgar's consciousness has the typewriter as its intermediary and this is perhaps analogous to the novel's use of the third-person position in its creation of a formal distance between subjectivity and language. It is also perhaps an integral part of the Indian experience of American modernity: like the railroad, the typewriter is something of an alienating incursion. Nevertheless, Edgar's possession of the Hermes Jubilee is central to his self-esteem and integral to his self-composition; he uses it to type against his impoverishment and dispossession, and typewriting informs the language of subjectivity in which he is able to express himself. The typewriter is also institutional in the sense that it contains the alphabet, the mint of words; a mint is a place where money is coined, and the typewriter is the means by which Edgar's subjectivity is minted, each of his typewritten pages represents a unit of currency in his self-composition. When Edgar first begins to type his name on the Hermes Jubilee he describes its keys as being 'as big as pennies' (57).

Edgar's story includes many expressions of the importance of the typewriter to his sense of identity. When he first moves to Utah, Edgar is carrying with him 'my Hermes Jubilee and the 11,789 pages that bore every last word and line of gibberish I had ever struck on paper' (239), and the physical weight of this transcript is a powerful antidote to that weightlessness which is Edgar's most pressing emotional anxiety. The therapeutic value of typing is also seen when Barry, the doctor who purports to have saved his life, tracks down Edgar in Utah:

> I went up to my room and typed nonsense on my Hermes Jubilee for awhile, really gave that typewriter a good pounding . . . I typed the same page over and over again until it was almost completely black and moist with ink, and I felt myself calming down. (299)

Again the physical activity of typing is emphasised in the production of a material commodity that attests to Edgar's existence. This physical evidence of Edgar's life is vitally important because without it his sense of identity would be precariously attenuated and contingent:

> I typed because it felt good, because I had nothing else to do, because I thought by getting it on paper, by turning the nameless into words, I might understand things a little better . . . I typed because typing, for me, was as good as having a conversation. I typed because I had to. I typed because I was afraid I might disappear. (139)

This idea of disappearance is especially important because of the spectre of the cultural disappearance of Indians from the American west. Because his Apache mother married a white man, Edgar is only half Indian; if Edgar married a white woman, then his children would only be one quarter Indian. This process could be repeated until the Apache nation was extinct. This anxiety about disappearance is a prominent theme in contemporary native American writing; it is seen, for example, in Sherman Alexie's *The Lone Ranger and Tonto Fistfight in Heaven* (1993), where the precedent of the Anasazi is used to articulate fears of contemporary annihilation: 'I know somebody must be thinking about us because if they weren't we'd just disappear just like those Indians who used to climb the pueblos. Those Indians disappeared with food still cooking in the pot' (Alexie 1997: 119). It is significant that Udall's novel ends with Edgar 'wondering what to do with all of these pages, bundled and stacked and useless, my zigzag life accumulated on paper' (422–3), because this is tangible evidence that he has now finally produced a material artefact that gives witness to his existence, a body of work that is a significant weight to counter the weightlessness of his childhood. As well as being a valuable aesthetic accomplishment, these accumulated pages, like the stories of Alexie, have a crucial social and political dimension in recording in a uniquely creative form the life of a marginalised American Indian culture.

The innovations of the formal written perspective of the novel are also integral to Edgar's bi-racial identity as a boy of both Apache and white parentage. Edgar is between cultures, and the result of this is to make him feel painfully excluded from both. For example, Edgar expresses his trepidation at going to school in these terms: 'Mrs Rodale had told me I was coming to Fort Apache to be among my own kind. If I was sure of anything, it was that these kids, these teachers, were *not* my own kind. *I'm the only one,* Edgar typed on his Hermes Jubilee, *I'm all there is'* (132). Edgar's profound isolation and loneliness is brought about by the absence of family and community, or as his friend in Utah, Brain, expresses it at one point, 'No father, a dead mother, a dead best friend and nowhere else to go' (316). Edgar suffers repeated crises in his sense of identity as a consequence of being neither white nor full-blood Indian; he is exposed as a child to the casual vindictive racism and stereotyping of white culture in Arizona, but neither is Edgar raised to feel that an Indian or specifically Apache cultural legacy is integral to who he is. Instead, Edgar is caught between two cultures that are often strongly antagonistic to each other in Arizona in ways that compound and intensify his sense of isolation. This feeling is succinctly captured in Edgar's exchange with an Indian hitchhiker: ' "You Indi'n?" the Indian said. "No," I said. "Yes" ' (376). Although Edgar's first response here is 'No', there are several points in the novel where he aligns himself with some idea of what it might mean for him to be properly Indian. For example, in the incident in which the stables that were formerly used to house the horses of the sixth cavalry are burned down, there is a cathartic energy that is expressed by the 'soprano keening' of the boys who celebrate the conflagration: 'Somebody let out a shrill war whoop which was answered half a dozen times and we began to move around the stables . . . our eyes full of fire, stomping and howling like the savages we were' (182). There is an important alignment here of the contemporary incarceration of these children with the historical harassment and oppression of the Apache by the U.S. Cavalry, especially by William Tecumseh Sherman (1820–91), who believed that the Indians should be exterminated. Edgar is hardly Geronimo (the most eminent Apache resident of eastern Arizona), but the act of rebellion is nevertheless an important assertion of a specifically Indian cultural history.

The issue of Edgar's ethnicity is also central to his isolation because it makes him feel that he is 'the lone survivor of a past I had lost all connection to' (186), but to some extent this is a form of existential despair at being constantly thrown back on his own meagre resources. Edgar feels that he is profoundly alone, and this is an expression of his desertion not only by his father but by God. Edgar's quest is to find a father in the form of the mailman, but this is also a search for The Father. Edgar's existential loneliness, what he terms 'lonesome little Edgar' (131), has a significant precedent in Huck Finn who uses the word 'lonesome' repeatedly to characterise his own personal predicament, and who remarks at one point 'I felt so lonesome I most wished I was dead' (Twain 1994: 13). What Edgar describes as 'this black depression that dragged at my insides' (216), is a familiar feeling for Twain's fourteen-year-old protagonist, who begins his textual life by staging his own suicide in *The Adventures of Tom Sawyer*. Edgar's beginning is also portrayed as a kind of death: he wonders if his near-fatal accident occurred because 'he might have considered suicide' (14). For both Huck and Edgar the textual starting point is a symbolic death, at the hands of an uncaring father, from which they are magically resurrected; Huck and Edgar then commit themselves to perilous journeys in which they search for a proper father and a true sense of themselves. As Harold Beaver argues, 'The whole of *Huckleberry Finn* is a parody of Christian death and resurrection. In this sense it is a secular fable' (Beaver 1987: 85). Udall's novel is also a story of the search for redemption, but, although it is occasionally critical of Mormonism, it is not a parody of the search for original innocence.

Death and resurrection become consistent structural features of Edgar's life; where Huck's coming of age proceeds in terms of a sequence of aliases by which, paradoxically, he becomes himself by impersonating other people, it is Edgar's shifting institutional contexts that inform his development. The novel is structured in terms of the hospital, the school, the Mormon Church in Utah, and finally the home of Rosa (the wife of the mailman) in Pennsylvania. In each case Edgar falls asleep on the journey and is born again in the new environment. Edgar sleeps so soundly on the bus from Arizona to Utah that the driver assumes he is dead; he also sleeps through the journey from Arizona to Nevada to visit his friend from school, Cecil Jimenez. In this respect, a fellow patient at Saint Divine's envies Edgar's quintessentially western narrative of American re-fashioning: '"All the terrible shit in your life, all the guilt, and regret, it would be gone, washed away. You take a little head trauma and – zap! – you're a new man" ' (38). This apparent celebration of historical amnesia is challenged by Udall's novel, though, because Edgar goes forward, however abruptly, in order that he might return to the historical circumstances of his beginning. This cyclical return is also typical of those contemporary coming-of-age novels (notably *Bastard out of Carolina*, *The Virgin Suicides*, and *Fishboy*), that dramatise their protagonist's attempt to historicise themselves. It is also characteristic of Twain's Huck, who ends, at least linguistically, as he began: 'The Widow Douglas, she took me for her son, and allowed she would sivilize me; but it was rough living in the house all the time . . . and so when I couldn't stand it no longer, I lit out' (Twain 1994: 11). 'But I reckon I got to light out for the Territory ahead of the rest, because Aunt Sally she's going to adopt me and sivilize me and I can't stand it. I been there before' (Twain 1994: 281). As one critic succinctly expresses it, 'Twain returns him exactly to square one' (Egan 1977: 18). This might not be entirely a coincidence: as a child Edgar Mint reads mostly westerns, but in hospital he does find 'a ragged copy of *Huckleberry Finn*' (52–3).

Edgar's existential despair or feeling of being deeply lonesome, is also associated with a strong sense of original sin. When he witnesses the abject condition of his alcoholic mother, Edgar comments that 'I knew without a doubt that it was I who had done this to her' (153). Edgar's guilt is closely associated with his ethnicity, because his mixed blood is a curse that he carries with him everywhere so that 'wherever I went, it didn't matter where, ruin would follow' (210). Edgar believes that his mother's pregnancy, the very fact of his existence, has destroyed her life, and this secular guilt is subsequently given a religious interpretation. The association between guilt and ethnicity is also made by Edgar's friend, Sterling, who tells him '"even if you got just a couple a drops a Indi'n blood, that's all it takes, it's like a disease"' (173). Edgar's quest for redemption is complicated by the proximity of ethnicity and original sin in ways that will become a serious problem when he joins the Mormon Church. Simultaneously, Edgar is marked out from the beginning not only by his Apache blood but by his miraculous survival, and this gives him a unique quality that is equally integral to his identity: '"There's something special about you Edgar, you've got some kind of destiny to fulfil"' (67). Edgar is not sure what this might be, but with the advent of the Mormon Elders he realises the strongly redemptive value of a search for the mailman who believes he has killed Edgar. This search thus becomes 'my purpose in life' (285), and especially after the death of Cecil, the Havasupai boy who saved Edgar, with a bow and arrow, from the school bully, Nelson, and was his close friend, Edgar is consumed with the idea of personal responsibility for salvation: 'I became obsessed with the idea that I could relieve him of that burden'

(312). The Mormon Church gives Edgar's search a specifically religious interpretation: '"God spared you from being killed so that you could find the person who almost killed you and tell him you survived?"' (228). In this way Edgar discovers that 'I could do a little saving of my own' (228).

The most serious expression of Edgar's crisis of faith occurs when he discovers the death of Cecil. The despair that Cecil's death brings upon Edgar is expressed again in terms that conflate the mailman with God: '*What kind of father*, typed Edgar, *could do this to his own son?*' (318). Nevertheless, however difficult God might be to interpret, Edgar has no doubt about His existence: 'God was out there. He had touched me and I had felt His presence, which was more than I could say about my own father' (311). The absence of Edgar's real father propels his search for a spiritual father, a search in which the mailman offers a redemptive focus and in which the doctor, Barry, acts as a phoney substitute. Edgar's spiritual quest brings the novel to the specific ideological institution of the Church of Latter Day Saints, and to the issue of how his belief is shaped by its doctrine. Edgar's interest in the Church is motivated as much by economic necessity and the desire for a family as it is by the prospect of 'having my sins washed away forever' (234). This ambivalence is matched by the unflinching dramatisation of the Church's racism, when Edgar is made an example of by the Elders:

> Brother Hughes made much of the fact that the Lamanites had not followed the will of God and had therefore been marked with a curse: dark skin . . . "Out in the world they might call him an American Indian, but we know better" '. (276)

This indictment of the Mormon Church does not diminish Edgar's faith, nor perhaps that faith's expression in the specific doctrine of Mormonism; it is even possible that it concurs with Edgar's sense that his Apache blood is an integral aspect of his original sin.

Barry Pinkley is a curious presence in Edgar's life, an apparently benign and benevolent doctor who seeks to provide a stable family environment for the orphan, but a man towards whom Edgar feels from the outset an unarticulated hostility. Barry claims to be responsible for saving Edgar's life (although the Phoenix neurosurgeon had a key part in it), and Edgar's antagonism to Barry starts here: 'like Dr Frankenstein who gave the monster life, I think Barry felt a kind of ownership towards me' (25). Edgar is suspicious of Barry's motives throughout because Barry wants to control Edgar's life regardless of what Edgar wants; having saved Edgar's life, Barry wants to use it to fulfil his own emotional needs. In particular, Barry has his own loneliness to assuage:

"I know what it's like to be alone, to not have anybody. I've dealt with it my whole life. It's terrible, Edgar, the worst thing in the world. You need someone who'll take care of you. That why I'm here now". (83)

The post-conversion Edgar confesses, 'I knew that he loved me, in his own way, more than anyone in my life ever had. And I knew that if I looked hard enough, I could find some small part of me that loved him back' (347). This is a very important quotation in the novel because it helps to characterise the ambivalence that Edgar feels towards Barry; it is an ambivalence that is faithful to the complexity of Christian trust. Barry is not a one-dimensional villain, not always simply 'some low-rent incarnation of Santa Claus' (76). Barry also has his own dream of a conventional family unit by which to achieve happiness and stability 'the white clapboard house on Maple Street with the wife baking cookies, and Edgar the coma-boy sitting at the kitchen table doing his homework' (326). Edgar is thus integral to Barry's narrative of his own heroism and saviour-status, a means to validate his own position and value and importance. Edgar tacitly recognises this from the beginning: he is principally a vehicle for the restoration of Barry's damaged self-esteem. Eventually Edgar finds the words to articulate his fear of Barry's desire for control: 'Every time I thought of him a panic would swell in the space behind my heart and lungs, like a tremor rattling up from deep underground' (323). This appropriately subterranean image expresses strongly the previously unspoken anxiety that Barry engenders in Edgar as a child; for the most part, the fact that Edgar is a child prevents him from naming this fear, and it remains something of an enigma. But it is clear that, having saved Edgar's life, Barry will not permit him autonomy and independence, and the stethoscope Barry gives Edgar on his birthday 'felt like an anchor chain around my neck' (329). Like an overbearing parent whose suffocating presence threatens the autonomy of the child, Barry must be vanquished if Edgar is ever to find some breathing space of his own. Barry's self-aggrandisement is especially evident in the myth that he has created of Edgar's miraculous saving: he 'recited the whole thing, as if it was an epic poem that he had written himself and memorised. On other nights, Barry would tell everything else he knew about me, dramatising quite artfully' (183). This epic poem is a repeat performance of a narrative that Barry created at the time of the accident 'and then he told the story, in full and painful detail, of my accident. He didn't leave out a thing', (68). It is here too that Barry tells Edgar 'In the end, that mailman tried to commit suicide' (69). It is even possible that Barry embellished the story to place himself at the centre of the drama, and it is clear that Edgar's sense of original sin is strongly compounded by the story of the mailman's remorse. Barry even throws into doubt the efficacy of his own stories when he reports to Edgar at one point that 'The Postal Service doesn't deliver to the reservation' (331). As a storyteller, Barry is someone who Edgar must push aside so that he can take possession of his own story and write his own 'epic poem', which becomes *The Miracle Life of Edgar Mint*.

Killing Barry is crucial to Edgar's coming of age. When he becomes a serious drug addict, Barry inadvertently gives Edgar the chance to do away with him. Edgar flees the Madsens in order to abort Barry's affair with Lana and in so doing alleviate the guilt he feels at having brought this trouble on their house, but he also takes the opportunity to terminate Barry: 'I slipped in the needle and pushed the plunger down' (373). At this point Edgar regains control, and the next chapter is entitled 'Edgar at the Wheel'. In the context of the emotional anxiety that Barry causes Edgar, 'rattling up from deep underground', it is appropriate that Edgar consigns his body to the depths of a disused mine shaft. Although fellow hospital patient Art Crozier assists in locating the drop site, it is important that Edgar disposes of Barry on his own, and that at the point of exhaustion Edgar finds the strength to do it when he is reminded that Barry has the mailman's address: 'It was that folded square of paper, like a piece of warmth against my thigh, that gave me the strength I needed to pick Barry up by the ankles and roll him into the dark tunnel of air' (385). Edgar rids himself of one phoney father so that he might pursue the man he thinks of as his true father.

Art Crozier is clearly an important figure in the novel, protecting and nurturing Edgar in a responsible and selfless way when they are both patients at Saint Divine's. Art protects Edgar from the hospital orderlies who tie him down, and also from Barry, whom Art recognises as a dangerous threat to Edgar. Art is a constant presence in Edgar's life, and he even writes letters to him from Willie Sherman. Like Edgar, Art is a survivor, and, against the odds, he is still alive at the end of the novel and Edgar still writes to him every week. Art is instrumental in disposing of Barry once Edgar has killed him, and the efficient and unquestioning manner in which Art helps Edgar to be rid of Barry is indicative of their mutual trust and understanding. This understanding is more than simply a surrogate father role: Art was responsible for the death in an auto accident of his wife and two daughters: 'all three drowned upside down in fetid water laced with insecticides' (34). Art's guilt at causing these deaths is the reason for his alcoholism, and also an oblique complement to Edgar's sense of guilt too, and this sense of guilt is the real reason for their mutual bond. Where Edgar feels unaccountably guilty for burdening the mailman with an imagined sense of guilt, Art's guilt is real. Where Edgar feels guilt for bringing about the destruction of his mother's life (another version of original sin) Art is directly responsible for the death of his family. It is interesting to note, too, that Edgar mimics Art's act of mourning: in one of the novel's most compelling scenes, a scene that is closely faithful to the fear and confusion of a child in the presence of inexplicable adult behaviour, Art spoons dirt from his family's grave into his mouth 'until black oozing mud began to seep from the corner of his lips' (80). When Edgar attends his mother's funeral, he too forces a fistful of dirt into his mouth 'until it dissolved into a gritty paste that began to seep past my lips' (167). The relationship between Edgar and Art is also vitally reciprocal: Art says of Edgar's letters, 'You can't know how much they helped me. They were all I had, is what I'm saying. They kept me going when I didn't have nothing left' (387). This scene, full of pathos, is also testimony to the value of writing; Edgar's relentless typing is not only a vitally sustaining act of self-composition, but an activity of communication that has life-saving and redemptive social power. While Barry wants to cling to Edgar forever, Art believes that he should forget his time at the hospital, and that forgetting 'would be the best thing for you' (387). This attitude is characteristic of Art's paternal selflessness, and it distinguishes him definitively from Barry. Art is still an important presence at the end of the novel, he still corresponds with Edgar and 'has become something of a surrogate grandpa' to the two boys of Edgar's new relationship (419). At the novel's end, Arnold Mint has absconded and Barry and the mailman are dead, but Art, like Edgar, is a survivor, and his survival in the novel attests to the unique emotional quality of paternity that he represents.

At the novel's end, Edgar is newly-minted, not in the west but in the east, where he returns to another version of American origins and to a place where he discovers not only the true story of his beginning but a mother rather than a father. This is an appropriately cathartic resolution of the anguish he has carried his whole life: he was seven years old at the time of the accident, the novel covers eight years until he arrives in Pennsylvania as a fifteen-year-old, and now a further thirteen years have elapsed to this final point at the age of twenty-eight. This final new beginning is also (like his other resurrections) an annihilation of the past that is necessary before he can begin again. For Edgar, the closer he approaches the mailman's house 'the harder it was to shake the sensation that I was disappearing' (395). The symbolic nature of this beginning is clear when Edgar describes this part of Pennsylvania as 'more lush and green and overgrown than the Garden of Eden itself' (416). It is here that Rosa tells Edgar that the mailman, Nicolas Petenko, has died; the death of the mailman before Edgar could trace him makes that final absolution impossible, despite

Rosa's poignant exclamation '"It's not your fault"' (410). Rosa also tells Edgar that his mother sold him to her, before his accident, for nine hundred dollars, and Edgar's interest in this specific sum of money (something of a mint in itself) is partly a throwback to the commodification of Apache slaves in the nineteenth century. This is also, in a sense, a double origin for Edgar, because it evokes the moment in his early childhood when his mother could no longer cope with him, but also the scene in *Huckleberry Finn* when the black slave Jim tells Huck that he is worth eight hundred dollars. In this narrative moment, then, Edgar is both Huck, in his coming of age, but also Jim, in his enslavement to ethnicity. Edgar's journey east also adds another significant turn to the novel's depiction of ethnicity. In Pennsylvania, Edgar discovers that 'a dark face was a dark face' (416), and therefore he might be able to escape the racism of the American west, but only at the expense of his Apache inheritance, which to a large extent now disappears from cultural view. The Apache Indian disappears, partly among the 'Ukrainian and Filipino dishes' of Rosa's cooking, but also in a more multicultural east where Edgar is not solely defined by his skin colour. Edgar's development also continues to take place in the supportive context of the Church, which embraces him while 'seeming not to notice that I was a stranger in that place' (416).

The end of the novel continues to be preoccupied by a concern with the nature and status of beginnings. Edgar claims that 'there isn't all that much to tell about these last thirteen years' (417), and this belief, contrary to the evidence of the novel's final pages, emphasises his conviction that the experiences of his childhood were formative or determining. Edgar has no final moment of absolution in a meeting with the mailman, but although this father-figure eludes him, he does discover a miraculous second childhood in the home of the mailman's wife. In this respect, Edgar's relationship of guilt with the father continues as strongly as ever, but he finds a nurturing mother to function in place of the one that he lost: 'there has been no greater blessing than Rosa' (420). In his relationship with Rosa, Edgar finds that 'I have lived my life in reverse' (417), a further claim that tacitly relegates the value of the experiences of adulthood, and which extends for him the importance of maintaining a concept of innocence well beyond childhood. This belief in innocence is principally a means to address the powerful sense of guilt that Edgar continues to struggle with. It is that feeling of guilt from which the whole novel is written, an extended confession which ends by questioning the emotional value of the confessional mode:

> could it free me of the nightmares I have of Barry tumbling through a dark void, never hitting bottom? Could it relieve the guilt I feel not only for Barry's

death but also for everything else, for my mother, for Cecil, for Nicolas, all of whom, it seems clear to me even now, gave up their lives on my behalf? (419)

The sacrifices of these figures are, for Edgar, earthly manifestations of the sacrifice of Christ, and Edgar's story acts as a confessional expiation for his sense of original sin. This is the true origin of Edgar's writing, a sinfulness that he strives to overcome, both by writing and by affirming a belief in the redemptive potential of symbolic rebirth. By the end of his story, Edgar has amassed a body of testimony to the ways in which his coming of age was defined by a particular form of spiritual quest, and he finds himself 'wondering what to do with all of these pages' (422). Simultaneously, the connection between writing and salvation is made in his new career as a newspaper reporter, a role which finds him attending to the confessions of others. The novel thus becomes an act of atonement, from which Edgar can finally emerge, like Lazarus, 'blinking and holding my hand to the sky, amazed at the light, like a man raised from the dead' (423).

Chapter 2

I Change Therefore I Am: Growing up in the Sixties

In terms of the social history of the United States in the late twentieth century, the decade that is most often singled out as exceptional is the 1960s. It is generally accepted that the 1960s was a time of unprecedented social upheaval in the United States, and that change had its focus in civil rights, the emergence of militant feminism, and the student protests against the war in Vietnam. The 1960s is typically characterised as a period when the radical challenges of the 'counterculture' were made to the social institutions of the United States, and violent confrontations of many kinds were symptomatic of fundamental political upheaval. David Burner characterised it as a time of 'a ferocity of debate, a challenging of conventions, and a testing of visionary hopes' (Burner 1996: 3). For the novelist at the end of the twentieth century, this was the decade whose unique character most strongly informed the identity of the United States.

Both of the novels of this chapter use a dispassionate third-person perspective to offer a critique of the legacy of the 1960s as they understand it from their different view points. Both novels ask: what specific features of the 1960s gave that decade its particular character, and how is the late twentieth-century the heir to those features in ways that it is now possible to evaluate? Both of these novels offer representations of coming of age that show how adolescence was informed by that historical moment, but which also suggest ways in which their contemporary moment is still finding ways to understand and come to terms with how modern adults are the product of that historic decade.

These novels also have a particular value because they use the genre to suggest ways in which the contemporary United States was coming of age as a nation in the 1960s. In particular, they dramatise ideas about authority and freedom that they hold up to scrutiny. For Mona this is an opportunity to experiment with a sense of identity that is dynamic and liberating and concurrent with the spirit of the age. *The Age of Consent* takes a darker view of the freedoms of the 1960s, punning on the word

'Age' in the sense of both its female protagonist's age, and the historical age which advertised its consensual nature. Both novels are in some important ways ambivalent about the forms of liberation that the 1960s made possible. In terms of authority, both novels recognise that challenges to authority made social change possible, but simultaneously there was a disconcerting tendency for young people to feel the absence of authority figures who could safely be relied upon to guide them through adolescence – and at a time when guidance was particularly needed. In this respect both novels raise issues about the place of social responsibility and the potential abuse of power; here, moral and ethical values are placed under a great deal of scrutiny.

Geoffrey Wolff, *The Age of Consent*

Geoffrey Wolff's *The Age of Consent* (1995) begins with the dramatic public spectacle of a girl called Maisie Jenks making a swan dive from a high ledge head first into a shallow pool at the bottom of a gorge. She is fifteen years old. Maisie's suicide attempt is witnessed by her thirteen-year-old brother Ted, who runs to her rescue with a crowd of onlookers that includes Maisie's parents. Maisie's mother cries out '"My baby!"', and when the family friend, known as 'Doc', attempts to breath life into Maisie's crumpled body she says to him bluntly: '"She's dead; you did it."' But Maisie survives, and she spends several months in hospital in upstate New York with a broken neck. Maisie's parents are devastated, and the whole community is shocked by 'some show-off teenager who decides to commit suicide in front of the whole town' (Wolff 1996:16). Maisie's dive is inexplicable; no one can understand why this intelligent and articulate teenager from a comfortable middle-class background should suddenly want to make a public spectacle of killing herself. *The Age of Consent* begins with this scene and these questions, and gradually works backwards through history to uncover Maisie's reasons for wanting to kill herself; her story becomes an indictment of the historical legacy of her family, a remarkable disquisition on the idea of innocence, a coming-of-age narrative of her brother Ted, and a compelling account of the unique choices and decisions of Maisie's path to adult self-determination. Like *The Miracle Life of Edgar Mint*, *Fishboy*, and *The Virgin Suicides*, the near-death experience with which Wolff's novel begins, initiates an aetiological narrative in which the idea of an origin and the concept of innocence are closely inspected.

Maisie, in a coma in hospital for three months, is symbolically dead, or at least, says Ted, '"She might as well be"' (9), and the secret of her suicide attempt is attendant on her symbolic rebirth. In the absence of Maisie's spoken explanation, the vacuum is filled by various, contested speculations (like those of *The Virgin Suicides*) and by a heightened self-consciousness concerning what can be spoken about. Neighbours do not visit Maisie in hospital because 'they don't know what to say' (14). Maisie cannot speak about what has happened, and her speechlessness is reflected everywhere in the novel's early scenes, where the issue of the spoken word becomes a significant and pervasive source of anxiety. While the narrative waits for Maisie to awaken, her younger brother begins his own story of coming of age; it is at this point, for example, that Ted's mother switches from calling him, at thirteen years old, 'Baby', to 'young man' (10). In his attempt to understand his sister, Ted looks back on the childhood that he shared with her, one he had always assumed was Prelapsarian. This view of the past has been abruptly shattered by Maisie's suicide attempt. The local newspaper covering Maisie's story looks back even further for explanations, specifically to the late 1960s, when 'trust fund socialists' arrived in the area, and the papers wrote scathing editorials 'crying shame upon the morals and family arrangements of the "homeless hippies"' of this Adirondack community (13). Ted's coming of age is a personal history lesson, a revision of his understanding of his childhood, and the beginning of an enquiry into the circumstances of his parents' own early adulthood. There is clearly something awry here which it is the purpose of the novel to uncover, and this has to do with innocence, language, and history. *The Age of Consent* is concerned with a secret history, but also with a language of history that is problematical in a way that is yet to be uncovered. The novel's arresting beginning initiates a search for historical points of origin, and the narrative reveals a heightened awareness of how any such origins are necessarily defined by the language that articulates them. Ted's search, and that of the newspapers, is depicted in a way that shows a particular sensitivity to the semantic units of stories of the past, and also to those specific ideas about power and authority that language underwrites. What adult language is it that the adolescent siblings Ted and Maisie have not yet acquired, and what important lessons about history will their coming of age consist of?

The novel's preoccupation with the veracity of the spoken word is augmented by a problem with naming; the family name of Maisie and Ted is 'Jenks', but their father is commonly known as 'Jinx', an unfortunate nickname that was given to him by his close friend Doc. The name 'Doc' is also a misnomer – he is not a doctor at all, but has acquired the name in historical circumstances that no one can remember. 'Jinx', like Dexter's nickname 'Hex' in Moody's *Purple America*, is a derogatory name that Jenks has learned to live with, and no one knows its proper origin. Jinx and Doc are wrongly named, and the question of their authority, and its relation to a trustworthy language, is hidden in historical circumstances of which the younger generation is innocent. The reticence of the novel's early chapters is broken by the significant speech acts of Doc and Jinx. Doc is characterised in terms of 'a stream of talk' (17); he is a man whose eloquence is underpinned by a knowledge of 'the etymology of the word *civic*' (18) and by an ability to quote Twain's *Huck Finn* in the service of an argument about American freedom. Doc's monologues are persuasive and authoritative, and they culminate with self-confident expressions such as '"you can take my word on that" ' (18). By contrast, Ted's father has no such self-confidence, and is, in fact, already composing a speech for a memorial service for Maisie, even though his daughter is still alive. This speech is preceded by quotations, from Jeremiah, Song of Solomon, and the poetry of A. E. Housman, all of which are inappropriate in different ways. Further, none of his quotations comes from their original context, but each is lifted from a secondary source; Jinx draws the Song of Solomon quotation, for example, from a 'newspaper clip about floods in India' (20). Where Doc's language is impassioned, full of conviction, and shows a knowledge of texts that can be used with tact and discrimination, the language of Jinx is ersatz, borrowed, and reveals a fundamental fatalism that seems to betray his daughter. The textual nature of these fatherly voices is crucial to Ted's coming of age, and it is his adolescent alertness to linguistic idioms and registers that brings about the first crisis of his young adulthood. Ted knows that 'it was natural to be in awe of his father' (19), but the memorial speech for his sister undermines his faith in Jinx. Simultaneously, Doc's speeches 'traded on Maisie's name' (21), and this too is a betrayal for Ted, one that is sufficiently serious to convince him that Doc, despite his eloquence, 'didn't know what he was talking about' (21). In these ways, *The Age of Consent* is a novel that asks what language do father figures bequeath to society, and what efficacy does it have? What interests and investments does that language encode, and how might the younger generation of Maisie and Ted learn to read it critically, so that they might create their own narratives of coming of age in some productive opposition to it? From the outset, Ted's coming of age is conducted in specifically linguistic terms.

The scenes dramatising Ted's emergent understanding of the power of discourse, take place during Maisie's prolonged and significant speechlessness; that speechlessness is suddenly broken by her emergence from her coma with the utterance of the word 'please'. Maisie is symbolically re-born by learning a new language and a new history. Like Ted, Maisie is encouraged to learn a history that is also her own, she has a mission of 'repossession and salvage' (52), in which her forgotten childhood is reconstructed and played back to her. Maisie is confused by this process, and she notes that 'Her brother was wary about her effort to rescue her past, seeming to prefer a clean slate' (52). Just as Doc has a personal investment in a particular narrative of history that lends him power and authority, the medical profession has personal investments in the history that they help Maisie to recover, 'making careers for themselves studying how to solve Maisie's problem' (53). For Maisie, to recover her health is to recover her memory, and the best way to do this is to 'write down everything she remembered' (53). The language of memory however, is a profoundly problematical issue for someone who has been in a coma: 'How could she remember what she couldn't remember . . . how could she know that she was using [language] accurately? These were tiresome questions' (56). To some extent, these are insoluble questions, but the novel is nevertheless devoted to addressing them closely. Her amnesia makes Maisie's childhood and adolescence a *tabula rasa* which needs to be recovered and rewritten, and in this respect Maisie, like Ted, finds herself attempting to compose an authoritative version of her own past, and that very process is the means by which her coming of age proceeds. Maisie is also characterised partly in terms of her special facility with language: 'Maisie could always get Ted to talk about the damnedest things' (59), and this precociousness is something that she shares with Doc, for example using the expression 'blow job' at little league (61). Maisie asks herself where she gets her interest in language, and the answer, like Ted's, returns to the language of the fathers; she remembers that 'Her dad would hang on Doc's every word and at dinner quote from Doc's Book of Wisdom . . . but Maisie had trouble with the logic of it' (63). Further, she finds that 'when she tried to write down what Doc was like exactly, she grew tired and slipped away to sleep' (64). Maisie begins to realise that there is something deeply enigmatic about Doc (his origins, his identity) even while his eloquence is powerfully seductive; this language usurps, for both Ted and Maisie, the language of their own father, and this is an indication that something is profoundly awry in this family and its specifically post-1960s cultural legacy. The coming of age of both Ted and Maisie emerges from the dramatic events of the novel as a struggle between rival languages of the past, in which the social politics of the relationship between Doc and Jinx are deeply implicated.

While talking to her therapist, Maisie remembers running away from home with Ted once because of their parents' arguments (in which Doc is closely implicated): 'She was almost fifteen . . . and maybe she was in a hurry to grow up' (82). The siblings decided to climb blackberry

mountain 'to run away from home' (83). Climbing the mountain is a rite
of passage, a journey of independence because 'Everyone who lived there
resolved someday to get to the top' (85). The wilderness is potentially full
of danger, bears and coyotes and snakes, and within an hour they were
higher than they'd ever been, Maisie leading the way. Most of their conversation en route is a struggle over words, particularly definitions, an
'erratic' (96), the name of the mountain, 'monadnock' (96), 'aurora bor-
ealis' (98), and the word 'hibernate'. Maisie believes that 'Ted made her
feel younger than she'd wanted to feel . . . like a vacation from being old'
(89). Here too, away from civilisation, Doc is present in his language:
'Doc claimed if you slipped a hemlock bough under the backpack straps,
they'd smooth the load and, as they were crushed by the weight of the
pack, give off a pleasing fragrance. Those had been Doc's words' (91).
The struggle between the teenage siblings is conducted through arguments about the use of language, the correct words for things in the
world. The siblings attempt to demonstrate their maturity in terms of
their diction, but at the same time they make fun of each other for it.
Here again Doc's influence is felt: '"he's an innovator" . . . "You've got
a pretty amazing vocabulary"; "Is that Doc's word"? "I guess. Maybe
Doc's"' (94). There is a strong sense here that Doc has usurped the
father's position and authority, and this usurpation is dramatised
through language. As a result, 'The ground was rumbling beneath Ted's
family, like tectonic plates' (95). This takes place at the same time that
Ted gathers new adult confidence in the activities of naming and
knowing, because, 'he liked the sound of himself pronouncing the words'
(96). Maisie also exercises power through the control of appropriate language, saying to her younger brother 'Let's not talk about it' (98). Sex,
too, is the subject of talk; they remember watching blue movies together
which were silent, but 'Maisie did most of the talking', and Ted is
impressed by 'her easy way with the jargon' (99).

The culmination of this adventure in the wilderness is the sex scene,
one in which talk about sex leads to physical sex between the brother and
sister, and where Maisie takes the initiative; she climbs into her brother's
sleeping bag and suddenly 'it was too late to pretend they didn't grasp
what was happening' (103). The description of the physical act, which
remains enigmatic, is matched by the importance of talking, and of being
able to control what is talked about; 'she was whispering in his ear, but
he couldn't make out her words' (104). Maisie silences Ted at crucial
points, and she therefore determines what can be spoken about and what
cannot. This is an extraordinary scene, punctuated twice by Maisie's
injunction not to speak, 'shush', as an abuser might enforce silence on
their victim as a further expression of power and control. This is part of

the novel's critical assessment of the concept of innocence, and the scene suggests that at an early stage of the novel, before adults are fully implicated in Maisie's coming of age, she is not innocent in the conventional ways. It is a scene that disrupts the idea of childhood innocence in an uncompromising way; the very idea of children as innocent becomes open to question. Part of this novel's audacious innovation with the coming-of-age narrative consists of its disruption of this category and the conventional views of childhood that traditionally accompany it. This sexual experience occurred a year before Maisie's dive; however, Ted has come to learn that it is not a significant point of origin, and that it is not the reason that Maisie attempted suicide. Ted believes, in his innocence, that Maisie simply lacks a natural curiosity 'about how we come to be who we are' (110). But in fact the structure of the narrative inhibits readers from access to Maisie's perspective at this point, and crucially foregrounds Ted's naivety. Maisie does have a knowledge of history, and it is a very unsentimental one; it is also a response to her father's phoney nostalgia: 'Jinx sighed and said it was just like the old days' (118). It is as if he has never properly grown up himself, a child of the sixties, and in some ways still a child. Maisie's view of the past is radically different from her father's, as the novel now sets out to reveal.

These ideas about social politics and language are brought together in a major way for Ted's experience of coming of age when he becomes a high school history teacher. Even though Ted is now twenty-two years old and calls himself Edward, he continues to be the dramatic focus of the novel's examination of innocence: although Ted is a teacher, it is emphatically his education that the novel dramatises. The agent of this education is a pupil called Laura who, although only fifteen years old (the same age as Maisie when she attempted suicide), is, nevertheless, very confident and daring in her behaviour towards Ted, and in ways that seriously disconcert him. Laura's particular offence is plagiarism, and it calls up the full force of Ted's moral indignation. Many important aspects of the novel's examination of coming of age converge here simultaneously. Ted's enthusiasm for teaching history through 'primary documents' is somewhat compromised by his use of photocopies and his flagrant violation of copyright laws, but, more importantly, he is something of a copy himself in his style of teaching. Ted 'apes the manners' and 'mimics the gestures' of his college professors (125). Ted's exaggerated moral indignation at Laura's plagiarism is therefore undermined by the novel's critical enquiry into the problematic nature of textual originality. From where, the novel asks, does Ted's moral piety itself originate? Part of the answer lies in the language of his father: 'Listening to his dad tell, as though they were his own, stories already told (and told better) by Doc'

(126). Textual corruption begins with the language of the father, which is, for Ted, ersatz, substitute, inauthentic; again Ted's father's authority is contaminated by the voice of Doc, and as we have seen, Doc's very name is a misnomer. Further, the sexual aspect of fifteen-year-old Laura's appeal to Ted, and its importance in terms of growing up, is ingeniously (or at least not innocently) mirrored by her own textual choice: Ted identifies immediately the 'Kosy Kabins' of Nabokov's *Lolita*. But Laura's response to Ted's accusation of plagiarism disarms him: 'Don't you think someone else stole from her before I came along?' (130). Laura also challenges her teacher's supposed maturity: '"I don't buy into your definition of young . . . Age is an arbitrary fiction"' (132). Further, when Laura writes an original diary in place of the plagiarised term paper, Ted is sufficiently appalled by its content to mail it to the authorities in the belief that she has been sexually abused by her stepfather. Here, in a remarkably economical form, the novel brings together ideas about textuality, originality, innocence, and moral education, that are profoundly important to the understanding of coming of age. Fifteen-year-old Laura is the agent of Ted's education, even while the reader is able to see her behaviour as a characteristically adolescent performance of adult sexual behaviour (and one that is itself closely imitative of Dolores Haze). That the text for this confrontation between two young people growing up should be *Lolita* is no coincidence for a novel that is centrally concerned with the relationship between education, innocence, and language.

In pursuit of these issues, the focus of the novel remains with Ted, not only on his examination of history, but on the ways that he is himself caught at a particular historical moment: 'too young for nostalgia' (135) and 'too old for his own good' (137). While these matters await a narrative resolution, Ted returns to a different form of textual account to discover what he is searching for in the past: the home-movie projector. Here, in his search for scenes from the day when Maisie jumped, the novel finally returns to the scene of its first pages. It is significant here that it was Ted's father, Jinx, who held the camera, and is therefore, in a sense, the author of this textual narrative, of this version of the historical events of that particular day. Ted's father chooses what to photograph and how long to hold certain images in focus for the attentive viewer. Quite simply, 'Dad saw everything' (173). This film is the father's occluded text, one that articulates his perspective of the past and, in so doing, recovers the crucial evidence that enables Ted to discover the truth. This is central to Ted's growing up, and it is clearly important that it is his father who facilitates it. Simultaneously, what Ted sees in his father's film is a dramatisation of Maisie's loss of innocence; as she expresses it: '"I did grow up, that's my sin isn't it?"' (142). The home movies also make it clear that there was something about the spirit of the 1960s that helped to make Doc's abuse of Maisie possible, and here and throughout the novel there is a particularly unsentimental depiction of that unique period in the history of the United States. This scene is reminiscent of the scene in Peter Hyams' 1978 film *Capricorn One*, in which the maverick investigative reporter played by Elliot Gould, discovers the truth about the space programme. In both cases the medium of film provides vital clues to a different version of historical knowledge. This aesthetic aspect of knowledge is important, because Ted's interpretation of the spectacle of the parade floats in the home movies, where 'Once again his father holds the shot uncomfortably long' (143), recalls the scene towards the end of Henry James' *The Ambassadors* (1903), in which Strether watches Madame de Vionett and Chad in a boat, and suddenly perceives the sexual nature of their relationship: 'What he saw was exactly the right thing' (James 1979: 348). The aesthetic properties of Strether's epiphany are analogous to Ted's; the interpretation of the text is a valuable form of knowledge of things in the world, a vital means by which naivety is overcome and innocence is lost. For Ted, this is a visual return to the novel's narrative origin, and one that facilitates coming of age by means of the authoritative text of his father.

When Ted confronts Maisie with what he has learned from the home movies, he discovers again that his moral certainties are not as secure as he would like to think. Ted insists to Maisie that ' "I did the right thing" ' (157), but even his visit to see Maisie in New York is strategically situated in the context of moral judgements that he has failed to learn from: his sudden departure from his high school at this point results directly in rumours that he is guilty of the sexual harassment of his student Laura. In a twist that owes as much to Bernard Malamud's *A New Life* (1961) as it does to Henry James' *What Maisie Knew* (1897), Ted discovers that his coming of age consists principally of revising the simple moral judgements that he has been accustomed to making. Ted is only now beginning to grow up, because 'All this time he's nourished a version of his sister as she was' (153), and Maisie (the real victim of abuse here) repudiates not only his version of the past but his methodology too; she does this with her physical injunction ' "Let your body tell your head what's what" ' (157). Maisie refuses to think of herself as a passive victim, and, in taking possession of her own story with such confidence, she makes her brother 'feel like a kid' (160). The satirical targets of the novel, then, belong not only to the 1960s and to a particular way of remembering, nostalgically, that decade's liberating energy, but include the specifically male form of Ted's enquiry into the past and its moral certainties and retrospective judgements. Ted's coming of age is a radical revision not only of his memory of his own childhood, but also of his very methods of thinking about the past, its language, its morality, and its relations to power. The critique of patriarchy here is not simply of Doc, but of Ted too, and it is in this respect that the novel is the story of Ted's coming of age as much as it is Maisie's.

It is not until the novel's end that Maisie is finally permitted to give her account of the past, and in this scene the dialogue emphasises repeatedly the intensely adolescent nature of Ted's experience while he is forced to listen to the uncomfortable details of his sister's adolescent experience with Doc. There is a particular reflexivity in the treatment of adolescence here that is characteristic of the novel's interest in a return to beginnings. Maisie upbraids Ted for his childish responses to her story, ' "Don't look like your pup died . . . I hate it when you pout" ' (162), and throughout her account of her relationship with Doc, Ted is still the child, uncomfortable with adult language, and pleading to his sister to ' "just indulge young Teddy" ' (179). Although it is Maisie who speaks about the traumatic consequences of her relationship with Doc, it is Ted who cries. Moreover, what might be interpreted as Ted's immaturity is given a specifically sexual inflection by the references to his own romantic confessions, to which his roommate once replied ' "shut up, I've been hearing this story since fourth grade" ' (175). Ted is now twenty-three years old, but Maisie's revelations about the past are for him a vertiginous descent into the unknown that completely disorientates him and makes him feel like a child listening to stories that his sister might 'bring home from middle school' (165). This schooling is, for Ted, extremely painful, and it brings him to a point where he feels 'as if he's about to dive off a cliff' (171). This is an audacious image, making a close analogy with what happened to Maisie in terms of a violent and traumatic partition from childhood. The implication is that Ted's loss of innocence is somehow analogous to Maisie's; this is perhaps an interpretation that readers should resist, because obviously the siblings' coming of age are not conducted in similar terms, and we should not lose sight of their crucial gender difference and its social politics.

There is no doubting, for example, the importance of gender to Maisie's experience, then and now; she is forced to refute again and again the imposition of Ted's interpretation of her story. Ted's interruptions are an annoyance, and Maisie upbraids him repeatedly for his reductive ways of thinking, ' "Don't be so literal" ' (167). Maisie's understanding of history is much more sophisticated than Ted's, and she has learned how it eludes definition in two crucial ways: 'it started *before* it started' (171), and, ' "I shouldn't say it *all* began, because I can't say what *all* is" ' (160). History is more indeterminate than Ted's view would allow; there is no

simple and definitive point of origin to which all subsequent events can
be attributed or ascribed, there is no easy way to designate cause and
effect in a simple linear trajectory. It is this attitude to history that most
disconcerts Ted, the young history teacher. But Maisie also repudiates
the easy moral judgements that might be made of her story, telling
Ted, ' "This isn't tragic" ' (175). Maisie's language of history refuses to
conform to Ted's ways of thinking; she is not a victim, and she argues
strongly that she was not a victim when she was a teenager either, but
that her experience with Doc was ' "something I wanted to do, and I did
it" ' (175). Maisie does not understand her past in terms of victimhood
or abuse, and she is remarkably self-composed and self-possessed in the
ways that she has accommodated what happened to her. This is especially
important to the politics of the novel, because in order to wrest possession of her story and to be properly empowered by doing so, she has to
resist strongly Ted's attempts to interpret it in ways that suit his views:
' "It's my life, I own myself" ' (174). In the struggle to have full authority over her version of her history, Maisie must reject Ted's interpretations of the past, and repudiate his protestations and challenges. It is this
power struggle in the present tense that the novel offers as equally
important to the relationship Maisie had with Doc: ' "Try to tell me how
to feel about my story and I'll shut up" ' (168). Maisie threatens a return
to the silence of the novel's beginning; the word 'feel' here is indicative
of the importance of their gender differences. Ted's coming of age is conducted principally in terms of historiography, but its abstract or purely
intellectual and moral character is undone by Maisie's emotional and
physical responses.

Further, refuting Ted's judgements, Maisie explains that she took Doc
as her lover partly because of the adolescent vulnerability that she found
attractive in him when they were intimate. Here, in a further inflection
of the novel's examination of innocence, Maisie explains to Ted that she
participated in a relationship with Doc partly because of the innocence
that she perceived in him: for example, the attractiveness of a scar that
Doc acquired in a motorbike accident ' "when he was my age" ' (177).
Here, in Maisie's reminiscence, Doc is himself transformed into an adolescent during Maisie's discourse about him, and, in a moment strongly
reminiscent of the temporal ingenuity of *Lolita* (Humbert's attachment
to Dolores is a reprise of his earlier relationship with a young girl in 'a
kingdom by the sea'), Maisie gives Ted a momentary glimpse of Doc's
first sexual initiation with a babysitter, one that took place ' "when he
was eleven and she was sixteen" ' (178). The age gap is significant here,
and so is Maisie's feeling that, for Doc, Maisie was an attempt on his
behalf to return to this defining moment in his childhood: ' "I was always

waiting for him to call me by her name" ' (178). At the very heart of the novel then, is the sense that Doc's predatory nature is founded upon an earlier baulked or interrupted experience from his childhood that he seeks to recapture and repeat. But the proximity of the textual power relations of *Lolita* remind the reader that in his relations with Maisie, Doc was not a child, and that he encouraged Maisie to think of herself, often in admonitory tones, as an adult: ' "Don't giggle Maisie, act your age. You're not a little kid" ' (167). It is worth remembering that Maisie is actually only fourteen years old at this time; Lolita was twelve. Doc plays upon Maisie's childhood precociousness to make her feel like a daring but appropriate sexual partner for him: Maisie is made to feel that ' "it wasn't a moment to act like a child" ' (164). But of course, Maisie is a child, and one who becomes complicit in a power game that distorts her real social relations with the adult Doc. Maisie's confusion about Doc's status is evident in the ways that she characterises him; while speaking to Ted she says, ' "He was younger than we were . . . he was also a fuddy-duddy" ' (178). But Maisie's confusion cannot disguise Doc's invidious manipulations, and, in a reprise of teenaged Laura's specious arguments, Maisie tells Ted that Doc argued that ' "A person's legal age . . . was an arbitrary convention" ' (170). Doc's argument here cannot disguise the moral accusation that he has exploited his position as a close friend of Maisie's father, and that he has abused her respect and admiration for him as an adult. Here, in a dry joke on the novel's disorientating temporal perspectives, the thoroughly disconcerted Ted calls, ' "Time out" ' (170).

In these ways, *The Age of Consent* is a novel about innocence, sexual forms of knowledge, and the language of history. Ted learns to read, and, simultaneously, the reader is encouraged to re-read *Lolita* and *What Maisie Knew* for their representations of innocence at particular moments of American literary history. Both Ted and the reader of the novel learn a fresh appreciation of what is at stake in reading, and of how innocence is a loaded term that is partly contingent upon a knowledge of language. These issues, of historiography and language acquisition, are underwritten by the social politics of gender: Henry James' Maisie, Nabokov's Dolores, and Malamud's Nadalee: it is the women who are presumed innocent, and this too is a male assumption about gender that *The Age of Consent* revises. Nevertheless, Doc ends up in the dock, where he is given a three-year suspended sentence for contravening the legal age of consent. But the 'age of consent' is also a reference to the 1960s, which Maisie's father characterises in these terms: ' "It was different up here before you kids started running all over the place. It was hard-core, and we tried new ways of doing everything. We had a rule:

No rules" ' (216). This is the intoxicating social ethos of the late 1960s, and Doc is a product of its cultural language. Coming of age at that particular time gave Doc and Ted's father a momentary opportunity to experiment with new freedoms, but this entailed a neglect of responsibility that infantilised them both; either, 'he's a victim of the youth culture into which all of them, if they will only be honest, have bought' (192–3), or, by another interpretation, 'Doc's just a kid himself and has no inkling he's fifty now' (193). Both interpretations of Doc's behaviour emphasise the ways in which he did not grow up, and that failure, like the failure of Ted's father, is an indictment of the social culture of the 1960s. For *The Age of Consent*, these judgements are never easy, because they are contingent upon a challenging, sophisticated, and compelling, interrogation of what is meant by the word 'innocence' in all its linguistic, literary, and social contexts.

Gish Jen, *Mona in the Promised Land*

Gish Jen's *Mona in the Promised Land*, first published in 1996, is a novel about a young Chinese-American woman growing up in Scarshill, New York, in the late 1960s, and it has several narrative features that are integral to the genre of the bildungsroman. The temporal compression of the novel, so that much of its action takes place during one long summer vacation, and its close attention to the events of Mona's sixteenth year, are characteristic of the genre. The summer absence of Mona's friend's parents provides a freedom that can be used to encounter, and to experiment with, forms of cultural difference, and the strategic visit of Mona's Aunt Theresa provides the adolescent protagonist with an adult figure who offers a valuable alternative to the authority of Mona's parents. When the challenges of coming of age become unbearable, and Mona decides to run away from home, she begins her journey at Grand Central Station, which is described as being 'like the Garden of Eden' (Jen 1997: 255), and she meets a benevolent adult who tells her 'we all have to go through this' (257). Chapter eleven is entitled 'The Fall Begins'. *Mona in the Promised Land* is thus a novel that is substantially devoted to dramatising the particular pressures of coming of age in a particular community at a specific historical moment, and its close attention to Mona's developing consciousness situates it within the coming-of-age genre.

   Recent studies of Asian American fiction provide a valuable interpretive paradigm by which to contextualise Mona's story. Although they do not refer to this novel, nor to Jen's first novel *Typical American* (1991), critical works such as P. Duncan's *Tell This Silence: Asian American*

Women Writers and the Politics of Speech (2004), P. P. Chu's *Assimilating Asians* (2002), J. C. Chang's *Transforming Chinese American Literature* (2000), and R. C. Lee's *The Americas of Asian American Literature* (1999), examine narratives of assimilation in ways that are closely relevant to Mona's coming of age. The assimilation narrative is, like the bildungsroman, a story of personal transformation, one that dramatises the cultural processes of becoming American through the struggles of a young individual. Narratives of immigration to the United States are closely analogous to the coming-of-age genre in the ways that they portray the challenges to individual subjectivity of particular cultural formations and institutions. Both genres, for example, often focus on the dynamic processes of language acquisition to show how the subjectivity of contemporary Americans is shaped by their knowledge and understanding of an English idiom that codifies semantically the ideology of the dominant culture (for example Eva Hoffman's *Lost in Translation* and Chang-rae Lee's *Native Speaker*). The bildungsroman is often addressed in studies of assimilation because it is in some respects a homologous field of discourse. Lisa Lowe, for example, argues that the bildungsroman is

> the primary form for narrating the development of the individual from youthful innocence to civilised maturity, the telos of which is the reconciliation of the individual with the social order . . . a narrative of the individual's relinquishing of particularity and difference through identification with an idealised 'national' form of subjectivity. (Lowe 1996: 98)

The coming-of-age genre is thus reinvigorated by these writers because they recognise its value in focusing on how cultural differences are negotiated. That focus on difference in turn dramatises the particular values of American culture at a specific historical moment. As another critic expresses it, 'the genre is inevitably transformed in Asian American literature because the Asian American subject's relation to the social order is so different from that of the genre's original European subjects' (Chu 2000: 12). There is a double historical process here: in *Mona in the Promised Land*, the central character is transformed by the process of growing up during a particular period in the history of the United States, but only as that history is imagined from the perspective of the 1990s, a decade with its own ideological priorities. Mona Chang is the American-born daughter of Chinese immigrants to the United States, and the account of her coming of age is fundamentally informed by a struggle between the values of her parents and the values of an emergent 1960s American multicultural society. In this novel, the conflation of the two genres (assimilation, bildungsroman) is augmented by the historical setting in the 1960s (as recreated from the 1990s), which also vitally shapes the circumstances of Mona's adolescence. It is partly this synthesis of formal and ideological narrative challenges that gives Jen's second novel its particular value.

Mona in the Promised Land begins by dramatising a symbolic fall for thirteen-year-old Mona, a fall into the knowledge of social class, of the opposite sex, and of the ethnic and national differences that will inform her whole life. It is 1968, and Mona's friend in junior high school, Barbara, tells her that 'To be popular, you have to have big boobs, a note from your mother that lets you use her Lord and Taylor charge card, and a boyfriend' (16). Mona's teenage susceptibility to this kind of peer pressure leads her into a relationship with Sherman, a Japanese boy with a very strong sense of his unique Japanese national identity, and one that is significantly different from Mona's American-born sense of herself. Sherman teaches Mona a history lesson: 'Atomic bomb dropped on only one people . . . The Japanese do not forget' (14). But Mona's Chinese-American mother also teaches Mona about the Second World War, 'She knows the Japanese were on the wrong side because they bombed Pearl Harbor' (15). Here is Mona's first dilemma about what it means to be fully or legitimately American, the old-world antagonisms carried over into the new world where becoming American means, partly, relinquishing cultural history. Mona is American-born, so of what value to her is a knowledge of this history? The question of the status of this historical knowledge to Mona's emerging identity is compounded by the question of her knowledge of boys: Mona has an adolescent crush on Sherman, and although she is made aware of important differences between them, she is also drawn to him because of the appearance of Asian similarities; she also befriends him simply because of high-school peer pressure. When Sherman eventually leaves the United States for Japan, instead of kissing Mona goodbye he unexpectedly floors her with a judo throw, and he accuses her of betraying him: 'You just want to have boyfriend to become popular' (21).

This is an important coming-of-age moment for Mona, a literal fall which dramatises an abrupt new knowledge of ethnic difference. Mona can adapt to becoming American, but Sherman retains a Japanese identity that resists Americanisation, and which he understands as very different from Chinese identity. This is Mona's first experience of the concept of 'switching' that will dominate her adolescence; it is a literal fall, one that sends her 'sprawling through the late afternoon' (21), into an abrupt new awareness that Sherman's poor English-language skills are not necessarily a sign of his naivety, and that ethnic affinities and differences are going to be the defining paradigm of her sixties American life. What Mona terms 'switching' will have its costs and limits; as Sherman says of her attempts at friendship, 'You will never be Japanese', (22; 82). The formative value of Mona's startling realisation here is emphasised by the structure of its representation; the account of the farewell scene with Sherman is interpolated with the scene in which Mona refuses to tell Barbara exactly what happened; she does this partly from embarrassment at her fall, and partly to show that she has already learned a valuable lesson about loyalty from her friendship with Sherman. The scene is thus managed retrospectively within the structure of the novel's first chapter, so that some coming to terms with experience seems to have been already accomplished. But the figure of Sherman returns throughout the novel like a repressed anxiety, to remind Mona of something that was never satisfactorily resolved, and the recognition of the power of otherness that he represents will haunt Mona throughout her life.

Following this experience with Sherman in chapter one, the novel skips forward two years and establishes its sixties credentials by reference to Polanski's *Rosemary's Baby*, to *Our Bodies, Our Selves*, and to Ken Kesey's 'Merry Pranksters'. Mona's emerging sense of identity as a fifteen-year-old is also situated in the context of struggles with the authority of her Chinese-born parents (Helen and Ralph from Jen's first novel *Typical American*), of her relationship with her Jewish friends Barbara and Seth, with her sister Callie who goes to Harvard, and with Alfred, the Afro-American employee at her father's pancake house. These relationships form the culturally diverse circumstances of Mona's coming of age, and they are all simultaneously conditioned by the novel's intense preoccupation with the nuances of social class that are presented here as being integral to a full understanding of American ethnicity.

For example, it is notable that despite being an American-born daughter of Chinese American immigrants, Mona appears not to recognise herself or her family as an ethnic minority; rather, she regards herself as part of her local Jewish community and not as an oppressed or victimised group. Blacks are the 'majority minority' (270), that is to say they are the first to politicise their social position, sometimes radically (as, for instance, in the cases of Eldridge Cleaver, Malcolm X), ahead of other minority cultures in the United States in the 1960s. For the black characters of the novel, this involves forms of social criticism that are regarded as un-American, especially by recent immigrants such as Mona's family who are eager to assimilate and who believe that conforming to established social values and demonstrating economic security are the most effective ways to become properly American. This is part of the challenging debate about what it means to be most legitimately American. The racial politics of the central chapters of the novel are far more important than its gender politics ('feminism' is a word not seen in the novel) and, in turn, racial politics is so intimately associated with social class as to be almost indistinguishable from it. This is all integral to the late 1960s counterculture identity crisis, in which new ideas about what is legitimately American can be explored, challenged, and developed, within the context of the coming-of-age genre. *Mona in the Promised Land* dramatises many different forms of cultural change, of various pressures on Mona's sense of identity: peer pressure, parental authority, and the culture of change germane to her historical moment. This synthesis of ideas about change is this novel's unique contribution to the coming-of-age genre.

Mona's conversion to Judaism might appear to be a superficial teenage gesture, but it is in fact an important part of her search for a structure of value that she hopes will give her ethical sense some social function and direction. Like Russell Banks' Bone, Mona is a teenager with a moral conscience, and, like Bone, she is in search of an appropriate cultural form in which to express her sense of social justice. This is precisely the ethical challenge which the commentators to whom I refer in the Introduction find lacking in the contemporary story of coming-of-age. Mona's conversion is in fact closely associated with, or indebted to, that moral sense which she has inherited from her parents during her childhood. As one critic argues,

> There is a notable historical parallelism between the Jewish and Chinese people, and between the Jewish and Chinese diasporas. In the United States, the Chinese are called the 'New Jews' because they seem to be living proof of the American Dream . . . Mona's conversion is not so outrageous: in becoming Jewish, she is reaching out for Chinese features she had not realised before. (Gonzalez 2001: 229)

The cultural paradigm here is characterised in terms of a struggle between some sense of ethnicity that can be termed 'authentic', and an ethnic identity that is created by the individual's story of American assimilation. Is the latter in some sense 'inauthentic'? The novel interrogates this question from a variety of perspectives in order to scrutinise the very idea of authenticity in the context of American identity. How, for example, is an American-born ethnic identity constituted as 'authentic', and from what sources is such an identity derived? These questions about identity in the 1960s are coterminous with Mona's search for some correspondence between her growing moral awareness and a social culture of equality, and it is in these terms that her coming of age is conducted.

The principal cultural difference that Mona experiences at a narrative level is a version of black America represented by Alfred and his friends. Mona's philanthropic impulse to help Alfred comes from an innate sense of the social injustice done to black people by the United States. The story of Mona's summer encounter with Afro-Americans is partly an examination of what the term 'racist' means; it is a shock to Mona's father Ralph that he can be accused of racism, let alone sued for it. In chapter twelve, Ralph is threatened with a law suit for racial discrimination as a direct result of something that Mona has said to Alfred about her parents' social attitudes. This threat is ultimately lifted, thanks to Mona's subsequent intervention, but not until her adolescent naivety has been tested: her mother tells her, 'You know where all the trouble started? All the trouble started from you become Jewish' (248). In fact, Mona's interest in Judaism is an expression of her desire for a cultural structure that articulates an ethical sense that must originate with the specifically Chinese values that her mother and father espouse.

Mona in the Promised Land is a novel with an almost forensic interest in dramatising the concept of change; Mona is not only changing from a child to an adult, but also attempting to cope with cultural change between the values of her Chinese parents and those of her American upbringing. Mona's relationship with Sherman tells her some important things about national identity, and about gender relations and social class. Mona's switching to Judaism is a further aspect of this dramatisation of the limits of mutability; it is also a form of peer pressure, from her Jewish friends Barbara and Seth, and perhaps also simply 'adolescent rebellion' (34). These forms of change are compounded and augmented by the great sensitivity to social class that is exhibited by this Scarshill community, and by Mona's parents' eager desire to fit in quickly and inconspicuously. Again, the late 1960s is a particularly appropriate historical moment to dramatise mutability because it has long been recognised by historians as a time of fundamental social rupture and upheaval. In *Mona in the Promised Land*, the changes of adolescence are situated in cultural and historical contexts that make the concept of the mutability of identity very sophisticated, complex, multiple, and diverse; the changes of adolescence are augmented by the principle of change in respect of every other aspect of identity. The coming-of-age genre is used as a vehicle for ideas about the coming of age of a culture and a historical moment in national identity, especially in terms of race relations and an emergent multicultural society.

This sense of a dynamic cultural environment, in which the individual's subjectivity is transformed by the pressures and opportunities of specific historical circumstances, is found also in E. L. Doctorow's *Ragtime*. This novel was published in 1975 and depicts the early years of the twentieth century; in many respects, however, and especially in its portrayal of militant Afro-American politics, it might be read as a creative response to the social pressures of the late 1960s. Indeed, as a novel that was written immediately at the end of that decade, it is difficult to interpret *Ragtime* as anything else. One of the epigraphs of *Mona in the Promised Land* is from Ovid, 'all things change', and Jen's novel shows how everything is part of a late 1960s culture of mutability, or what the novel terms 'a mysterious energy such as can turn one thing into another' (101). *Ragtime* also cites Ovid's *Metamorphoses* as an important literary expression of the principal of change, and in language closely reminiscent of Jen's, the narrator senses that 'the forms of life were volatile and that everything in the world could as easily be something else' (Doctorow 1985: 90). Both novels dramatise the radical transformation of subjectivity, and they use the idea of transformation to interrogate the idea of an original or authentic self. In *Ragtime*, for example, is not Baron Ashkenazy's emergence as a film industry entrepreneur, with the metonymic statement 'I have become a company', a travesty of the authentic Jewish socialist that he once was (Doctorow 1985: 191)? In Tateh's story, and many others in Doctorow's novel, the opportunities of change are placed alongside its costs and losses. Further, *Ragtime* demonstrates starkly how American society denies such opportunities to blacks because of their skin colour: Tateh becomes a film director, but Coalhouse Walker dies. *Mona in the Promised Land* is also keen to dramatise the limits of American self-fashioning: Albert makes this point: ' "And nobody is calling us Wasp, man, and nobody is forgetting we're a minority, and if we don't mind our manners, we're like as not to end up doing time in a concrete hotel. We're black, see. We're *Negroes*" ' (137).

For the Chang family, the desire to conform and to fully Americanise (principally through economic security) suddenly becomes, in the 1960s, an anomalous or anachronistic desire. The 1960s' anti-establishment zeitgeist is at odds with Mona's parents' determination to establish themselves as legitimately American. This critical approach to the United States' cultural identity (illustrated in part through Seth) is very disconcerting to recent immigrants like Mona's parents, Helen and Ralph. This non-conformity of the late 1960s becomes, to some extent, another kind of conformity, but it is one that is difficult for the Changs to judge and attune to; its apparently anti-American critical stance seems anarchic to people like Mona's mother, who has already experienced radical cultural upheaval in China. Seth, for example, is attracted to Mona for her difference, he calls her 'a regular Yoko Ono' (63), even while Mona herself is striving so conscientiously to be the same as him and his friends. Seth's intellectual questioning of American society is disconcerting for Mona, and even more so for her mother Helen, because it represents a desire for radical change where the Chang family seek security and social stability.

In the context of the novel's depiction of the politics of ethnicity, the figure of Naomi is as important as Sherman to Mona's coming of age. Naomi is Callie's roommate at college, and she introduces the Chang sisters to radical ideas about forms of American cultural identity, 'in this, our country the melting pot – no, mosaic – no, salad bowl' (129). Naomi encourages Callie to think more critically about her identity and her place in American society, 'She says we should stick to our guns, like the Jews' (41), and she helps Callie to reverse the process of Americanisation that was begun by Callie's parents; she encourages her to engage more fully with what it means to have a Chinese cultural heritage. To this surprising development in her sister's adolescence, Mona can only ask sardonically, 'And can Naomi teach me to be Chinese too?' (168). This idea of recovering a sense of identity, or more properly of American self-fashioning, is a talent that Naomi learned at an early age:

> Naomi herself claims for her ancestors a number of people not related to her – for example, Harriet Tubman and Sojourner Truth. These are famous people of whom Callie is just now learning. Luckily, another ancestor is Roberta Flack. Callie and Naomi attempt to discuss in Chinese what a moment it was for Naomi, seeing a natural on an album cover. (129)

Naomi creates for herself a sense of Afro-American cultural identity from those icons that she believes are most useful for her to appropriate, and, in so doing, she claims an intellectual and artistic heritage that becomes vital to her own sense of self-definition. This creative self-determination has always been part of Naomi's way of interpreting American personal freedom; she is characterised as a 'Renaissance woman' (169) who comes from a working-class family and has re-invented herself in order that she will not be the victim of American prejudice as regards either race or gender. It is interesting that the narrator's framing of Naomi's background takes the form of a rhetorical question, because it is perhaps suggestive of some narrative or authorial uncertainty: 'Is this what happens when you take a pom-pom girl from Chicago and set her to reading Lao-tzu in a fancy New England prep-school?' (168–9). To some extent the coming of age of Mona is shaped by the chance to 'invent herself the way Naomi has' (179), as much as it is by her political experiences with Alfred and Seth. Callie and Mona both learn from Naomi the potential of taking possession of one's identity at this particular historical moment, even if it is purely in terms of images. This process involves scrutinising closely the rules of the game, and of learning, occasionally, to be invisible: 'Naomi says Mona must learn to make herself invisible' (171). Naomi's ability to act out a role, to perform, is something that surprises Mona greatly: 'this is an aspect of Naomi that she literally has not seen before' (179). Blackness and invisibility have been associated at least since Ralph Ellison's *Invisible Man* (1952), but in Naomi's story of self-determination invisibility becomes empowering, an opportunity to be strategically covert, and this is an important part of her repertoire of performance.

Naomi is also a teenager, and her invention of herself within this particular late 1960s paradigm is a part of her unique experience of coming of age too, one that is more politically conscious than Mona's; this is why it is such a valuable foil to Mona's experience. Naomi's narrative of identity is a significant counterpoint to the ideas about the mutability of identity that are represented by Sherman (or the 'Sherman' figure as we should properly say). The novel suggests, paradoxically, that Naomi's identity is in some ways authentic, where Sherman's is an act or performance by Andy and Seth, even though Naomi's sense of identity is shown to have been constructed partly in terms of images. The very question of the authenticity of identity is thus central to Mona's adolescence; Seth himself argues that he is in the process of becoming an 'inauthentic Jew' (112), and Barbara points out that Seth's Jewish family 'didn't exactly hail from a shtetl in Galicia' (196). The impact of Naomi's ethos of self-definition is seen in the designation 'Callie/Kailan' that Mona's sister ascribes to herself as 'her original name' (302–3). Callie was born in the United States, but seeks to recover a sense of Chinese cultural heritage that was lost or renounced by her parents' cultural assimilation. The proximity of the compound form of this name to the form of the name that the novel gives to Mr Matsumoto, 'Sherman – Andy – Seth' (277), suggests again the multifarious aspects of 'authentic' identity. These compound names show that learning to dissemble is an integral part of American coming of age, and perhaps playing at being Jewish is a useful but temporary part of Mona's experience of growing up. What, after all, is the nature of Mona's real knowledge of, or commitment to, Judaism? One critic argues: 'It is the temerity of Gish Jen's approach, rather than her conception of the American identity per se, that strikes me as dazzlingly original. Jen's characters brazenly flout their prerogative to adopt or eschew ethnicities at their convenience' (Furman 2000: 226). This is true (with the exception of Sherman) but the novel also questions the degree to which such 'convenience' can be credited as truly authentic.

Another significant role model in Mona's adolescence is Rabbi Horowitz, and he too is subject to the novel's mutability theme. 'The Big R. H.', as he is known, begins the novel as an important authority figure for Mona, although an unconventional one, and he helps her to recognise that her interest in Judaism is partly 'adolescent rebellion' (34). But the Rabbi is fired for his unconventional views, and he disappears from the novel for eight chapters, only to turn up at Harvard, where he has re-invented himself as 'Dan' and acquired a wife and a new image. Significantly for the novel's interest in identity as performance, 'he is more theatrical than he used to be' (268). The Rabbi also has a more explicitly articulated personal philosophy, one that he has learned from his own experience of coming of age: 'It's not so easy to get rid of your old self. On the other hand, nothing stands still. All growth involves change, all change involves loss' (268). This statement goes to the heart of the novel, and is strongly reminiscent of Jen's choice of epigraphs from the *I Ching* and from Ovid. The gains and losses of change are dramatised in the novel's epilogue, where Rabbi Horowitz emerges again as 'the presiding authority' at Mona's marriage to Seth. Rabbi Horowitz is by this time married to Libby who is committed to women's liberation. Libby does not have to change her maiden name, however, because her maiden name is already Horowitz: 'and what was she going to do, change it to something else?' (297–8). The vital paradox here is that something appears to have changed, and especially to have compromised Libby's feminist politics, but actually no such change has occurred. The paradoxical nature of this use of the doppelganger is succinctly expressed by Dan: '*I put up with this Rabbi Horowitz like I put up with myself*' (298). The important point here is that where a crucial change appears to have occurred in the individual's politics, none has in fact taken place. This dramatises the elusive nature of the very concept of mutability with which the novel is centrally preoccupied: if mutability can be this enigmatic and mercurial, then how can any sense of personal identity be understood as 'authentic'?

Despite the novel's dispassionate third-person perspective, the anguish of Mona's growing up is not absent from the novel. For example, when Mona discovers eventually that the character called 'Sherman', to whom she has been speaking on the telephone, is not Sherman, but an act of mimicry by Seth and Andy, this is a complete revelation to her:

> Mona tries to keep her tone light. 'Ha ha ha'. She is not surprised to hear a skin of ice in her voice, though; and in a way, this is what breaks her heart, to hear her own bitterness. Bitterness – the very word so bitter to utter, what with that *b* and double *t*, not to say its associations: Decrepitude. Bunions. Gout. (276)

This moment of discovery about Sherman's identity (and simultaneously her own naivety) is also a crucial moment of language acquisition; Mona's knowledge of things in the world is here concomitant with a new and urgent knowledge of language. The linguistic peculiarity of the word 'bitter' recalls Mona's discovery of the silent 'g' in the word 'diaphragm' that she learns from reading Philip Roth's coming-of-age narrative

Goodbye, Columbus in chapter three. Mona's discovery is also reminiscent of the scene in which the Chang family discuss the semantic distinction between the words 'indigenous' and 'native' (41). Moreover, Seth comments directly on the structural importance of this revelation to the novel as a whole, characterising it as 'the big recognition scene' (277). Mona, however, is clearly ambivalent about how exactly this experience is supposed to constitute, for her, 'some kind of comedy' (277). This coming-of-age moment is particularly important to *Mona in the Promised Land* because it is one in which the novel's sense of its own generic affiliations is temporarily discomforted at the same time as Mona makes her disconcerting discovery. This is a further example of how the structure and technical features of the novel dramatise formally the coming-of-age experiences of its central character; at the point at which Mona is surprised out of her innocence, the novel itself experiences an identity crisis in which its formal conventions are disconcertingly shifted. This too is a formal innovation that is reminiscent of *Ragtime*, where the identity of the narrator, and his relation to the aesthetic of ragtime as a musical genre, has a vital shaping influence on the narrative form of the novel.

Although Mona discovers in chapter fourteen that the character on the Temple hotline calling himself 'Sherman' is in fact an act of impersonation on the part of Andy and Seth, this does not necessarily diminish the importance of the composite Sherman figure to Mona's coming of age. In chapter eleven especially, when Mona has lengthy telephone conversations with 'Sherman' (who we subsequently discover was Seth at this point) his disquisitions on the nature of national identity do have an important bearing on Mona's changing sense of identity. The comments that are made here, about the nature of social responsibility in different national cultures, are fundamentally important to Mona's moral awareness, and even an integral part of her appropriation of Jewish culture. It is during these telephone conversations that Mona begins to articulate a new sense of herself, and begins to feel that 'she almost does not know who is this Mona Chang' (234). Mona also articulates to the man on the telephone her pervasive sense of homelessness, that feeling of 'what it's like to be not Wasp, and not black, and not as Jewish as Jewish can be; and not from Chinatown, either' (231). While 'Sherman' distinguishes between American and Japanese in terms of their respective sense of civic duty, Mona is led to ponder how the Chinese and Japanese 'are as opposite as their geographies' (236). Sherman tells Mona about the Japanese word 'honne', which he defines for her as signifying 'the world of true feeling, and intimacy – the world without words' (236), which is akin to the Chinese word 'xiu'. These further valuable lessons about language complement Mona's reading; this includes Sinclair Lewis' *Babbitt* (229),

James Joyce's *Dubliners* (69), and the moral fiction of George Eliot and Jane Austen, which she finds especially valuable because 'those were people who knew what was right' (121). Mona's subjectivity is constituted in the synthesis of these different linguistic idioms, and her novel is partly an account of the significance of language acquisition to the processes of coming of age.

The importance of the telephone conversations to Mona's developing consciousness is not diminished by the subsequent revelation of Andy and Seth's impersonation. In fact, it serves to emphasise their value, not only to Mona but to Andy and Seth too, who are also teenagers at this point, and yet who find Sherman's Japanese identity relatively easy to impersonate. As Seth says of Andy's mimicry, 'it was weird how much he liked having an alter ego' (276). An alter ego can be a valuable vehicle for personal development, especially in a diverse and dynamic culture, and alter egos, like doppelgangers and name changing, are endemic in this novel. 'Sherman' is part of Andy's coming of age too, an experiment in successfully mimicking the language of the father: 'his father is a Japanese expert' (276). This is why Sherman's ideas are from a book, because thinking about difference, and its relation to a specific linguistic idiom, is one way to become fully American. The 'Sherman' character that Andy and Seth create is, for them, an important act of the performance of the self, and this does not diminish its impact on Mona, nor its value as 'play' to their own coming of age. Mona unwittingly confirms the value of such play when she runs away to Harvard and hides in her Sister Callie's room. Her mother calls, and Mona pretends to be Callie; the success of this ruse further demonstrates the ways in which Mona's coming of age is informed by a conception of subjectivity as a kind of performance. Further, the mutability of the performance is emphasised by Callie's mother's expression of anxiety about her daughter's experience of growing up at Harvard: 'Is she turn something else while she is there?' (264). Performance is part of the repertoire of experience that is integral to coming of age. But the concept of change, although pervasive, is not always as easy to interpret as it might appear. The most significant realisation that Mona experiences when she loses her virginity is that it changes no one. Libby Horowitz has not changed her name at marriage. Most importantly, in terms of racial politics, not everyone can choose to change in the ways that Mona tries to. Barbara gets a nose job, but Albert and his friends will always be black. The ability to recognise and interpret change correctly, is a form of cultural language-acquisition that is as important as learning to read.

Mona in the Promised Land uses the coming-of-age genre to dramatise debate about what is culturally sanctioned as legitimately American, and about what the words 'legitimate' and 'authentic' might mean in a particular historical and political context. To what extent can an individual citizen retain a strong sense of their native culture, or assert its difference from the dominant culture, and yet still be accepted in the United States as American? What is the origin, value, and status, of the concept of an origin here, and what efficacy does such an origin have for American-born citizens? *Mona in the Promised Land* suggests that the social conditions of the 1960s permitted examination of these ideas about national identity in new ways, and, for Americans who came of age in that decade, that political freedom became an integral part of their social conscience. This dynamic was still germane in 1996 when *Mona* was published. Although Jen's first novel, *Typical American*, was published during the 'relatively multi-ethnic 1990s' (Grice 2002: 205), it is a novel that returns to the Cold War 1950s to interrogate the origins of late twentieth-century American multiculturalism. *Mona* was also published in the 1990s, and its return to the historical circumstances of the 1960s is a fundamental aspect of its attempts to examine the coming of age of late twentieth-century multiculturalism.

The novel's epilogue shows a strong desire to bring the narratives of its characters to some form of resolution; here, the sudden temporal shift (a close formal parallel to the one between the novel's first and second chapters) has the effect of putting Mona's coming of age in a new perspective, and her experience of adolescence becomes subordinate to her new responsibility as a parent. Mona's relationship with Seth, and especially the birth of their daughter outside the sanction of marriage, has alienated Mona's mother, and, as a result, they have not spoken to each other for many years. In the meantime, however, Mona has learned from Aunt Theresa a new understanding of her mother as a young woman who was once very much like herself, 'a young woman not sure what mattered' (299). This fresh appreciation of her mother is augmented by a new recognition of Mona's sister:

> She says she's proud to be Asian American, that's why she's using her Chinese name (her original name, she calls it). But what in the world is an Asian American? That's what Ralph and Helen want to know. And how can she lump herself together with the Japanese? The Japanese *Americans*, insists 'Callie/Kailan'. After what they did during the war! Complain Ralph and Helen. (301–2)

Callie's parents are appalled by her historical amnesia, but Callie is an American-born second-generation product of the cultural politics of the 1960s who has learned, partly from Naomi, that modern American ethnicity is created by means of appropriation and performance. This too is the legacy of *Ragtime*, which ends with the image of 'A bunch of children who were pals . . . a society of ragamuffins' (Doctorow 1985: 236). This image might be a fiction, a fantasy of harmonious multiculturalism, but it is one which becomes, through its compelling representation, an integral part of the mythology of the United States.

This is Mona's cultural heritage too; on the eve of her marriage to Seth she considers changing her name, and her husband's, to 'Changowitz'. The wedding is a further opportunity to celebrate the principle of change, but it is tempered by Mona's new sense of adult responsibility, and so the novel draws short of depicting Mona's marriage. The novel's conclusion also omits Naomi and Sherman, but their legacy for Mona is very strong. Seth's impersonation of Sherman becomes an integral part of why Mona finds him attractive, even to the extent that one critic argues 'Mona does, in fact, get married to "Sherman" after all' (Lin 2003: 57). Sherman's adherence to an idea of ethnicity that is emphatically not performative is itself finally absorbed into the politics of American multiculturalism. The novel's final scene is a coming-of-age epiphany which is as important to Mona's development as anything that occurred in her adolescence. The final reconciliation with her mother, '*until death do us part*' (304), is a crucial aspect of Mona's moral education as an adult, and one that dramatises the ethical responsibility of mother and daughter's commitment to each other.

Chapter 3

Citation and Resuscitation

Both of this chapter's novels are dedicated to dramatising the profound long-term consequences of experiences that occurred in adolescence. In particular, traumatic experiences such as bereavement are shown to be impossible to overcome, and to have lasting effects that resonate well into adulthood. These novels offer adolescence as a defining moment, but in ways that are never satisfactorily resolved. For these adult protagonists, the failure to come to terms with adolescent experiences has resulted in an adulthood characterised by atrophy, arrested development, and pathology. These conditions in the protagonist are then given a sense of national significance by the ways in which both novels show the individual to be symptomatic of a moribund culture. Both novels are also strongly characterised by their attempts to contextualise their protagonists in terms of an analysis of recent American culture: the paralysis of adolescence is a symptom of a paralysed culture: Moody's Hex is 'stalled between consonants', and the narrator of Eugenides' novel is similarly transfixed by adolescent experiences that have traumatised him. Further, both novels seek to locate the origin of this contemporary malaise in a specific historical moment, that is to say, they identify a point in the history of the United States in the late twentieth century at which the contemporary predicament began. It is this cultural and historical analysis that gives these two novels their distinctive value.

Both of these novels are also broadly postmodern in the way that they problematise ideas about knowledge, epistemology, and representation. They both ask: what can be known about the past, how is it known with any degree of certainty, and to what extent is that knowledge predicated on a language that might be untrustworthy? The efficacy of forms of historical enquiry is thus called into question. In trying to address the processes of coming of age, both novels are acutely conscious of simply creating another language of adolescence that is not itself exempt from the forms of criticism that they bring to the language of history. These novels are also characterised by the self-consciousness and irony that they bring to this problem. In this respect, both novels are characterised by a particular aesthetic style, one which calls attention to its own forms of artful contrivance; these are novels that are often self-regarding and self-advertising, because their knowledge of themselves as texts is part of the problem that they seek to address. The novels are therefore formally static, pausing at obsessive length over brief temporal periods that seem in retrospect to have acquired disproportionate significance. This is their vision of coming of age: anguish, loss, and a neurotic preoccupation with points of origin that are curtailed, but for which there is no remedy.

Jeffrey Eugenides, *The Virgin Suicides*

Jeffrey Eugenides' first novel, *The Virgin Suicides* (first published 1993), is an account of its narrator's fascination with the five sisters of the Lisbon family, each of whom commits suicide while still a teenager. The novel is set in suburban Detroit in the late twentieth century, and the narrator remembers vividly how, as an adolescent, he was held in awe by the five Lisbon girls. The novel attempts to reconstruct an image of the girls, and in doing so it tries to understand what they meant to the narrator and why they died. The narrative is deceptively slight: Cecelia Lisbon commits suicide inexplicably at the age of thirteen, and her parents become increasingly protective of their other teenaged daughters. The girls are permitted one unchaperoned date, as a group, but Lux Lisbon does not observe the 11.00 p.m. curfew, and all of the sisters are subsequently confined to the house by their parents. On the anniversary of Cecelia's earlier suicide attempt, the four remaining Lisbon sisters encourage the narrator and his friends to rescue them from confinement, but on the brink of escape that night, all of the girls commit suicide. Mary Lisbon survives briefly (for three months) before killing herself just over one year after the death of her sister Cecelia.

The novel's unnamed narrator has devoted himself to detailed research into the circumstances and motivation for the girls' self-destruction. The novel is largely an account of this research, recalled by a narrator who is now an adult, ransacking his memory of events that occurred twenty years earlier. *The Virgin Suicides* is a catalogue of the fruits of this research. In this respect it is important to recognise the novel as both a search for a point of origin and a historical explanation. The narrator looks back to his own adolescence and tries to understand the circumstances that brought about the Lisbon girls' deaths. Simultaneously he tries to express a sense of the power that his memory of them has on his imagination, because it is a power that he has not yet come to terms with. The novel thus becomes a monument to its narrator's attempts to come to terms with his memory of adolescence. The year of the girls' suicides has become a defining moment, for the narrator, the community, and perhaps even for the nation. The girls die in adolescence and the narrator's own adolescence is crucially marked by their deaths in ways that continue to shape his adult life and consciousness. Thus the novel attaches a special significance to adolescence as a defining period: the girls are remembered forever as teenagers, and the narrator's adult life is crucially affected by his memory of his time with them and his postmortem enquiries. *The Virgin Suicides* seeks to define a specific historical moment, one that has an explanation that can be recovered and comprehensively known and documented. In this search the narrator expresses above all the need for manifold forms of knowledge of the past.

Although the novel begins with the death of the last Lisbon sister, Mary, it quickly turns back to the death of the first, Cecelia, and even then not strictly to her suicide but to her earlier unsuccessful suicide attempt. This temporal structure is characteristic of the whole novel: it begins with a dramatic event, and then tries to trace back and to recover the circumstances that led to that event, and, beyond that, the historical conditions that brought about those circumstances. The contemporary American coming-of-age novel is often aetiological in its search for origins: it goes back in a process of historical enquiry that recedes beyond the horizon of its protagonist's knowing. This process is particularly valuable because it defines an epistemology while simultaneously scrutinizing the efficacy of that epistemology. This is a process that creates a document of historical analysis, the novel, which then stands as an historical record in its own right, a finished or accomplished aesthetic record of a search for a legitimate historical beginning. This search for a satisfying origin begins again and again in the contemporary American coming-of-age novel; almost every search ends in the full knowledge of the inadequacy of searches, every methodology results principally in an understanding of the limits of methodologies.

The original question for *The Virgin Suicides* is why does Cecelia commit suicide? The narrator does not know, he can only assemble the evidence as best as he can from a distance of fifteen years. Cecelia was the youngest of the Lisbon sisters; in response to the incredulity of the doctor who patches her slit wrists, she says, '"Obviously, Doctor . . . you've never been a thirteen-year-old girl"' (Eugenides 1994: 7). What clues to her suicidal world-weariness can the narrator find? Her death might be associated with her sense of the brevity of the lives of the region's fish flies, or to a response to the virgin Mary, or even that it was, in her own words, 'a mistake' (21). It is possible that Cecelia jumped from her window in imitation of Dominic Palazzolo, a teenager who made a dramatic gesture of jumping from the roof of a house when his beloved Diana left the neighbourhood for Switzerland. All of these theories compete with each other for our attention and are variously discredited. For example, Cecelia's diary comments on Palazzolo's gesture, 'How stupid can you be?' (33). On the only occasion that the narrator ever heard her speak Cecelia was just thirteen years old and he was 'surprised by the maturity of her voice' (29). There might be a clue here that is more credible than others. After her suicide attempt, on the advice of a doctor, Mr and Mrs Lisbon throw a party for her. This party is chaperoned. In radical opposition to the parties that the narrator is more familiar with, parties of 'musical vomiting' (27), it is possible that the strictly circumscribed conditions of her parents' leniency are the final straw for a thirteen-year-old girl who is more mature than her parents allow. We cannot know definitively if this is the reason for Cecelia's second, successful, suicide attempt, but there is other evidence in the narrator's account of the past that lends this idea credence.

For example, although Mr Lisbon is a teacher at the high school that his daughters attend, he is characterised not in terms of his authority but of his emasculation. Mr Lisbon is 'boyish'; he has a 'high voice', and the narrator can easily imagine 'his girlish weeping' (8). At the party for Cecelia, Mr Lisbon 'opened his tool kit', and he plays with these symbols of masculine endeavour as if they were symptomatic of his impotence, until 'his lips grew moist' (28). When the narrator is conducting his enquiries many years later, he discovers that Mr Lisbon is now divorced, and he tells us that Mr Lisbon admitted that he felt occasionally overwhelmed and oppressed by his daughters' combined femininity, even to the point where he 'longed for the presence of a few boys' (23). As the significance of his daughter Cecelia's suicide sinks in, Mr Lisbon recedes into the background, and when he is later spotted by the narrator 'he had the sheepish look of a poor relation' (62).

Mrs Lisbon is consistently remembered by the narrator in terms of her control over her daughters, and her mortifying presence strictly regulates the girls' appearance and behaviour. Mrs Lisbon is characterised in terms of her 'rectitude' (120) and her 'surveillance' (117), even to the degree that she will not permit the television channel to be changed until the *TV Guide* has been consulted 'to judge the program's suitability' (84). Mrs Lisbon has forbidden women's magazines such as *Cosmopolitan*, and even the bookshelves are 'bowdlerized' (124). Lux Lisbon is compelled by her mother to destroy her rock music because of its subversive and licentious potential (143), and all of the daughters attend their only 'date' dressed, at their mother's design, in 'identical shapeless sacks' (118). Mrs Lisbon's punitive vigilance is such that this occasion is 'the first time she had allowed the girls to go out' (135). Mr Lisbon explains that the household is governed by 'certain rules' that cannot be changed, and 'even if he wanted to his wife wouldn't let him' (113). So extreme is Mrs Lisbon's need to govern her daughters' liberty that even when Therese dies, and is carried out of the house on a stretcher, Mrs Lisbon utters the single word command, as one might to a dog, 'Stay' (218).

It is difficult for the narrator to know, from his limited perspective, why Mrs Lisbon is like this, or for the reader to trust entirely his partial presentation of her. At one point the narrator observes that the family photographs 'virtually cease about the time Therese turned twelve' (229). Therese was the eldest of the sisters, and she was seventeen when she died. As the eldest, Therese would have been the first to experience menarche, and it is possible that the onset of puberty at the age of twelve was coincident with Mrs Lisbon's most extreme exercise of control. Many years later, when the narrator interviewed Mrs Lisbon at a bus station, he finds that she is still baffled as to the reasons for her daughters' suicides; nevertheless, she makes a comment that might be revealing: 'Once they're out of you, they're different, kids are' (143). This 'difference' from the parent is difficult, perhaps impossible, for Mrs Lisbon to come to terms with, especially as her daughters become women. It is possible that her daughters' emergent autonomy as teenagers was something that made Mrs Lisbon fearful, and that her response to that fear was a severity of control which was disproportionate or even neurotic. If this is true, then it might help to explain the significance of the idea of difference in the novel. Mr and Mrs Lisbon, for example, are 'leached of color, like photographic negatives', in opposition to their five daughters who are seen as 'bursting with their fructifying flesh' (8). The sometimes voluptuous and sumptuous abundance of the girls' vitality is radically different from the austerity of their mother, with her 'brutally cut steel wool hair' (8). Moreover, the idea of difference is a powerful component of the way that the girls are presented to the reader; the narrator's infatuation with them, and his distance from them, makes it often difficult for him to distinguish between them. For example, at the party for Cecelia when the narrator first gets to meet the girls personally, he registers his sudden surprise that the Lisbon girls 'were all different people', and not, as he had previously believed, 'five replicas with the same blonde hair' (26). At the novel's second party, when the narrator and his friends meet the four remaining sisters, 'the boys weren't even sure which girl was which' (122). At the ensuing dance 'the Lisbon girls looked identical again' (132). Mrs Lisbon is responsible for the girls' appearance, for the unfashionable dresses that 'homogenized them' (122), but even Cecelia's diary makes the five different daughters appear as a uniform group:

> Cecelia writes of her sisters and herself as a single entity. It's often difficult to identify which sister she's talking about, and many strange sentences conjure in the reader's mind an image of a mythical creature with ten legs and five heads. (42)

This is partly a function of the narrator's desire, a desire that informs everything in the novel; nevertheless, that the Lisbon sisters should be undifferentiated even in Cecelia's diary is very surprising. It is perhaps indicative of Cecelia's profound feeling that the girls are simply not permitted to be different, from their mother or from each other. This denial of difference, of individuality, leads to a despair that is suicidal. Cecelia is the daughter by whom this sense of the undifferentiated is most strongly expressed, and she is the first to commit suicide.

The girls' desire to be different is associated with their emergent personalities as young women. As a boy, the narrator cannot understand 'why the girls cared so much about being mature' (43), but he does recognise that the daughters were already in some respects 'women in disguise' (44). This sense of maturity is also confirmed by Cecelia's diary, 'an unusual document of adolescence', because it reveals a maturity beyond her years: 'The standard insecurities, laments, crushes and daydreams are nowhere in evidence' (42). Again the intervention of Mrs Lisbon is partly to blame for the denial or repression of this emergent maturity; her exaggerated response to her daughters' burgeoning sexuality is a violent prohibition: 'Mrs Lisbon had soaked her things in Clorox, bleaching all the Kevins out' (43). This image of bleaching is reminiscent of the image of the Lisbon parents as 'leached of color like photographic negatives', and it suggests that Mrs Lisbon is the agent of a mortification that is sometimes pathological.

Once again the novel is in search here of an origin and an explanation that lies just beyond the limits of its narrator's knowledge; again, the form of his enquiry is as important as its subject. It is impossible to determine whether Mrs Lisbon's austerity and denial are solely to blame for her daughters' unhappiness, or whether simply the narrator's baulked desire for the girls finds a convenient satirical target in the dominant parent's authority. For example, it is possible that Mrs Lisbon's regime of prohibition is an aspect of her religious faith; Mrs Lisbon is a regular church-goer, one who denounces the practice of cremation as 'heathen', and is able to support this belief by reference to 'a biblical passage that suggested the dead will rise bodily at the second coming' (36). Mrs Lisbon disapproves strongly of dances and proms in the conviction that they lead inevitably to teenage sex, and she is an avid fan of the kind of church music that is characterised principally by its banal piety. Cecelia, who dies with a picture of the virgin Mary clutched to her chest, dismisses such music as 'that crap' (136).

The testimony of Trip Fontaine is especially valuable here because he is the only one of the neighbourhood boys to have direct personal experience of the girls, and a relationship with the most seductive of them, Lux. Trip is the product of an unconventional family upbringing that is very different from the Lisbons': his mother is conspicuously absent, and his father is gay. Trip gives the appearance of having crossed the rubicon of adolescence, 'of having graduated to the next stage of life' (77), and he is sexually experienced in ways that distinguish him from the narrator as having undergone a 'transformation' (69). Trip loses his virginity in Acapulco to a thirty-seven-year-old Las Vegas croupier who takes him in hand; it is a teenage initiation that changes Trip fundamentally, and it is imagined by the narrator in an image that is significantly maternal: 'We looked on it as a wonderful initiation by a merciful mother' (71). Women then, are the guardians of sexual knowledge, and it is by admitting boys to this knowledge that boys become men. The word 'merciful' is evidence of women's bounty, of their power to bestow, but also of their quasi-religious connotations. Virgin Mothers, however, are perverse in their sexlessness: 'No one could understand how Mr and Mrs Lisbon had produced such beautiful children' (8). An austere virgin mother who advocates abstinence, or who does not interpret sex as the proper means to attaining male masculinity, is one who is feared and stigmatised by adolescent boys. By withholding sexual experience, women can thus prevent boys from coming of age in the only way that the boys recognise or understand (or have been taught by their male elders). Mrs Lisbon's parental anxiety about raising teenaged girls is therefore augmented by a religious doctrine that the narrator regards as pernicious. The Virgin Mary epitomises this, and images of her are a constant motif in *The Virgin Suicides*. The greatest antagonism is reserved for the mother who will not permit access to sex; as Kevin expresses it, 'The old bitch had locked them up again' (139). These views are sanctioned by the entirely male community of the novel, its collective 'we' is a group of boys whose ideas about relationships are inherited from the sexism of 'our fathers, brothers and uncles', who tell them that 'no one was ever going to love us because of our good grades' (69). Once again here the novel's real subject is epistemology; sex is interpreted by the narrator as a form of knowledge that he needs to experience in order to become a man, and the virgin deaths of the Lisbon sisters are a catastrophic and calamitous failure of knowledge that has scarred him for life.

One consequence of this is a paralysis and inertia that is often gothic in its exaggeration. The Lisbon house in which the girls are confined becomes 'one big coffin' (163), an edifice that collapses around them in ways that are symbolic of the atrophy and degeneration of their adolescent vitality. The Lisbon house becomes a darkly romantic symbol of a corrupt and disordered subjectivity that is permitted no outlet, and which disintegrates slowly as a result of the disease within. Here the novel inherits a nineteenth-century mythology of ruined cottages and derelict homesteads, where stagnation is symbolic of morbid and pathological states of mind. Tennyson's 'Mariana' for example, is trapped in a moated grange, paralysed by the absence of her lover, and repeating a death wish among rotting fruit and marish mosses that threaten to overwhelm and suffocate her. On Eugenides' suburban American street, the Lisbon house is conspicuous for its 'moss blackened windows' (186), and its gothic shadings and overtones are so strong that 'Bats flew out of the chimney in the evening' (88). Meanwhile, Mr Stamarowski (from Poland) stands on his balcony next door in a black turtleneck like a latter-day Dracula:

> At sunset he let us roam his big lawn, and once in the flower bed we found a dead bat with its face of a shrunken old man with two prize teeth. We always thought that the bats had come with the Stamarowskis from Poland; they made sense swooping over that sombre house with its velvet curtains and Old World decay. (89)

Further, the Lisbon house begins to emit a smell that pervades the neighbourhood, and Paul Baldino interprets this as the odour of 'trapped beaver' (165). Other evidence that it is specifically the prohibition against physical movement, of liberty, that ails the Lisbon house, comes from Trip, who tells the narrator: 'You would have killed yourself just to have something to do' (84), and from the girls themselves, who complain at one point, 'we just want to live, if anyone would let us' (132).

These characterisations of the Lisbon family by the narrator and his friends reveal as much about them as it does about the girls. Looking back on the suicides from a distance of twenty years, the narrator is himself paralysed by the memory, as much stuck in the moment of his adolescence as the girls were frozen by death in theirs. His collection of ninety-seven exhibits amassed in 'five separate suitcases' (246), is still held as a monument to their mourning in a 'refurbished treehouse' (246), which is as incongruous as the Lisbon's gothic entrapment and suffocation. The narrator's interest in the girls is extraordinarily fetishistic, an often prurient desire to objectify and commodify through the accumulation of tokens by which the girls can be known. The collection of exhibits becomes a 'strange curatorship' of artefacts and icons that is symptomatic not so much of the girls as it is of the boys' desire to know and to possess them. In this respect, the novel is principally a depiction of a particular kind of adolescent male desire, one in which its unrivalled intensity is as morbid and pathological as the supposed causes of the deaths themselves. This desire has a prurient focus on the female body, for example on the tampon 'still fresh from the insides of one of the Lisbon girls' (10), on the documents of Lux's gynaecological exam that include a photograph of 'her rosy cervix' (155), and on the Lisbon family thermometer, which was discovered to be 'oral, alas' (228). These fetishes are deeply revealing of the narrator's own paralysis and pathology, one that is shared by, shaped by the other boys: Joe Conley for example: 'Nearly two decades later, the little hair he has left remains parted by Bonnie's invisible hand' (134). Adolescence remains the defining moment for these boys, as much as it is for the Lisbon girls who died when they were teenagers.

The morbid internalising of these anxieties about knowledge and the body find expression in one of the novel's most significant moments:

> On a regular basis we're forced to explore with clinical detachment our most private pouch and, pressing it, impress ourselves with its anatomical reality: two turtle eggs bedded in a nest of tiny sea grapes, with tubes snaking in and out, knobbed with nodules of gristle. We're asked to find in this dimly mapped place, amid naturally occurring knots and coils, upstart invaders. We never realised how many bumps we had until we went looking. And so we lie on our backs, probing, recoiling, probing again, and the seeds of death get lost in the mess God made us. (170)

Here we see the narrator searching for the seeds of a disease that is deeply embedded in the fabric of the body, its potential fruitfulness somehow gone wrong, and the adult narrator's awareness of mortality bringing about an anxiety that cannot be alleviated. This forensic self-examination is carried out with a clinical exactness and detachment but is nevertheless inward-looking in ways that can only serve to heighten his anxiety. The focus, too, is specifically on that part of the body that makes him a man; his sense of mortality is closely associated with his gender, just as the Lisbon girls' suicides are associated with being female. The authority of forms of knowledge is also important here: the self examination is carried out at the recommendation of doctors, but their ability to know is deferred to the authority of God, the original maker of the body, and therefore beyond the secular, human limits of knowledge. Here the narrator expresses, perhaps inadvertently, a paradoxical but nevertheless close affinity with Mrs Lisbon, in her association of sex and death and religion. It might be proposed that in this scene the authority of doctors and of God is also in competition with Mrs Lisbon's authority as a guardian and with the narrator's authority as the character who author- ises this particular narrative of adolescence. The narrator shares a vestige of a religious faith that he recognises in the authority of Mrs Lisbon, and her authority as a mother clashes with the writer's claim to knowledge. Gradually, images of the Lisbon girls begin to fade 'no matter how reli- giously we meditated on them in our most private moments' (186).

The narrator's use of 'we' gives the novel's enquiries a general currency for the depiction of male sexuality; the novel is a depiction not simply of a lone aberrant individual, but of a community and a culture. The fact that the novel is set in suburban Detroit is also important in this respect. As it broadens the scope of its commentary beyond the immediate neigh- bourhood, the novel searches for contributory factors that include the decline of the automotive industry, the pollution of Lake Erie (234), and the migration of people from what became known as the rust belt, to places like Florida and the American south west, or sun belt. The novel is set during the period of 'extensive layoffs at the automotive plants', when many families suffered under 'the tide of the recession' (93). This was a period of serious economic decline and transition in the region, when, 'our last great automotive mansion was razed to put up a subdivision', and when, 'after deserting the city to escape its rot' (245), families also deserted Detroit's affluent Grosse Pointe in a mass exodus that was closely associated with the new industrial competition that General Motors faced, especially from Japanese car manufacturers. In this context, the explanation for the suicide of the Lisbon girls that is put forward by the high-school English teacher acquires some credence: Mr Hedlie 'put the whole thing down to the misfortune of living in a dying empire' (231). This empire is the empire of American heavy industry, and the identifica- tion of this industry and American national identity is made at Alice O'Connor's debutante party: 'People said our industry was coming back, our nation, our way of life' (236). It is also worth noting that the histor- ically strong Catholic population of Detroit went into serious decline post 1991, and that a crisis in Detroit's heavy industry is understood by the narrator as being concurrent with a crisis in faith.

In opposition to the (terminal) decline of American heavy industry, to the stagnation of the manufacturing recession of the 1970s, the narrator envisages escape, and the novel is consequently full of images of flight. The alternative to dereliction is to abandon that which has failed, and to begin over again in a new place. It is perhaps revealingly American that something as historically recent as the decline of the American auto industry can be regarded in a contemporary novel as a kind of Old World atrophy, and that its response to this development is not renovation but abandonment. Here again the adolescence of the Lisbon girls acquires a national significance, because it is as if the youthful energy of American life must always seek out new opportunities and horizons, and its native restlessness must not be inhibited. In this respect the novel presents the very identity of the United States as adolescent; it is a nation whose dynamism is principally a function of its youthfulness. The American answer to a project in serious decline is to flee, to escape, and to begin again elsewhere. For example, the narrator expresses a yearning for 'the pure, free desolation of back roads we didn't even know yet' (212), a romantic desire to escape history and to pursue the unknown frontier, fresh fields and pastures new. When Mr and Mrs Lisbon leave the suburbs 'they drove away. Fast. Got the hell out' (241). Mrs Lisbon's mother, the Lisbon girls' grandmother, has already moved away, to New Mexico, and she tells the narrator that 'the best thing I ever did was get out of that town' (144); she moves not simply to the American south west, but specifically to Roswell, a town that is notorious for having been the site of an alleged visit from the final frontier, outer space. Even here, and at her mature age, she admits the ways that adolescence permanently determines one's life: '"You never get over it", she said, "But you get to where it doesn't bother you so much"' (144).

The Virgin Suicides is a comic study of the ways in which innocence can be understood, where the narrator's methodology is indicted as much as the historical circumstances of the girls' deaths. The search for origins and for original innocence becomes a morbid project that only reflects the serious emotional anxieties of those who cling to a belief in Eden. At what point was the Lisbon household, or the narrator, or the United States, ever really innocent? The forensic analysis of such questions reveals principally the anal nature of those who investigate them; innocence becomes a projection of the narrator's fear of loss, absence, and death. These too are subjects that cannot be definitively known, only speculated upon and worried over. But the desire for a knowledge of innocence comes from the fear of mortality, and it is from that conflation of fear and desire that *The Virgin Suicides* is created.

Rick Moody, *Purple America*

Rick Moody's *Purple America* (first published in 1997) is a dramatic account of one weekend in the life of Hex Raitliffe, a thirty-eight-year-old man who lives at home in Connecticut with his severely disabled mother Billie and his stepfather Lou Sloane. Hex's father died when he was a child, and the gradual deterioration of his mother's health has led to his increasing responsibility as a carer for her. Billie's illness is now sufficiently serious as to bring her to the verge of despair and even to suicide; she longs to release herself from dependency on others and her son from a role which has circumscribed his freedom as a young man, and she appeals to Hex to end her life. At the same time, Lou Sloane has reached the point where he can no longer cope with the demands that he feels Billie's illness make on him. On this particular weekend, Lou abandons Billie and Hex and, forced to accept early retirement, he flees towards a new life. However, a serious incident at the nuclear power plant where he worked summons him back, and Lou begins to realise that he cannot simply run away from responsibility. Hex, meanwhile, encounters a woman named Jane Ingersoll on whom he had a crush in ninth grade, and he now embarks on a brief but intense relationship with her. The family situation reaches a crisis as Hex tries to suffocate his mother with a plastic bag, 'the logo [covering] her eyes so that he doesn't have to look at them' (280), and when this fails, he takes up an antique shotgun which he turns upon the now repentant Lou. The novel ends as the police arrive, and Hex escapes on foot across a neighbouring golf course and into 'the irradiated waters of the Long Island Sound one Saturday in November just after dawn' (295). *Purple America* is a black comedy on these subjects, pursuing the anguish and entrapment of its major characters with uncompromising acuity while also offering historical glimpses into how this particular situation arose in the first place. It is a novel about the travesty of coming of age, of innocence gone badly awry, and it offers a vision of modern American history that tries to account for this contemporary malaise. In particular, *Purple America* is a search for origins and a dramatisation of the crucial importance of adolescence.

The fiction of Rick Moody has shown a consistent interest in the subject of adolescence from *Garden State* (1992) to *The Black Veil* (2002). It is in adolescence that Moody dramatises important points of origin that come to define the unique predicaments of adulthood. Not only does Moody's fiction locate adult problems in the experiences of adolescence, but it is often marked stylistically by an intense self-consciousness which is also characteristic of teenagers' struggles to define themselves as individuals. For example, in *The Ice Storm* (1994), the teenager's voice is used in the first-person to frame an omniscient narrative and to provide a vital personal element to Moody's otherwise clinically dispassionate social satire of the early 1970s. *The Ice Storm* is a form of coming-of-age novel where the teenager's journey over a single weekend gives an adolescent intensity to the narrative. This temporal compression (often characteristic of the modern bildungsroman) is also a notable feature of *Purple America* as it dramatises the predicament of adults who are 'stalled', and whose lives are revealed to have been crucially determined by childhood experiences that are impossible to overcome. Both *The Ice Storm* and *Purple America* are novels about paralysis and death, and they use adolescence as an origin myth that has both personal and national significance. But where *The Ice Storm* is notable for its use of both first-person and third-person narrative voices, *Purple America* abandons the idea of a unified narrative voice altogether in favour of something much more complex in its linguistic ingenuity. *Purple America* is characterised by a radical self-consciousness about the language of narrative voice, and by a formal self-reflexivity that acts as a commentary on the novel's multiple, Joycean languages, even to the point of anticipating critical paradigms that might be used to interpret it. One of the vital formal questions that *Purple America* asks is where does a novelist find the authority beyond existing linguistic structures by which to challenge authority? Simultaneously, *Purple America* is concerned with situating that crisis in a specific national narrative (the emergence of nuclear power) in order to facilitate much wider social and political analysis of the contemporary United States than the bildungsroman might usually allow.

Purple America is a novel about crisis and failure, especially failing powers of speech and crises of articulation; it sets out to provide a historical account of the domestication of nuclear power, while simultaneously offering a disquisition on the ability of language to speak about such things, and to create an aesthetic artefact from them; *Purple America* is a novel that self-consciously asks 'how did we get here?', and that question is directed both at technology and at the language that might be used to articulate the history of technology. Most of all, the novel parodies a variety of linguistic registers that it clearly deems to be redundant or trite, and it sets them alongside other forms of creative language by way of evaluative comparison. In this respect, *Purple America* is a form of metafiction, deploying a range of linguistic styles as part of the wider aesthetic strategy of asking of itself 'what is the appropriate language with which to speak of these subjects?' It is a novel that comments on its own linguistic identity, and self-evaluation is an integral part of its parody of those linguistic registers that it deems to be exhausted. In 1967 John Barth argued that 'exhaustion is just an invitation to administer artificial resuscitation to the apparently dead' (Barth 1967: 32), and *Purple America* is a novel that takes up this invitation and constitutes itself from it. The idea of exhaustion is central to the drama, narrative, and theme of the novel, and central also to a concern about the nature of its own aesthetic style.

Such postmodern pre-emption was already a convention when *Purple America* was published in 1997, and it is a narrative strategy that is integral to the genre of metafiction. Moody is the inheritor of a very considerable metafictional legacy here, the canon of which goes back as far as Gaddis's *The Recognitions* (1955), and which might briefly include the fiction of Nabokov and Donald Barthelme, Barth's *Lost in the Funhouse* (1968), Coover's *Pricksongs and Descants* (1969), Sorrentino's *Mulligan Stew* (1978), and Philip Roth's *The Counterlife* (1986). These novels, among others, had already made narrative self-reflexivity a familiar feature of innovative American fiction. Moody's novel is the inheritor of this particular formal genealogy, a legacy of works that discover ingenious ways to anticipate and to internalise the methodologies of critical inquiry. The aesthetics of metafiction have received a lot of attention, both from novelists and critics. In particular, metafiction has been defended against Tom Wolfe's charge that its characteristic strategies 'are merely decadent forms of self-absorption which deprive the novel of significant energy' (Currie 1995: 17). Mark Currie has argued that a definition of metafiction as a borderline discourse between fiction and criticism 'gives metafiction a central importance in the project of literary modernity, postmodernity and theory' (Currie 1995: 2). Metafiction's value is that it derives a creative energy from its internalisation of critical practice. Simultaneously, of course, metafiction can be seen to valorise the practices of those who would seek to interpret it. Metafiction endorses and promotes the importance of the critic's role and the critic's professional skills. Although metafiction has been around at least since *Tristram Shandy* (1759–67), it has a heightened value now, it has been argued, because in the postmodern period 'the most authentic and honest fiction might well be that which most freely acknowledges its fictionality' (Hutcheon 1980: 49). Metafiction's paradoxical 'authenticity' consists of its readiness to advertise itself as fiction, to make a narrative virtue of self-analysis. In the late twentieth century particularly, this willingness to concede the constructedness of texts led to a profusion of metafictional experiment, and attention from critics who were informed by post-structuralist theories of the problem of language's referential dimension. If it is true that 'metafiction has enjoyed an international boom' (Hume 2000: 286) it is because writers in the vanguard of creative innovation have been alert to those changes in the humanities contemporary with the advent of post-structuralism since the late 1960s. Post-structuralism's recognition of the contingent nature of all linguistic genres and modes (that paradigm shift or fundamental change in value attendant upon new theories of the textually-determined world and the structures of representation), suddenly gave self-reflexivity a special importance as a creative quality. Post-structuralism (among other things) radically problematised the relationship between knowledge and language; in an infinitely textual world, what metalanguage can speak competently of that which we profess to know? Is self-reflexivity the only reflexivity that is possible or credible? Critical self-analysis has led to a valorisation by critics of the same strategies at work in contemporary novelists. It has been argued, for example, that Philip Roth's fiction dramatises the belief that 'the test of novelists' worth is the degree to which they can challenge their own beliefs and expose them to destruction' (Wheeler 1999: 19). Has creative textual self-annihilation become a measure of value since post-structuralism, or is self-conscious fiction the only fiction that critics can applaud since post-structuralism? Metafiction will always be important because it can be read as an account of the practices and problems of interpretation. The question then becomes, what contribution does *Purple America* make to the lexicon of self-reflexivity, and how does the novel constitute itself aesthetically while speaking about itself evaluatively?

Part of the answer to this question is that the novel contextualises the practice of self-interrogation in the historical period of the advent of nuclear energy, thus attempting to redeem what might otherwise seem a solipsistic enterprise. Self-referentiality might then be understood as more than simply the means by which the aesthetic product advertises itself as a commodity and be seen as part of a political as well as a formal legacy. Moody's novel shows how the Cold War made a significant contribution to that change in attitudes to language which metafiction set out to explore and exploit. In a sense, it is an attempt to historicise is own postmodern aesthetic, and that effort is one of the things that makes *Purple America* such an ambitious novel. Simultaneously, *Purple America* is another novel in the line of American end-of-innocence narratives that goes right back to the birth of the nation; it is a national bildungsroman that posits the discovery of the United States' nuclear capability as a decisive coming-of-age experience. The depiction of Hex's adolescence is coterminous with the advent of both nuclear energy and the aesthetic innovations of metafiction, and this convergence of coming-of-age narratives gives the novel's depiction of innocence a particular value.

The problem of the appropriate metalanguage with which to approach metafiction is compounded by the novel's black humour. *Purple America* is a gothic fiction: visceral, monstrous, and pathological; it functions within the broad parameters of American gothic with a canny self-consciousness about the linguistic peculiarity of its own literary inheritance. Further, many of its central narrative characteristics conform uncannily to gothic conventions. The novel visits scenes of horror and lurid spectacle with a black humour that seems to acknowledge its own literary belatedness. The novel feasts on the past, and it seems to know that feasting is what the gothic does best. In *Love and Death in the American Novel*, Leslie Fiedler formulated an outline of an American gothic tradition that characterised it as having a penchant for 'transcending the limits of taste and endurance', a particular attitude to the past as 'something lapsed or outlived or irremediably changed', and an interest in 'certain special guilts' that are quintessentially American (Fiedler 1966: 118, 115, 127). These gothic conventions are singularly characteristic of *Purple America*, and they might lead us to conclude that the novel is a contemporary parody of the gothic, or even a gothic parody of the gothic. But how is it possible for the novel to speak in such an idiom, and what is the value of its generic self-consciousness? By what aesthetic strategies does the novel speak about the difficulties of finding a language in which to speak?

The idea of speech is a crucial issue from the beginning of *Purple America*. The novel's first chapter is a rhetorical tour-de-force of four baroque sentences, structured by the word 'whosoever' and framed by the phrase '*he shall never die*' (Moody 1999: 3). The novel begins by calling attention to itself as a linguistic conceit, by speaking uncompromisingly of shocking subjects in an outrageously self-advertising style. Simultaneously, this opening chapter is packed full of questions about the nature of aesthetic judgements, and these questions make the reader's judgements about the style of the novel a central issue. Further, the novel's anxiety about its own style is matched by that of its characters, embroiled in a 'drama of anguished communication' (9) in which Billie's voice is replaced by the technological incursion of Handispeak with its vocabulary 'culled from one of those inferior college dictionaries' (12). Billie's loss of the power of speech has an analogue in her son's stammer, which the text reproduces typographically, so that while the drama of her approaching speechlessness is enacted, he can only ask her '*Is there something you want t-t-to say?*' (14). Hex's contribution to the care of his mother is represented in terms of the failures of communication; he strives 'to anticipate her needs, to prempt her need for words, to eliminate a language based on need, and thus to eliminate language' (9). Hex's stammer is a further dramatisation of the failure of powers of speech; his nickname is coined because it reduces his real name, Dexter, to a one-syllable sound that 'was easier for their boy to pronounce' (35), and which signifies both his ineptitude (Hex means curse) and the fact that he is the victim of a disabling legacy. This name Hex is his father's 'last word' (35), and Hex's anguished exclamation at witnessing his father's death 'never did amount to a word' (35). Billie's written request to die is printed out and signed, with a graphic 'X', and she appeals to her son to end her life at that point in the future 'when I'm no longer able to communicate' (56). In a scene that dramatises the suppression of speech, Billie's last will and testament is used as scrap paper to light the fire, and chapter seventeen of the novel ends with the poignant image of her final request going up the chimney in ashes. The failure of the ability to communicate is a central narrative theme of *Purple America*, and it is pursued with remorseless energy through every detail of the text. Simultaneously, the novel is anxious about its own ability to find a language in which to express itself appropriately, and to articulate a contemporary aesthetic from the failures of communication and the deteriorations of style that it regards as endemic to this contemporary America.

The novel's depiction of the difficulty of summoning the power to speak is analogous to its own ethical and aesthetic concerns about the best way to write about difficult subjects such as nuclear accidents and multiple sclerosis. Part of the novel's response to this issue is to offer a plethora of styles, registers, and idioms (and there are dozens) that compete with each other and challenge the reader's criteria of aesthetic judgement. *Purple America* is a novel in search of an appropriately contemporary creative language, and an aspect of that search is its parody of exhausted languages and styles. The baroque style of the first chapter is another aesthetic response to the degeneracy of outworn idioms that is parodied throughout the novel. The text derives its energy and wit partly from its ironising of exhausted languages as well as from its determination to discover and articulate an aesthetic style that does justice to contemporary life. The novel's forensic interest in questions of aesthetic judgement gives rise to a pattern of citation and resuscitation in which the novel's critical evaluation of its own language becomes a central feature of the text. Some of the novel's most acute comic moments derive from our recognition of empty language; Hex's phoney desire for fatherhood is expressed in ersatz diction: 'He would like to lavish his surfeit of feelings on her adorable little naysayers, would love to be called *Dad* by some moppet who refuses to do any kind of chores' (236). The language of Hex's father is similarly lampooned when he tries to give his young son some advice on courtship: 'You are a ladykiller, fella, and don't forget it. They'll fall at your feet. Your day will come. They'll want what you have. Don't worry about the lean years' (33). With the burden of empty rhetoric like this, it is not surprising that Hex approaches Jane with questions such as '*what k-kinds of international c-c-c-cuisine excite your p-p-palate?*' (130), and the banality of his conversational gambit is matched by Jane's deployment of 'blowoff codes' (130) that are equally learned from fatuous sources. Lou Sloane's narrative is similarly impeded by his entrapment within an empty rhetoric of romance and masculinity: his return to Billie and his determination to 'win her back' is as ludicrous and bathetic as the trite fantasy of escape by which he erroneously believes himself to have left her. Lou's telephone message ('I know some things about myself now, some dark things', 284) is an empty cliché by which genuine self-knowledge is emphatically impeded. Worse still, Lou lacks the critical self-consciousness that might help him to discover a more authentic sense of himself: 'He doesn't know where he gets these commonplaces' (284). These hackneyed and mendacious idioms have an invidious and corrosive effect on the acts of communication that they inhabit, and the satirical impulse of the novel shows how they contribute to the characters' profound loneliness and isolation. Billie's plight is given a general currency thanks to the bankrupt nature of much of the characters' language: '*Oh, Hex, I am alone*' (15).

The metafictional analogue here is the novel's determination to speak uncompromisingly of difficult subjects as a way to preserve its readers against the debilitating effects of trite platitude, for example in the paragraph in chapter eight, which begins with a parody of the rhetoric of Manifest Destiny and ends with the ludicrous exclamation 'Save the West! Eat a burger!' (81). It is not simply the language of the novel's characters that is haunted by redundant idioms but the language of national identity too; the omniscient narrative perspective is likewise profoundly anxious about its narrative ability to find a register that is not already outmoded and outworn, and it often takes refuge in acts of ventriloquy that treat a wide range of social and professional idiolects with irony, and in so doing dramatise a profound loss of faith in language's communicative ability. Thus the novel mocks the language of interior design, Sunday school instruction, medical discourse, and police bureaucracy ('with the perpetrator or other inhabitants residing therein' (287)). Although the local effects of this are often comic, their cumulative effect strongly suggests the corrosive disintegration of the efficacy of language as a medium. The narrative dramatises the serious human isolation that is a consequence of failures of communication. None of these is as interesting *in itself* as the way that they cumulatively compete for the reader's attention, and thereby engage us in a process of critical evaluation of languages. As with all good metafiction, the central subject of the novel becomes the interrogation of the status of language itself. It is not just Billie who is stranded by the deterioration of communicative media, but this whole contemporary culture. But what metalanguage might enable readers to discern an aesthetic hierarchy in the novel's styles, or does its plethora of styles constitute an aesthetic in its own right, perhaps one that might be designated 'an aesthetics of the gothic sublime' (Martin and Savoy 1998: 9)?

Since Joyce and Beckett, this strategy is reasonably common in serious fiction, but in Moody's novel it is traced back to the corruption of language that occurred during the Cold War, and with Spencer Murphy's promulgation of the rhetoric of Eisenhower that was contemporaneous with the advent of atomic weapons. In other words, the loss of faith in the language of the father that is dramatised by Allen, is given a national resonance by the specious propaganda of the Cold War. In this way, both fathers, Allen and Lou, are contaminated by their proximity to forms of corrupt and degraded language that they pass to future generations with the dubious gift of the technology of new forms of energy. This is partly how *Purple America* gives its metafictional disquisition on the importance of coming of age a specific political target, and is careful to redeem itself from formal solipsism. The accident at the nuclear power plant (significantly called 'Millstone') is therefore integral to the novel's social satire. This whole industry is characterised by incompetence and failure: 'Misfits and idiot savants, coveters of weapons-related data, fundamentalists, borderline personalities, potsmokers, people who fell through the cracks of a franchise-fuelled economy; these were the guardians of the atomic age' (105). These guardians are not trustworthy, but for *Purple America* that is not as important as the way the powers of language have deteriorated through irresponsible use. The Code Two Unusual Event of the novel, so closely reminiscent of the Airborne Toxic Event of DeLillo's *White Noise* (1984) with its emphasis on spectacle and representation ('This day would be written about' (104)), is an 'event' in terms of narrative drama, but also an occasion for disinformation and the mendacious public relations spin of managers like Stanford Warren who need to 'keep a tight rein on who's talking' (102). Moody makes an explicit connection between this accident and the first strike detonations of Inter Continental Ballistic Missiles (111), but also between the contemporary language of the media and the national rhetoric of the Cold War. Both are characterised by the novel in terms of corruption, duplicity, and mendacity, and so *Purple America* traces the crisis of language back to this crucial coming-of-age moment when the word of the fathers was depleted of its communicative efficacy.

This interpretive paradigm suggests that, in terms of a psychoanalytical reading of *Purple America*, Hex's absent father leaves him feeling responsible for the care of his dying mother, and this crisis of parenting is fundamentally important to both Hex's coming of age and the novel's aesthetic legacy. Hex witnessed the death of his father while he was trying to pronounce Hex's name, and this trauma is the origin of Hex's stammer. The death of his father leaves Hex searching for a language that will help to authorise his narrative. The son's predicament is also the consequence of his father's technological legacy, and it is no coincidence that while Allen was involved in atomic tests the step-father Lou is implicated in the accident at the power station which threatens to devastate southeast Connecticut. Thus the sins of the fathers are visited upon the sons; the novel's last sentence articulates this inheritance as 'crimes', and the novel's final utterance is the letter 'A', the (scarlet) letter standing at the beginning of the alphabet that signifies the father's name, Allen. Dexter's own middle initials, A. A., satirically remind us of his disabling alcoholic dependency. Thus the name and the word are the novel's points of origin. It is significant too that the accident is the result of corrosion, because according to *Purple America* the corrosive deterioration of language in history is the most heinous crime that fathers are responsible for.

The father is present in *Purple America* in the texts of his letters and in the text of his obituary, which he wrote himself and in which he lied about everything 'even his own middle name' (64). This obituary is a bogus personal history that dramatises the duplicity of American self-authorship. Like Jay Gatz, Allen is a mid-westerner who 'left his parents behind' (64) and systematically reinvented himself to disguise the nature of the activities that made him who he was. The obituary is a public document that exposes Allen as 'a liar and a fraud' (64). Paradoxically, it is the national importance of his work 'in the south west' (The Manhattan Project at Los Alamos, New Mexico, in 1945) that makes it necessary for him to invest in the fiction that 'his roots were entwined with the origins of the nation' (64). These public deceits are essential to protect the secrecy of the real story of modern American coming of age, the making of atomic weapons. Allen is complicit in this deceit, but he is also the victim of its authoritative rhetoric. His real history is articulated in the two private letters to Billic from 1946, in which he immediately confesses to difficulty in communication: 'this is hard to write but I'll do my best' (70). The history of the accident and its far-reaching consequences for the contemporary United States is the secret history of the novel, a history that has been silenced: 'the censor, who's made an exception here, reminds you to destroy this' (72). Allen's letter of three months later, the text that ends the novel, is offered posthumously 'in the hopes that it'll explain a thing or two later on' (296). Thus the novel presents a conflation of the American national coming of age, the language of the father, and the transmission of contamination through bogus rhetoric. It is from precisely this aesthetic and political conflation that the novel wrestles its own artistic identity, and it does so in the shadow of the gothic genre to which it knows such a conflation to be integral. The psychoanalytical struggle with the authority of a father's language thus extends to the novel's own knowledge of itself as a gothic text. The impossible question that the novel posits here, as with most metafictional novels, is what is the horizon of its knowledge of itself? Can there be an aesthetic language above and beyond the knowing self-reflexivity of metafiction by which *Purple America* can articulate something individual that escapes the suffocating dominance of its parental geneaolgy?

The answer lies in the novel's depiction of Hex's coming of age. Hex is paralysed in history: his sexual encounter with Jane takes place in the bunkbed of his childhood where it replicates the 'mammalian procreative posture' (122) that he learned from the surrogate fathers listening to Frank Zappa in 1967. In psychoanalytical terms it dramatises his inability to take possession of the mother: 'Jane Ingersoll is polite enough, or queasy enough, not to mention the symbolism of Raitliffe's request, but she's alert to it . . . She'll be immobilized. Paralyzed' (205). This sexual moment is starkly revealing of Dexter's entrapment: without an authoritative language of the father, history for him can only be a regression to points of failure where he can repeat the past, but not conquer it and progress to adulthood; he is 'stalled between consonants' (134). This psychoanalytical interpretation is consonant with the novel's political satire. Hex's step-father Lou is the willing victim of deceitful public rhetoric; his willingness to subscribe to the public account of the accident entangles him in a form of public relations discourse ('the physics of spin', 98) that corrodes his integrity and implicates him in a disabling narrative. Lou, 'a skimmer of techno-thrillers' (20), is also in search of a language that can do justice to his contemporary predicament. Lou's note to Billie, 'your poverty has tired me out', is a further expression of that sense of exhaustion that is endemic in the novel, thematically and linguistically. The function of CEO Spencer Murphy's language here is to dramatise the pressure on individuals of coercive public discourse, especially when it is underwritten by the rhetoric of national progress: 'Ike said it best don't you think, "Moving out of the dark chamber and into the light"' (47). This connects the Eisenhower administration (1953–60) with Allen's letters as the central satirical target of the novel, but it is their forms of language that interests the novel most.

When Lou finally speaks about his relationship with Billie it is a solipsistic leakage: 'he can hardly believe it when it starts coming out, the language of his marriage, a ten-foot swell, past the mechanisms that stifle talk' (221). It is significant here that Lou thinks he is talking to himself because this momentarily facilitates a freedom from the commonplaces of social dialogue that enables him to speak honestly. In this struggle to get beyond the exhausted language of cliché, Lou confesses himself to be, like Hex, infantilised: '*not like a man ought to be . . . but like a child*' (222). Thus, the novel's critique of logocentrism and its interest in the female body are part of the same analytical agenda: 'whosoever knows the folds and complexities of his own mother's body, *he shall never die*' (3). The mother's body takes the place of the lost word of the father as the guarantor of meaning in Moody's contemporary America. As we learn of Hex's intimate contact with his mother: 'He can't resist the opportunity here for *knowledge*' (5). It is significant that these forms of psychoanalytical and historiographical interpretation are also integral to theories of (American) gothic. But is it possible that the novel knows this and is it haunted by the narrative practice of gothic haunting? The intensely solipsistic nature of the question is inevitable because of 'the incipient or tacit "gothic" preoccupations of a variety of poststructuralist theories' (Martin and Savoy 1998: viii). Further, it is hardly surprising that a psychoanalytical interpretation seems plausible, because as one critic has argued 'Freudian theory and Gothic sensations are "homologous realms" of discourse' (Williams 1995: 94), or, as another writer succinctly expressed it: 'psychoanalysis is a late gothic story' (Kilgour 1995: 221). This is more than a question of metafiction then, but of the problems of reading a novel that is so paradigmatic that it seems to outrun the critical apparatus by which we would interpret it.

The problem with the theoretical paradigm does not lie with its appropriateness to the novel, but with the value of the paradigm itself. *Purple America* strives towards a vision of American coming of age that is expressed in a metafictional semiotic, and the origin of this semiotic can be seen in the crucial representation of Hex's adolescence in chapter eleven. Here, in the 1960s, two beatnik decorators function temporarily as substitute authority figures, following the death of Hex's father. They suggest to Hex a radically different lifestyle from the values of his mother. It is a formative moment, one of 'initiation' (the word is used twice), a coming-of-age moment for Hex, but also for national history, 'the lost Eisenhower years' are pushed aside for an era of social ferment; Hex's bow ties and tweed jackets are suddenly incongruous in a time when, as Frank Zappa put it, 'Brown Shoes Don't Make It'. The importance of this chapter lies in the ways that it reveals the degree to which Hex is 'stalled between consonants' (134), a belated adolescent who is 'initiated into the derangement of senses' (126) that becomes the fundamental condition of his beleagured adult life. This chapter of the novel dramatises a key moment in Hex's adolescence that he has never really outgrown: in the experience of the Vulcan Forge he hears a voice '*like the g-g-g-guy who p-p-p-played the v-v-v-voice of G-god in the T-ten C-c-c-commandments*'

(126) and, although this is only a disembodied voice from a movie, it has a sudden compelling authority for Hex in the absence of the voice of his father. It is here, and only here, that Hex's stammer temporarily disappears, because his proximity to an authoritative male voice (even such an ersatz one) temporarily relieves him of the anxiety that causes his impediment: '*without stammering. A miracle!*' (127). This adolescent flashback is the vital point of origin in *Purple America*, one that complements the other key scene from Hex's childhood in which he witnesses his father's death (in the house of God) while his father was struggling to pronounce Hex's name. The Lacanian Name of the Father is substituted for the voice of God in 'The Ten Commandments'. This chapter's depiction of adolescence is crucial to *Purple America*: the girl he dotes on is Jane, and the lower mammalian procreative posture that the beatniks mimic is the one that Hex will assume with her twenty years later in the very bunk beds that they are assembling (they make the bed he lies in). Simultaneously, the novel is characterised by forms of ventriloquy in which the idea of a single unified voice has gone; the voice of God is a mere disembodied echo, distant, attenuated, ersatz, and somewhat comic, but it is the absence of a single authoritative narrative voice that paradoxically facilitates the 'contemporary eclectic' (115) which is the novel's formal hallmark. John Barth's call for narrative 'resuscitation' in 1967 is coincident with the novel's reference to Frank Zappa's *Absolutely Free* (also 1967); this neatly situates Hex's formative exposure to youth culture at precisely that historical moment when the aesthetic legacy of *Purple America* was burgeoning. Important ideas about the nature, status, and authority of 'voice' are given an origin in the 1960s, and are therefore contemporaneous with the very moment of the origins of the novel's own creative matrix.

The novel's most obtrusive stylistic device is undoubtedly its use of italics; they are often used to parody redundant language, to make readers pay attention to certain linguistic forms, and to emphasise their ridiculousness. Italics give us a heightened awareness of diction and locutions that are trite, banal, or clichéd. This is certainly how David Hollander interprets Moody's use of italics: his excellent coming-of-age novel *L. I. E.* (2000) deploys italics in exactly the same way, and his novel is dedicated to Moody. But this is not their only use in *Purple America*: sometimes italics signal a shift to interior monologue, sometimes they designate reported speech (in lieu of inverted commas), sometimes they serve as a form of emphasis where no satirical intention is clear, and sometimes they are used in all of these ways simultaneously as if to challenge our ability to interpret the purpose of their use. This might be very frustrating as a reading experience, but italics are one of the ways in which readers are drawn into a critical engagement with the text. The novel encourages readers to identify a creative unity and consistency in the use of italics, but their value lies in diversity, multiplicity, hybridity. This is a playful aspect of the novel's drawing attention to its own formal properties, and that strategy is integral to the business of metafiction. This can be interpreted as ludic or irritating depending on one's sense of humour: compare Paul Auster's use of his own name in his fiction, or even anagrams of his own name, as in the character called Trause in *Oracle Night*. To some extent the novel's use of italics can also be understood in terms of Jameson's theory of pastiche, a formal illustration of postmodern narrative's entry into 'a field of stylistic and discursive heterogeneity without a norm' (Jameson 1991: 17). Further, italics could be regarded as part of the novel's theme of technological contamination, an effect of the technology of contemporary writing media that infects the language of the novel like a virus; it is a technological malfunction, a formal invasion of the text by the keyboard functions made available by contemporary writing technologies.

As a signifying practice, italics function in a similar way to the use of purple in the novel, and there is a certain affinity of structure in the way that italics and purple are used as integral aspects of the novel's interest in aesthetic issues and in forms of hermeneutic engagement. For example, in terms of the semiotic of *Purple America*, the excessive or hyperbolic tendency of purple prose is seen often in the novel's evident delight at the infinite resourcefulness of language, which is itself an attempt to resuscitate a degraded aesthetic for contemporary uses. Purple prose is a disparaging term for over-elaborate writing, but in Moody's novel the baroque is made to work as a counterpoint to the exhausted. The style of the novel occasionally indulges in excess and hyperbole, in an elaborate linguistic showiness that is dramatically self-advertising, such as using three words where one would suffice: Kowalski's eggs are 'zesty, tasty, savory' (214), lovers are like 'primates, anthropoids, prosimians, protohominids' (200). The novel's ironic deployment of incongruous registers is part of its evaluative linguistic strategy, and its passages of purple prose demand aesthetic judgements of the reader while simultaneously showing everything post-Joyce to be a function of the style that expresses it. Paul West would probably concur; in an article called 'In Defense of Purple Prose', he argued that it represented 'the world written *up*, intensified and made pleasurably palpable, not only to suggest the impetuous abundance of Creation, but also to add to it by showing – showing off – the expansive power of the mind itself' (West 1987: 47).

To adopt the obvious metaphor here, everything in the novel knows itself to be 'colored' by the language that expresses it, and shades of purple contaminate the novel's three central characters: Lou's suitcase is 'royal purple' (16) and Hex has an eye injury that is 'swollen and purple' (270), but principally the colour is associated with Billie who has purple pom poms (128), a purple welt (88), purple wrapping paper (11), a fondness for '*colors in the purple family*' (25), and something that her son characterises as 'this dumb obsession with purple' (124). It is significant, then, that the origin of the colour in the novel is with man-made technological interference with nature: when Allen describes the accident at the lab in 1946, he writes 'It was a prompt burst . . . blue at first, anyway, and then a lavender color' (71). This is the incident in which Allen and his colleagues are dangerously exposed to radioactivity for the first time, and they have to be isolated immediately: 'It was the loneliest feeling I've ever had' (72). Allen's second letter also makes this association between the colour and atomic energy: 'The sky was luminous and gray and violet while all this swept over us. We were fifty miles away with the whole sky the color of purple' (297). Further, the interior of the club that Hex and Jane occupy has 'purple vinyl booths' (240), and it is here that the novel makes its most direct statement about the importance of purple: 'it's the color of monarchs, of the gods, the color used to trip up Agamemnon' (240). This is an allusion to the Greek myth in which Agamemnon, returning home from the Trojan wars, is seduced by the solicitous welcome of his wife Clytemnestra; she spreads for him a purple carpet (literally 'sea-red'), and he accepts her invitation not knowing that it will lead directly to his death. Purple becomes for this novel the colour of hubris, of duplicity, and of death: America, having purpled the skies with the most apocalyptic detonation known to mankind, has become, and continues to be, self-polluted, the victim of its own vengeful contamination. Having taken the genie out of the bottle, the fathers of contemporary America have bequeathed to future generations a murderous purple fall-out.

Further, it is tempting to speculate whether the word 'of' in Allen's phrase 'the whole sky the color of purple', was added to disguise the locution 'the color purple' and, therefore, direct allusion to Alice Walker's novel of 1982. In both novels the precise significance of the colour is less important than its function as a signifying system, because in both novels purple denotes an ethical and aesthetic quality that is multiple and diverse: 'I think it pisses God off if you walk by the color purple in a field somewhere and don't notice it' (Walker 1985: 203). Shug Avery's pantheistic doctrine is only part of a wide variety of uses that the colour is put to in Walker's novel: it is the colour of sex, the colour of black African skin, the colour of bruises (Allen too describes 'this bruise in the sky'), but above all, Shug's injunction is to engage and to participate. Moreover, *The*

Color Purple dramatises the transformative capacity of aesthetic forms in the processes of historical and political awareness: in Walker's novel, Folkespants, the blues, the epistolary novel. It is hard to imagine that a novel as erudite as *Purple America* could be unaware of *The Color Purple*, and it is likely that Walker's use of purple and its variant shades is a further aspect of Moody's knowing and playful textual indebtedness.

To conclude with a synopsis of these arguments: the practices of metafiction, the conventions of gothic, the device of italics, and the semiotic of purple, all of these are signifying practices, and the novel comprises itself of them even while it interrogates their value, and this is what makes the novel such an ambitious and challenging text. *Purple America* thus dramatises the predicament of a metafiction that seeks to create something new from its own intense self-consciousness while simultaneously operating at the limits of representation where even its attempt to historicise contemporary language failure knows itself to be merely a function of the linguistic protocols of historical narrative. The novel uses Hex's adolescence, and the significant failure of his coming of age, to dramatise a vision of a contemporary origin that is both political and artistic. *Purple America* thus places itself self-consciously in the context of a literary or aesthetic line, parasitically feeding off the past to keep itself going. Pollution, disease, contamination: these central themes have their aesthetic analogue in the novel's generic legacy. The novel's critical interrogation of a variety of signifying systems is a remarkable aesthetic response to the status of metafiction in the late twentieth century, one that enables it to articulate something of both formal and social significance while retaining a sense of creative self-reflexivity in the face of mendacious American languages.

Chapter 4

Language Acquisition: Life Sentences

The coming-of-age novel is a reasonably well-established genre with certain conventions and characteristic habits that have been in evidence at least since Twain's *Huckleberry Finn*. Some contemporary novels are aware of this heritage and constitute themselves in part by negotiating a relationship with existing forms of narrative language that are perceived as having the power to shape their own story at a fundamental level. These are novels that ask: how can I create an individual voice that does sufficient justice to my story but in forms of language which are already written and which I can only appropriate? These are novels that acknowledge that the story of the self can only be conducted in a language which is to some extent prescribed. An awareness of this issue, and a willingness to confront it directly, makes this chapter's two novels particularly compelling and innovative. These novels manage to conduct an analytical commentary on the form of the narrative while telling their respective stories, and this makes them both particularly subtle and sophisticated interpretations of the genre. Further, these novels are also characterised by a form of journey narrative that has gone wrong. Conventional ideas about the journey of self-discovery are refuted by baulked narratives of loss, failure, and defeat. This feature in turn becomes central to each novel's particular form of social criticism. Coming of age here is simply not possible, or at least traditional ideas of personal fulfilment and social integration in this genre are refuted by the very conditions of the different American societies that they represent.

In addressing these specific challenges, these novels create the unique voice of their respective first-person protagonists. In both novels, that male voice has a particular interest in the body of the mother; these are male narrators who find ways in their respective texts to acknowledge that the mother is crucial to their identity and their aesthetic formation as voices. In both cases this interest in the mother emerges partly as a consequence of, or in relation to, a deeply patriarchal society. For these novels, the very idea of creative language, of speaking, of self-expression, is related to the mother in ways that are fundamentally important. Both novels are marked by the male protagonist's sense of possession by the mother, or of the mother, and this is in direct opposition to the predominantly male environment in which they find themselves. Both novels end with a symbolic death in which the authentic voice of the narrator is subsumed by the environment and by an adult culture that is mortifying. In this respect they both offer forms of social criticism that are particular to their region.

Scott Bradfield, *The History of Luminous Motion*

Scott Bradfield's *The History of Luminous Motion* (1989) is the first-person narrative of Phillip Davis, a seven-year-old whose parents have separated. Phillip's mother has fled the marital home taking Phillip with her, and the novel is Phillip's account of their nomadic existence in various towns along route 101 in southern California, living in motels and eventually resorting to petty crime to survive independently of Mr Davis' financial support. 'Mom' has a brief relationship with a man called Pedro, until Phillip attacks him and mother and son return to the highway. Eventually Dad tracks down his wife and son and the family is briefly reunited. Mom is now pregnant, and Phillip spends much of his time with his new friends, Rodney and Beatrice. But once again Phillip's resentment that his relationship with his mother should be interrupted by a man leads him to attack Dad, and this attack is severe enough to warrant Phillip's confinement in a California correctional facility for juveniles. The novel ends with Phillip, now aged eight, briefly revisiting the house he shared with Mom before Dad's return and experiencing a moment of epiphany. These narrative events are subordinate to the revelation of Phillip's psychological development, but some important aspects of the novel emerge from this synopsis, principally the closeness of Phillip's attachment to Mom and a corresponding hostility to male adults who intervene in that relationship. Further, through the separation of his parents, Phillip is exposed to radically alternative versions of the world and of history that Mom and Dad represent to him, and this division, firmly based on gender, is very difficult for the child protagonist to reconcile. The real drama of the novel takes place here, in the protagonist's awareness that his understanding of things in the world is dependent upon his knowledge of the different languages that are used to represent the world to him.

The History of Luminous Motion is thus an account of Phillip's child-hood as an autonomous human subject but also as a child who is uniquely alert to the ways in which he is the subject of languages that are already spoken when he enters the world; Phillip must learn these lan-guages in order to articulate that sense of self which is the traditional ground of the genre. Phillip begins to learn that these languages (that are anterior to his emergence as a subject), are languages that define him, both in terms of how he is able to understand his world and how he is able to express himself. Phillip learns too that these various languages are not innocent. In other words, this is a novel of the drama of language acquisition. This is a difficult and complex subject for a coming-of-age novel, and the work's ambition lies in its attempts to dramatise the sub-tlety with which Phillip's knowledge of things in the world becomes a function of his knowledge of language. This process occurs to some degree in all good novels in this genre (and especially in *Fishboy*, *Rich in Love*, and *Housekeeping*), but Phillip is uniquely sensitive to the processes of language acquisition, and he makes it the principal story of his upbringing in ways that most other novels in the genre do not. *The History of Luminous Motion* is a book that often seems to play know-ingly on a pun on the word 'subject': Phillip is a subject in the sense of being a citizen that his parents have jurisdiction over, but also in the sense of linguistics, where he is subject to the devices of language that talk about him. Phillip's novel is always an account of his subjectivity in this double sense, and his narrative dramatises a struggle between various idioms or discourses that offer to Phillip different ideas of the world and of himself. The pun on 'subject' is a Lacanian one, that is to say it is derived from the psychoanalytical theory of Jacques Lacan, and espe-cially from his interpretation of Freud's Oedipus complex. Lacan offered a revision of Freud's concept, a revision in which language is vitally situ-ated as an integral and determining aspect of childhood development. For Lacan, human subjects are interpolated into the structures of society, or the Symbolic Order, principally by initiation into forms of language that profoundly influence consciousness.

The pertinence of ideas about language and identity to Phillip's coming of age can be seen with the advent of Pedro. Pedro is one of 'Mom's men', and one of the first to be specifically named by her to Phillip. At the same moment as Pedro is named, Phillip is also named for the first time in his novel: unlike Philip Pirrip, the protagonist of Charles Dickens' classic bil-dungsroman *Great Expectations* (1861), Phillip Davis does not begin his first-person narrative by naming himself to the reader. The moment when Mom simultaneously confers names on Pedro and Phillip, coincides with 'that first staggering cessation of Mom's body and her voice', (Bradfield

1989: 10), and it thus signifies more than just a name because it both stills and silences Mom; this moving and speaking is, for Phillip, fundamental to her identity. But, as Mom names Phillip and has her own identity called into question by her new attachment to Pedro, the drama of naming and identity is further complicated when Phillip discovers that Pedro's real name is in fact Bernie Robertson and that in his house, 'Pedro's real unvoiced name was everywhere' (10). The ubiquity of this real name, Bernie, monogrammed to everything he owns, compromises the spoken name 'Pedro' and thus reveals him to Phillip as a sham. This written name is still a threat, however, because one day 'it might very soon attach itself to Mom and me' (11). Moreover, Pedro's speech is as phony as his name, and is almost entirely characterised by its banality: 'he didn't speak so much as erupt in aphorisms' (13). From Pedro Phillip learns the duplicity of adult names, adult speech, and the threat of the Lacanian name of the father that promises to come between him and Mom. Pedro's arrival signals to Phillip that 'I wasn't mom's baby anymore' (24), and the distress this causes him is expressed in images of entrapment and paralysis. Phillip decides to alleviate this threat by doing away with Pedro. These psychological conflicts are conventionally oedipal, but they are Lacanian in their emphasis on the role of language in the formation of the child's consciousness.

Phillip's violent physical attack on Pedro is precipitated by an exchange between them which is all about language and its various discrepancies: between speaking and writing, between naming and knowing, between language as an autonomous system and the social consequences of language in the world. Pedro's banal language is seen in expressions such as 'That's just the breaks' (35), and 'I'm going to hit the hay' (36), and he repeatedly addresses Phillip as 'Kiddo'. Pedro makes the mistake of trying to use this linguistic idiom to chastise Phillip for his apparent indolence:

> All this teary-eyed feeling sorry for yourself childhood crap just doesn't work – doesn't work for long anyway. I can promise you that, I mean, your mom wants you to have this idyllic childhood and all. She thinks this is Camelot or something, your childhood. Well, I want you to know, kiddo. I looked up 'idyllic' in the dictionary and I wouldn't hold my breath. I wouldn't lie in bed all day just waiting for some idyllic childhood to come along. (35)

It is especially revealing that Pedro, an adult, needs to look up the word 'idyllic' in a dictionary. This monologue of Pedro's brings about Phillip's attack on him, and the drama of their antagonism is a fierce conflict over language in which Pedro is no rival to Phillip's linguistic proficiency. In an earlier scene, Phillip is depicted reading the dictionary for pleasure: 'Words in a dictionary have a rhythm to them, a dry easy meaning I can

assemble in my head like songs, or caress like pieces of sculpted wood'
(11). Phillip has an aesthetic appreciation of words for their own sake,
and a much more sophisticated vocabulary than Pedro, and while he is
exasperated by Pedro's language and frustrated by the suffocating torpor
of their new lifestyle together, Phillip's fertile and energetic inner life
advances towards a violent confrontation: 'my secret internal motion
however couldn't be so easily disavowed' (23).

After the attack on Pedro, which the text of the novel significantly
represses, mother and son return to the road. In oedipal terms, Phillip is
successful in defeating the father and taking renewed possession of the
mother: the father is abandoned in favour of an exclusive and newly
intensified relationship with Mom. In Lacanian terms, these scenes
demonstrate the failure of the name of the father to come between the
child and its mother; the taboo of incest is not enforced, and Phillip is
not initiated into the symbolic order of his culture, partly because he
rejects its language as that language is articulated by Pedro as the male
agent of its systems of signification. Pedro's word is no guarantor of
meaning, and therefore Phillip rejects it. But the apparent victory over
Pedro condemns Phillip to continue to be Mom's baby, that is to say to
be infantilised, and to defer the inevitable conflict until a more authoritative male figure attempts to come between him and his mother, in this
case Dad.

One problem with the scenario outlined above is that it enacts literally
that which is only supposed to occur symbolically. The oedipal challenge
to the father is, according to Freud, a symbolic process by which the child
learns the taboo of incest – that he is *not* to take possession of his mother.
But Phillip appears to vanquish Pedro literally, and his newly intensified
relationship with Mom does indeed have occasionally erotic moments.
This mistaking of the literal for the symbolic is partly a consequence of
Phillip's understanding of language: for example, Mom introduces her
son to Pedro as 'the only important man in my life' (10). Phillip is determined to prove this literally true, and Mom appears to sanction that
interpretation when she flees from Pedro's house taking Phillip with her.
Mom's language has also been contaminated by a bankrupt Californian
culture, and, for Phillip, her relationship with Pedro is merely part of 'her
own tragic and naïve compromise with the world of Pedro' (22), and one
which necessarily embroils her in 'some vaster scheme of lying' (23). This
'scheme' is clearly Phillip's recognition of the codes and regulations that
shape his self and society, or what Lacan termed the symbolic order, and
Phillip is determined to repudiate it because he recognises the duplicity
of its languages and the power of those languages to intervene in his relationship with Mom. The symbolic order in this novel is synonymous with

patriarchy, with the word of the father and national culture of the United States: when Phillip meets one of Mom's other men, he comments, 'The next time I saw him I was supposed to have memorized the names and chronologies of all our presidents' (10). The name of the president is that name which guarantees the meaning of all (male) names in American society, and learning the names is a valuable initiation into that knowledge. As a child, it is Phillip's business to internalise the name of the father as part of the process of becoming a properly socialised adult. It is precisely in his resistance to that process that Phillip's unique voice is created.

On the eve of Phillip's attack on Pedro he appears to say to him 'Death is the hard song, Pedro, we only sing it once, and none of us ever gets it exactly right' (37). This enigmatic statement is an important expression of Phillip's understanding of a relationship between mortality and aesthetics. Death is a form of creative and artistic expression of subjectivity, a swan-song, and an awareness of the aesthetic imperfections of it becomes part of the elegiac consciousness of life's particular challenges. This first 'hard song' is the lesson Pedro learns from Phillip by underestimating him with his patronising and banal language, but significantly the phrase is repeated as the title of the novel's final section where it becomes the artistic designation for the enunciation of Phillip's symbolic death as he moves from child to adult in the conflict with Dad. Phillip's idiom is infinitely more subtle and compelling than Pedro's, and it is the father-figure's language that Phillip repudiates as much as his corporeal presence. This repudiation, however, is something of a double-edged sword; Pedro might only be 'the man whose name she taught me once to say' (50), but nevertheless, he remains a vestigial presence in Phillip's consciousness because of the important lessons about language and identity that he teaches him. Phillip cleaves himself to Mom, but this can only be a temporary respite from confrontation with the true name of the father.

These struggles with specifically male voices are contrasted with the language of Mom and with what her language signifies to Phillip. Where Pedro's language is associated with a kind of death, it is immortality that Mom's language represents to Phillip. When they flee Pedro's house for the exhilarating mobility of the open road Phillip comments 'God, I was filled with light that night. I was filled with Mom's voice and the very light of her. We were moving again. We would never die' (42). The sense of a profound connectedness with Mom (almost identical to Hex's closeness to his mother in Moody's *Purple America*), is associated by Phillip with energy, movement, and light, and the perpetual expansions of horizons that are both of the self and of the world. This sense of infinite possibility is associated with a transcendent energy that is inviolable, and from which Phillip generates his sense of himself, his text, and the world. It is a power, a history of luminous motion, that he is extremely reluctant to surrender because it drives his creative ability to tell his childhood story and thereby constitute himself as a subject – both in the world and in the book of his self that becomes *The History of Luminous Motion*. Mom's voice is profoundly seductive to Phillip, and it seems to speak exclusively to him in unique ways. Mom comforts him, in their nomadic and increasingly desperate lifestyle, with comments about how special he is, and Phillip interprets that voice as an intensely romantic expression of his special qualities. It is, in fact, the product of the exclusivity of the attention that she appears to give him, and that attention inspires his imagination: 'You are immaculate. You endure for numberless centuries. You persevere in a world of pure gravity and sound' (30). Phillip's messianic imaginings originate with a sense of never being separated from Mom: 'we could live together forever and ever, again and again, life after life' (43). The power of Mom's voice, of what she seems to say to Phillip, is closely associated with the defeat of that mortality he sees in both Pedro and Dad: 'I felt Mom's voice rising in me, strong and intrepid for the first time in months. I would never die, Mom would never leave me' (175).

But Mom's voice does not stand in some uncomplicated opposition in which Dad is simply and wholly demonised. Mom is variously portrayed as an alcoholic, as promiscuous, as a criminal, and as an irresponsible parent, and most significantly as a narcissist. For example, at one point Mom's voice speaks of 'the freedom we can only live inside ourselves' (28), and it is useful to recognise this as Phillip's interpretation of her solipsistic withdrawal from a California culture from which she is in beleaguered retreat. At the outset Mom is depicted as having a tendency to become 'self-involved' (20), and as 'gazing aimlessly at her own reflection' (20), or 'lost in endless dialogues between herself and her own reflection' (21). In his embattled antagonism to the circumstances of his upbringing Phillip also withdraws into himself for protection, or as he says to the imagined figure of Pedro at one point, 'I only care about me now, Pedro, because now I'm like mom. Because now I'm never thinking about anybody except myself' (150). This is an explicit statement of his indebtedness to his mother, but at an early stage in the novel there is a scene in which it carries far greater psychological freight:

> I could feel her breath warm in the air around me; I could taste its warmth against my skin and face. Sometimes her nipples grew more prominent and stiff. She would remove her left hand from the table and place it against the inside of her left thigh. Lying on my side of the bed I watched her, and my body filled with strange, smoky sensations. (45–6)

Mom's narcissism includes an element of auto-eroticism; her attention is fixed on herself and is explicitly sexual, while Phillip is the voyeur, watching but not watched. This is not the only scene in which adults are perceived by Phillip as profoundly self-regarding: 'I wondered if in Pedro's dreams there were visions of Pedro dreaming, like the way angled mirrors reflect one another infinitely in department-store dressing rooms' (50). Pedro's imagined narcissism is an expression of Phillip's belief that all adults are narcissists, locked into their own private worlds and unable to communicate properly with others because of something that has gone profoundly wrong with the languages of their culture. California, in this novel, is a deeply narcissistic place whose subjects are dedicated to the satisfaction of private desires and where other people are simply the vehicles for that personal satisfaction.

An important dimension of the novel's analysis of this cultural narcissism, and one that has a crucial bearing on Phillip's coming of age, is provided by the story of Mom's childhood. Mom's attempt to escape, which vitally sets Phillip's narrative in motion, is articulated in terms of a bid for autonomy and self-determination: 'Before your dad came I was beginning not to be afraid anymore. The spell of my own blood actually made sense to me' (130). Mom learns, away from Dad, to be attentive to her own desires, and she experiences a new sense of freedom that she expresses in terms of her body, or 'blood'. At one point Mom's delirium precipitates memories of her own childhood in which she recalls that her father took her to doctors often, and that he usually had his hand on her knee: 'I was never really sure if I liked my father's hand there on my knee or not' (131). Mom's memory of her father, then, is characterised by an ambivalence about the nature of his touching her in which he becomes like 'one of the dark men' from the psychic landscapes of *Apocalypse Now* (131). Mom's visits to the doctor are not explained, but the darkness of Mom's memory of her father is associated in another scene with a form of depression that she suffered as a child: 'I could feel this sort of moving black cloud slowly engulf me. Inside the black cloud, I couldn't think about anything' (51). Depression, solipsism, alcoholism: the problem of her childhood becomes a serious adult malady in which her father is darkly implicated. Mom explains to Phillip that 'your father took me away from all that' (52), but in California there is no escape from patriarchy. Dad rescues Mom from abuse and then becomes the abuser, not simply because these men are misogynistic, but because they are the agents of a culture which is itself patriarchal, and which therefore permits no space for women to be different from the standard that is dictated by the word of the father. As Mom expresses it: 'Sometimes it's hard to tell the difference between your conception of the world and the world's conception of you' (51). Mom's experience of 'culture', then, is difficult and painful, partly because she cannot conform to its expectations, and her attitude to culture is therefore an expression of defeat: 'Culture's got our best interests at heart' (28). This surprisingly male language (patronising, patrician) is indicative of Phillip's recognition of Mom's failure to come to terms with a male-centered society that has no place for her, and on which he becomes determined to wreak revenge. Phillip intuitively understands the gender politics of this culture and its relations to power: because she was a girl 'Mom hadn't stood a chance from the very beginning' (136). Here again Bradfield's novel anticipates Moody's *Purple America* in its depiction of a son who recognises his mother's paralysis and who creates a remarkable account of his fall from innocence through fidelity to her predicament.

Mom's childhood memories are a crucial point of origin for *The History of Luminous Motion*; they help to account for her flight from father and husband, for her later difficult relations with men, and for her estrangement from society. Most importantly, it is her alienated voice that Phillip finds so absorbing and which in many ways he seeks to be faithful to in his own account of coming of age. It is, after all, Phillip's mother who both inspires his imagination and encourages him to express himself in language: 'Mom had recently determined I would be a writer someday' (53). Phillip assembles pens and paper as the tools of his trade, and he is dimly aware of the inchoate unconscious desires that they represent: 'there was something submarine about them, even anxious' (53). This anxiety stems from a sense of the importance of what is at stake in writing, an investment in the business of language choice that has the power to define him both for himself and for us as readers of the text of his self. But Mom's voice also expresses a specific theory of aesthetic value: 'Take words and make them useful she told me. Drain them of all the crappy meanings they *used* to mean, and make them mean something useful instead' (53). The pragmatic emphasis here on 'making' and on 'use-value' (rather than on words that are 'beautiful', 'philosophical', or 'true') suggests a belief in the social value of language, in its communicative capacity to serve important civic purposes. This quotation also shows an awareness of the degraded and outmoded languages of men like Pedro and of the broader contemporary culture of the United States. Mom perceives language to be derelict, and she envisages Phillip to be the agent of its restoration. Phillip's account of coming of age therefore strives to be 'useful' in new ways, partly by satirising the banality of 'crappy meanings' and partly by creating a new language of subjectivity and a fresh interpretation of the genre of the coming-of-age novel. But because this aesthetic project is derived from a sense of the alienated voice of his mother it is at odds with the culture, and it is therefore extremely challenging for Phillip to find a voice that can exist in an imaginative space outside the languages of that culture. Nevertheless, his novel tries to create that separate space in language which his mother seeks on the road, a freedom which is both linguistic and spatial, a dynamic horizon of the self. How can Phillip find a language of subjectivity beyond the empty idioms of this culture? One answer is again provided by Mom, who makes the novel's only explicit literary allusion: 'Emily Dickinson said she could find the entire universe in her back yard' (7). In the coming-of-age genre, Phillip's back yard is his own consciousness, and in writing about the challenges of finding the appropriate language in which to express the drama of his developing mind, he defines his own aesthetic, albeit a perilously self-regarding one. The cultural authority of Dickinson's art sanctions Phillip's dedication to the drama of his self, but it is to some extent in the nature of the genre to be deeply solipsistic.

Phillip's sojourn with Mom temporarily defers the negotiation with Dad. Dad represents the true power and authority of a capitalist society in the vanguard of technological innovation. Doing business by telephone and laptop computer, Dad is at the frontier of financial development with his finger on the pulse of world markets. Unlike Pedro, who owns a hardware store in San Luis Obispo, Dad can do his work anywhere as an agent of a global economy that governs the prices of commodities worldwide. This is the very grammar of a free-market system, and it is integral to California and to American national identity. Again, Phillip can recognise the authority of this idiom, understanding Dad as 'not a fact of data but a quality of interpretation' (54), and recognising that 'Dad spoke words not with other people but with the entire system of language itself' (123). Dad's identification with capital is dramatised by his arrival at Christmas and his desire to bestow on Phillip an excess of goods. Dad's power is further exemplified by his ability to take control of Mom and to subdue her by force in ways that Pedro could not. Phillip recognises the advent of Dad as momentous, saying 'This is history. Today I grow up' (114). Phillip is also enthralled by Dad partly because Dad calls him not 'Kiddo', as Pedro did, but by his own name: 'I had never answered a phone before to the sound of my own name' (55). Because the voice of Dad speaks the language of the system it seems inevitable that 'one day the world's Dads would prevail' (134), and that one of the commodities they should prevail over is the body of the woman. Mom is subdued, paralysed by injections that are administered by health professionals whom Dad employs. Mom becomes once again completely dependent upon him. This exercise of Dad's power is brutal and violent but sanctioned by Californian society. Only Mom's screams communicate to the reader the horror of her powerlessness and subordination: 'screaming until Dad finally gave her one of her injections, a sedative prescribed by one of Dad's "specialists" ' (128). Dad embodies the true name of the father, and Phillip recognises the association of the phallus with the system of language when he comments on his own body: 'Sometimes it felt hard, but it also felt remote and slightly detached, like a heavy steel pipe or a dictionary' (138).

There is, however, something significantly ersatz about Dad. First, his language, which is reported directly rather than understood intuitively like the language of Mom, is phony. The only conversation that the reader overhears between Dad and his broker is characterised by its banality: '"I can't make a living on theories, Harry"' (122). This is typical of the clichés in which Dad speaks, and it is a language that immediately aligns him with Pedro. Similarly equivocal is Dad's appearance: he dresses formally for work although he works at home in the apartment and only leaves home in his leisure time. Phillip has a closely critical perspective on his father's behaviour and speech. Phillip is exiled from the sustaining voice of Mom by Dad's intervention and, as we have seen, it is that voice that informs the unique character of his subjectivity. Phillip's resentment begins to accumulate: 'I could step into the high weeds and actually feel the language out there, like a human body, like Dad's firm words. Broken cinder blocks, decomposing garbage . . . Forgotten civilizations I had read about in books' (135). This quotation records Phillip's sense that the authorised male language of this culture is redundant and outmoded, and that initiation into its grammar is a form of death. At the end of this scene Phillip is depicted trying to imagine another world, another language of space that might permit a more authentic and compelling expression of the self. Again that idea finds a spatial metaphor: 'Dad was a house. Mom was just infinite space which Dad's house isolated and defined' (136). Isolation and definition are synonymous with narcissism and death; the circumscribed limitations of male language must be breached if some authentic expression of Phillip's subjectivity is to be permitted.

It is at this point in the drama of Phillip's developing consciousness that other voices begin to compete for his attention. Phillip meets Rodney, who initiates him into a life of house-breaking, and who provides a shocking alternative to how young men regard their mothers. Phillip holds Mom in awe, but Rodney treats his mother Ethel with abusive disdain. This attitude is a revelation to Phillip; Rodney's aggressive subordination of his mother is a brutal expression of power over her that Phillip can only marvel at: '"Do me a favor Ethel . . . Just sit down, read your comics, and shut the fuck up"' (73). The discomfort that these scenes cause Phillip is considerable, and this is commensurate with the disorientation of values that he experiences when he is exposed to compelling voices. Such voices represent both a serious challenge to Phillip's sense of personal identity and a threat to the integrity of the book that his own textual voice is in the midst of composing. Powerful expressions of 'otherness' in his text are therefore a literal threat to Phillip's self-composure because of the ways in which they intrude upon the integrity of that narrative voice he is striving to sustain. Rodney, too, is aware of a particular association between women and orality:

> 'That's the illusion that women prefer. That everything can be reduced to talk . . . Men do things. They get things done. That's what men do. Women, on the other hand, talk about things. Why they weren't done quite right. How you might want to go about doing it better *next* time'. (214–15)

This opposition between talking and doing is one of the means by which women are excluded from participation in the world, but it is a spurious opposition for Phillip, who has been attentive to his mother's voice from the beginning and who understands that 'talk' is integral to his sense of identity, and that her voice and Beatrice's are valuable constituents of his sense of who he is in the world. Rodney brutally silences his mother and devotes his adolescent attention to voices from the underworld, partly from frustration at the voice of Beatrice: ' "She never shuts up does she?" he said. "All day and all night. Yap yap yap. Even in bed when you're doing it to her, she talks right through it. She doesn't shut up for one minute" ' (196). Although the scenes in which Rodney tries to solicit a response from the voices of the underworld are principally a parody of a kind of male adolescent behaviour, it is nevertheless significant that, in the novel's drama of opposing voices, the underworld does not speak back, even while Rodney repudiates the voices of those around him who do speak. In this respect, Rodney serves as a classically male counterpoint to Phillip's shrewd attentiveness to the female voices of Mom and Beatrice.

Beatrice is an unlikely character in some ways, a twelve-year-old post-structuralist Marxist from a trailer park in Encino whose speech is punctuated by comments such as ' "My old man loves valium" ' (141). Phillip comes to know Beatrice during the period of his estrangement from Mom, and his friendship with her is a vital form of emotional support. The reader learns very little about Beatrice; she appears to be much more self-sufficient than either of her male friends, for whom she acts as a means to define themselves. The voice of Beatrice induces in Phillip another form of discomposure, because it speaks to him of the importance of another kind of language. She articulates some ideas that have serious implications for Phillip's coming of age; these ideas are sometimes inchoate or contradictory (as a twelve-year-old, she is coming of age herself) and do not necessarily constitute an integrated theoretical paradigm, but many of her comments (taken from cultural theory of the 1980s) are impossible to ignore as an interpretation of certain aspects of Phillip's childhood. Beatrice is another strong voice in Phillip's textual world, but one that is intellectual, analytical, and based on wide and challenging reading; her voice is also significantly female and offers an alternative to the voice of Mom. Where Mom spoke of culture as ' "a scheme of rules and regulations we've all quite happily agreed to" ' (28), Beatrice's critical stance towards culture is an informed oppositional perspective that has great value for Phillip's coming of age. For example, in opposition to Mom's attitude to society, Beatrice observes: ' "The culture industry is vast and incredibly articulate. It knows exactly what it wants to say all the time" ', and she describes the culture industry's attempt to control ' "how we think, who we *be*" ' (88). Where Mom retreats into herself as a defence against patriarchal culture that has successfully estranged her from herself, Beatrice's critical discourse contextualises Phillip in terms of the symbolic structures of society. Also, Beatrice's remarks are consistently directed outwards towards the world (unlike Mom, she rarely speaks about herself) where Phillip's discourse is directed, like Mom's, inward towards himself. Beatrice's feminist appraisals of Phillip's upbringing have resonance for him, therefore, because analyses of the United States' culture in terms of gender and capital are closely relevant to Phillip's troubled childhood. Phillip tacitly recognises this, partly because he too is a precocious reader and partly because he has already learned to pay particular attention to the voices of women.

Most importantly, Beatrice offers Phillip a fragmentary theory of that alternative aesthetic of subjectivity which he intuitively recognises in Mom, and in which he strives to express himself in opposition to the outmoded masculinist discourse of Pedro and Dad. For example, Beatrice tells Phillip ' "Your Mom's what men's words wreck" ' (132), and, further, that ' "What you really want to destroy is women, that story of yourself you can't control" ' (171). Although Beatrice appears not to have read Kristeva (who is not cited directly), her comments often come close to articulating that sense of the 'semiotic' which Kristeva proposed as an alternative to the language of the Lacanian symbolic order. For example, Kristeva had argued that there are 'non-verbal signifying systems that are constructed exclusively on the basis of the semiotic' (Kristeva 1984: 12). It is this sense of the semiotic that Phillip tries to express in this text of himself, and which Beatrice comes close to articulating through her knowledge of contemporary theory. At one point she accuses him of being 'so goddamn penile' (194), and at another she proposes that the alternative language that Phillip needs is French: ' "You should learn to speak French too Phillip, then we could talk French to each other over the phone" ' (171). This is part of Beatrice's search for an alternative to the grammar of gender politics and capital, and an important part of Phillip's text too, as we shall see later with the importance of Spanish in the novel's final scene. It is also Beatrice who identifies Phillip's central emotional problem: ' "You're a patent narcissist, that's what *you* are. You gaze at the world and expect the world to gaze dreamily right back at you. You've got to grow up, Phillip" ' (251). Phillip is a narcissist in the clinical sense of not recognising the reality of phenomena outside his consciousness, but also perhaps in the textual sense: Phillip composes his narrative in a prose genre that is necessarily devoted to the processes of emerging subjectivity, and it is therefore by its very nature principally self-regarding. When Phillip depicts himself reading the dictionary, it is not simply a coincidence that all of the cited words begin with the prefix 'auto' ('autodidact, autoecious, autogamy, autoimmune', 11) – because, of course, the word means 'of the self'.

Phillip's attack on Dad is accompanied by a profusion of texts, and this is evidence of Phillip's intensely heightened sensitivity to 'voices' at this critical moment. Phillip's susceptibility to textual signals, to the languages and lexicons of different forms of communication, contributes to his psychosis, to his feeling at this point that 'I'm not really in the world at all' (231). These texts are multiple and diverse (television, Rosemary Clooney) but there is a far greater urgency to their appearance here because of Phillip's confusion about their nature and their value. They intrude into his consciousness to such an extent that he can hardly distinguish or discriminate between them; here the novel dramatises in Phillip's mind the issue of what's real and what's imaginary. These voices are silenced by a further text: the text of his father's suicide note. The ludicrous resignation of this piece of writing ('All parents fail their children and we all have to get used to that, I guess',) precipitates Phillip's violent frenzy precisely because it reminds him of that sense of abandonment and neglect that he felt from his father as a child: 'I called his name but he didn't turn around' (229). This feeling, 'a solitary moment from my childhood', is offered by the novel as the point of origin that is crucially antecedent to the novel's beginning, a sense of loss that cannot be remedied, and which his father threatens to repeat by abandoning Phillip before Phillip can kill him. Phillip's father deprives him of agency, and thereby disempowers him again in the psychological drama of coming of age. For Phillip this is intolerable, and the attack proceeds until Phillip experiences a sense of messianic elevation: 'Dad's hot life on my hands and my clothes and my face' (237). The attack fails, however, because again it is literal rather than symbolic. Although Phillip terms this 'the night of my stark ascension' (233) no such accession to power takes place because in psychological terms, possession of the phallus is symbolic rather than literal. It is the novel's final scene that dramatises the failure of Phillip's attack on Dad, and it does so in terms that return again to the arena of language, not to the body of Dad but to the languages of this American culture.

Chapter twenty-eight begins with the line 'I was going to grow up', suggesting that the novel's final scene is the last scene of his coming of age, the final moment before this world is lost forever to the corruptions of a Californian adulthood of the kind Phillip wanted to avoid. It is a kind of symbolic death, a 'hard song' that Phillip is now about to sing himself. What is especially important here is that the language he has imbibed as a child now becomes, on the verge of adulthood, a whole discourse of culture, a narrative of personal history that is already prescribed, even laid down by law, and to which Phillip must now inevitably conform. Phillip can predict his own future with great assurance, and the deathliness and suffocating entrapment of it is conveyed in his language: 'I had a future now, as firm and incontrovertible as my house and my family' (269). The suffocating predictability of this narrative has its origin in the language struggles that Phillip's upbringing dramatises. The claustrophobic conformity, the certain knowledge of even its specific emotional details ('we would start to grow more anxious and uncertain') is a kind of death, the hard song of 1980s Californian culture that every individual is forced to sing. Phillip's future is guaranteed by the surveillance of hired professionals who monitor his movements and behaviour, just as his mother was previously subdued by health workers paid by Dad. The word of the father is the word of the state, and the institutional and legal edicts of this society are rigorously governed to manage the initiation of its subjects into a specific social language. This is the uncompromising social critique of Bradfield's novel, and its originality consists partly in its sophisticated and compelling portrayal of the processes of language acquisition.

The loss that growing up entails in this culture is registered finally in the novel's style. Phillip's tone and language have changed 'since I have settled down to a more normal childhood' (270). Phillip now speaks in a flat and unexpressive language that is purged of the linguistic inventiveness of his earlier years. His social behaviour, too, is now conventionally Californian: he drives a little red sports car up and down the coast road and he comments tritely, 'It is always nice just to drive and relax and not feel in a hurry to be going anywhere' (270). This is the banal language of Dad, who might recognise and approve of what Phillip has finally become. Tragically, Phillip has internalised the moribund platitudes of Dad and can comment with tired banality 'Sometimes children make mistakes which they regret later on in their lives' (272). This is part of the rules that Phillip has been coerced into accepting, and is a very long way from the semiotic language of Mom.

However, Phillip does retain a vestigial but important memory of his life before he became a dutiful subject; he returns to the house where he once lived with Mom and he breaks in. This is a significant return, and it is full of important information. The house is now occupied by a Hispanic family, and Phillip meets a little girl who momentarily mistakes him for her father. This is a moment of great emotional intensity for Phillip, one in which he is reminded acutely of 'the sound into which Mom had vanished' (272). The girl, of course, speaks Spanish, and this is a language that Phillip does not understand. The intensity of this moment brings his coming of age to a specific crisis that is again all about language: 'this was it' (273). Phillip feels that if only he could speak the language then everything would be remedied, he would return successfully to that Eden from which he has been cast out. But what Eden is it, what language is it that he seeks desperately to remember and to return to? In this moment Phillip realises 'the words wouldn't come, and I couldn't make them' (274). The return is the return to the language of the mother; in the place that he previously shared with Mom, Phillip finds another family devoid of a father, one where the mother's voice, 'growing larger and more distinct', precedes her physical appearance. The voice of maternal concern is heard at the point where Phillip is banished, once again and forever, from the realm of the mother's language. Thus the novel ends by dramatising Phillip's anguish and pain at being separated from the lost language of the mother, which is doubly occluded by its representation in Spanish.

By now, of course, the story is complete, the depiction of subjectivity is finally composed, and this last scene can record, with an intensely elegiac power, the costs and losses of coming of age. The finished novel is an acerbic social satire, a black comedy of Ronald Reagan's California, and a brilliantly sophisticated dramatisation of the vicissitudes of language acquisition in its child protagonist. Its particular contribution to the coming-of-age genre lies in its creation of a language of subjectivity that is completely original and unique, and which simultaneously accommodates an analytical commentary on the shaping cultural factors from which that very language emerges. *The History of Luminous Motion* is finally a hard song; none of us gets it right, but we are all sentenced to sing it.

Mark Richard, *Fishboy*

Mark Richard's first novel, *Fishboy*, was published in 1993, following the success of his short story collection *The Ice at the Bottom of the World* (1989). *Fishboy* is the first-person narrative of its eponymous protagonist, and his innocence is exposed to a particularly uncompromising adult world. *Fishboy* is a coming-of-age novel in the tradition of sea-faring narratives that goes back as far as *Robinson Crusoe*, and which might briefly include Coleridge's 'The Ancient Mariner', many of the novels of Joseph Conrad, and, in the United States, Melville's *Moby Dick* and Poe's *The Narrative of Arthur Gordon Pym of Nantucket*. Whether or not their narrators are adolescents, these are all stories of personal development and moral education in which the trials and adventures of life at sea, like Huck Finn's journey down the Mississippi River, have a transforming effect on the individual. *Fishboy* is a novel that participates in this tradition, especially in its depiction of the story-telling of the ship's crew, and in its dramatisation of this oral culture as a repository of knowledge. *Fishboy* is also a distinctly southern novel, particularly in its appropriation of the genre of black comedy that has come to be known as the southern grotesque, and which can also be seen at work in the novels of other contemporary writers such as Cormac McCarthy, Katherine Dunn, and Harry Crews. This genre has a special interest in macabre violence and various forms of damage to the body that is appropriate in the depiction of an all-male ship's crew in life-threatening situations. Yet *Fishboy* also announces itself in its title as 'A Ghost's Story', and this calls up another genre with a distinctly weighty lineage. *Fishboy* is an interpretation of a ghost story like Toni Morrison's *Beloved* (1987), a ghost story with a particular interest in the (gothic) haunting of the racial history of the United States. These generic parameters (sea-faring, southern, ghost story) are not mutually exclusive, but are suggestive of possible ways in which *Fishboy* might be understood and interpreted. Most of all, *Fishboy* is an innovative and experimental interpretation of the coming-of-age genre, one that draws on the conventions of the other traditions and synthesises them in its account of the rites of passage of its child protagonist.

Black comedy is not an easy style to assess, partly because it depends on impulses of laughter and horror that seem incompatible. But that kind of black comedy known as the grotesque does have a distinct lineage as a genre that can be seen at work in *Fishboy*. Most commonly, the grotesque can be identified in a text by the presence of elements that invoke disgust or horror but which, at the same time, are sufficiently ludicrous or exaggerated in their presentation as to appear comic. This synthesis of the humorous and the appalling causes a discomfort in the reader that is strategically deliberate, and often formally aggressive or uncompromising. Freud designated this feeling *unheimlich* or 'uncanny', and he identified it in the story by E. T. A. Hoffman called 'The Sandman' in which a young man is driven to insanity and suicide by a childhood spectre of dread. Freud interpreted the story as being expressive of an infantile castration anxiety. There is an association, then, between the uncanny recognition of horror and the experience of childhood that is germane to an understanding of *Fishboy*. As one critic points out, 'the grotesque is first encountered in the dreams and fantasies of childhood' (McElroy 1989: 182). This particular stylistic synthesis of the monstrous and the laughable is an indication of an ambivalence which is in turn expressive of a violent disorientation of values; the grotesque is the stylistic expression of powerfully conflicting or opposing values that cannot be reconciled. In this respect it has been argued that 'The grotesque is the expression of the estranged or alienated world' (Kayser 1981: 184). The use of the child as protagonist in *Fishboy* is therefore integral to the grotesque style of the novel and helps to facilitate the depiction of an adult social world that is profoundly disturbed and disrupted. Michael Steig has also argued that the grotesque style expresses the twin impulses of 'a desire for a liberation from fear and a liberation from inhibition' (Steig 1970: 256), and this characterisation is also pertinent to the child protagonist of *Fishboy*, for whom fear and inhibition are central emotional experiences. The grotesque is also characterised by physical injury (Bosch, Breughel, Goya), and by the presence of the abnormal or freakish in fictional characters. More specifically in American literature the grotesque can be seen in writers such as Nathanael West and Flannery O'Connor, to whom Mark Richard is clearly indebted, especially in their depiction of violence to the body. Witness, for example, the appalling violence done to the letter-writers of West's 'Miss Lonelyhearts', and the extremes of Hazel Motes' self-laceration in O'Connor's *Wise Blood*. The dark and ludicrous outrages of William Faulkner's *As I Lay Dying* are also part of this tradition of southern grotesque, a tradition which is often said to have originated with 'The Book of The Grotesque' that opens Sherwood Anderson's *Winesburg, Ohio* (1919), and which was interpreted by Flannery O'Connor in 'Some Aspects of the Grotesque in Southern Fiction' in terms of 'characters who are forced out to meet evil and grace and who act on a trust beyond themselves whether they know very clearly what it is they act upon or not' (O'Connor 1972: 42).

These writers' interest in physical damage to the body is often combined with the depiction of children or young people, or by characters who are specifically marked by a naivety or innocence that comes into violent confrontation with a fundamentally problematical adult world. Balso Snell, Hazel Motes, Enoch Emory, and Faulkner's Benjy, are all children in worlds in which is it impossible to come of age in the conventional ways. In fact, because he is already dead and this is 'A ghost's story', Fishboy might be said to join 'the long line of grotesque life-in-death figures in American fiction' that includes Hawthorne's Wakefield and Melville's Bartleby (Meindl 1996: 142). *Fishboy* therefore announces its generic affiliation when it tells us that its characters are 'a crew of criminals, mutants, idiots, freaks and murderers' (Richard 1993: 76). This is a microcosm of the world in which everything is awry, and the conventional teleological processes of coming of age are suspended by a sense of grotesque 'cosmic pointlessness' (O'Connor 1962: 13). For example, the ship's captain is a man who has the appearance of someone whose body has been turned inside out, and he instructs Fishboy specifically *not* to call him 'Captain' (47). One crew member is known exclusively as 'the weeping man who said *Fuck*', and another is an idiot with a toe fetish on a string around his neck. The novel is full of scenes of bodily disruption, such as disemboweling and mutilation, stabbing and vomiting, and some of its most inventive powers are put to the portrayal of barbaric practices; in one scene, two men take turns punching the face of the sheriff they have already murdered: 'the sheriff's nose shifted back and forth from cheek to cheek like a movable festering boil' (58). In another scene we are told the crew member called Lonny was once offended by a man in a bar and 'Lonny slipped his knife into the man's ankle and brought it all the way to his crotch, the man's leg open perfectly along the inseam through trouser and muscle so that in his first step the man's skeleton stick of bone walked right out of his leg' (124). The violence of the novel is often gratuitous and inexplicable; Fishboy, who is himself a 'fish freak' (55), with a limp, a lisp, and an evil appearance, is knocked on the head at the novel's beginning and thrown from a car in a weighted burlap sack into a side-road swamp. This original act of attempted murder is beyond Fishboy's comprehension but it is nevertheless indicative of the world into which he is born. Scenes of parental abandonment are subsequently repeated throughout the novel.

Fishboy is also a novel about the importance of narrative; its characters are defined by their relationship to a specific story, and especially a story that tells of their creation and their history. This is part of the sea-faring tradition in which telling stories is a special activity with a particular authority. In this genre, yarns and mythology are integral to the business of being a mariner, part of what Arthur Pym describes as 'the thousand superstitions which are so universally current among seamen' (Poe 2006: 93). Narrative is the principal means for mariners to organise and to preserve knowledge, and being able to tell a convincing tale, to participate successfully in the culture of tale-telling, is the principal means of proving one's value in this environment. Fishboy has very limited success in this respect; he makes only two important utterances to the crew and they are attenuated and ineffective. Fishboy acknowledges his failure to become part of the adult society when he observes 'I didn't know any stories. I hardly knew my own' (72). This is especially significant because it reveals the importance of the story of the self to social acceptance. Unable to tell his own story, Fishboy is unable to participate in one of the principal activities aboard ship; he is perpetually the auditor and not the teller of tales, and this contributes to his status as a junior. However, the novel called *Fishboy*, which becomes the story of its protagonist's emergence as an experienced member of the crew, is itself comprised of each of the stories that are told to him by adults who have similarly traumatic personal histories. By providing an account of how he heard these tales, Fishboy composes his own tale, both from them and in relation to them. Fishboy thus becomes the character who survives to tell the story of the stories that he has heard, and of the dire circumstances in which he heard them. In this way the novel is a collection of narratives of rites of passage, told to a child protagonist whose coming of age consists partly of being their auditor.

The stories of the adult crew members are almost exclusively stories of macabre violence, of murder and death, of barbarism and privation, and they are uniquely inventive and unconventional in the ways that they find to appall their auditors. These stories are also a cathartic unburdening for men whose lives have been defined by violent, catastrophic, and traumatic experiences. Like Coleridge's ancient mariner, their lives are defined by painful experiences that they are compelled to recount, often to unwilling listeners:

> I had known men who were strangers to each other gather at my cartonated encampment just to sit by my cypress-knot and fish-wrapper fire to get in out of the dark and burden each other with things on their mind, things they would never tell anyone in daylight, things that made them, in the morning, shake off each other like they shook off the frost that had grown on them in the dark before the dawn, avoiding each other, taking separate paths out of the fishhouse lot even when the night before in the camaraderie of the road they had promised to travel together against scavenging animals and maybe even against men like themselves. (141–2)

The compulsion to confess is often followed immediately by a murderous hatred of the auditor, who now possesses the secret of guilt that the teller has unburdened. In the cook's tale the act of telling a story is twice followed by a powerful desire to murder the person who was forced to listen to it. The narrative of *Fishboy* is structured by the tales of the crew members to which Fishboy is compelled to listen. The process of attending to these stories becomes integral to his coming of age because they encode for him, in oblique and enigmatic ways, knowledge of the adult society that he struggles to become part of, to integrate with, and to survive in. These stories are as important to him as his material experiences aboard ship, indeed they are a material experience for him, and attending to their meanings, as to the proper interpretation of dreams, is a vital way of understanding the adult society into which he has been born. Further, it is notable that the stories themselves are often tales of violent initiation and therefore they have a special value for Fishboy the initiate.

In many ways, then, *Fishboy* is a novel with orality as its central subject; it is a novel about the importance of speaking and telling oral tales (writing is merely illiterate fragments of much less significance or value). *Fishboy* is also about the value of eating, of consuming by the mouth, of cooking, of the idea of oral sustenance which is both story and food. In many of the stories, hunger leads to the consumption of detritus, waste, indiscriminately unappetising ingredients; the crew's food is often something abject that they are forced to eat in the face of various forms of oral privation. Yet, simultaneously, it is the oral tale that defines the identity and the personal history of the tale-teller in ways that nourish a sustaining sense of identity. In both cases orality is vital to survival because it defines and sustains, but it is also associated closely with violence, guilt, and horror and pain. Orality is connected in *Fishboy* with violent bodily trauma, stress, shock, and nausea; oral consumption and oral tale-telling are associated with profound psychological anxiety. Both the food of the crew members and their tales are vestigial remnants of something gone wrong that has become corrupt and rotten. Food and stories become commodified and exchanged in an adult world that is often characterised by privation, famine, and abject lack. Julia Kristeva, in *Powers of Horror*, has theorised this area most thoroughly, arguing that 'food loathing is perhaps the most archaic form of abjection', and drawing attention to the importance of orality: 'I expel myself, I spit myself out, I abject myself, within the same motion through which "I" claim to establish myself . . . "I" am in the process of becoming an other at the expense of my own death' (Kristeva 1982: 2–3).

For *Fishboy*, this lack is closely associated with cooking and the mother; cooking is a conventionally female activity which, in this novel, inexpert men are forced to carry out but which they associate with death. Fishboy is thus eager not to learn how to cook because he understands its connection with absence, loss, and death. The repudiation of cooking by the male crew is part of their rejection of that nurturing function of mothers of which all of them have been deprived. Being forced to eat waste is symptomatic of their abjection, and this is brought about by their rejection and denial by their respective families. The oath of allegiance to which the crew swear is a fundamental expression of this estrangement from family and self:

> John said *if any come aboard and hate not his father and his mother and his wife and children and his brothers and his sisters, and his own life too, he can not be a shipmate serving on this ship.* (70)

This is characteristic of this male community's violent self-division, an unequivocal statement of self hatred that originates with their perceived repudiation by the mother and with the profound disruption of family bonds. Fishboy attends to the crew's tales of family division but the tale of his own family origin is unknown and unspoken. Nevertheless, his narrative hurtles toward a confrontation with the mother figure known as Miss Magine, and to that symbolic return to her body by which his original separation from his family is addressed.

Each of the shipmates' stories has an important bearing on the story of Fishboy because they are all reflections on traumatic initiation that are darkly analogous to Fishboy's unknown origins. The tale of Mr Watt, the ship's captain, is typical: he is a freakish outcast from his family and from society, like Fishboy, and they recognise an affinity with each other in terms of their histories and their grotesque appearance. Mr Watt's injunction to 'get a good look at me' is a command to Fishboy to pay attention but also to recognise what kind of adult Fishboy has the potential to become. Fishboy's empathy with Mr Watt is expressed by the unflinching look that he gives him. Mr Watt was a child whose appearance so offended his family that he was completely ostracised by them; his mother was blamed by his father 'for bringing such an abomination into this world' (52) and she was subsequently murdered for the offence of childbirth. This has a parallel with the early childhood of Fishboy, who was abandoned by the father that he dimly recalls in 'the smell of cigar and shoe leather'. Fishboy is similarly rejected by his family because of physical differences that made him, 'a whispering lisp and the silken tipped fingers of another class'. Both Mr Watt and Fishboy suffer violent estrangement from fathers who wish them dead because of their physical difference; the very condition of their birth makes their lives anguished and wretched, and it condemns them perpetually to be the victims of society's murderous hostility. Again, orality is important here: while Fishboy begins by vomiting up his own symbolic re-birth, the murder of Mr Watt's mother brings about macabre scenes of famine and privation in which his family are forced to eat vermin, insects, and tree bark while the freakish child survives 'by sucking minerals from the mud of the bin bottom' (53). Mr Watt ultimately murders all of his family, and makes a bonfire of their home in a scene that dramatises the terrifying return of the monstrous to wreak revenge on those who abuse it. Where Fishboy buries his knife in the flesh of Miss Magine, the woman who would possess him, Mr Watt eradicates his family and thus commits himself, like Fishboy, to a life of complete exile. In both cases they offer allegories of being born into a world that does not want them, an adult world that is murderously hostile to their very existence. Estrangement is a necessary condition of being alive, and the very consequences of birth are denial, rejection and violent abuse.

The closeness of the tacit sympathy between Fishboy and Mr Watt is expressed in the latter's final phrase: 'I, too, began as a boy' (54). Although it is hard to believe that a man with such a frightening appearance and such a traumatic history could once have been an innocent child, this phrase echoes directly Fishboy's opening statement 'I began as a boy'. It is as if Fishboy has learned from Mr Watt the language of autobiography. Thus they share a similarity of narrative language and of personal history. Mr Watt's fate, in which the violent alienation of birth is something that can never be fully overcome, is the fate that awaits Fishboy. Their affinity is a birthright of violent repudiation by the very figures that have an obligation to nurture them: mothers and fathers. That repudiation can never be remedied or come to terms with because it lies at an originatory point to which they can never return. The consequences of Fishboy hearing Mr Watt's story are important to his development and education. There is a measure of Fishboy's acceptance and social integration in Mr Watt's expression 'like I had been part of the crew all along' (54), and Ira Dench registers the shock recognition of the similarly outrageous appearance of Fishboy: '*Boy, you gave me a fright,* he said. *You some kind of fish freak?*' (55). Fishboy's oddity makes him at home in this ship's crew, each one of them more monstrous and appalling than the next. The stories that they tell become an integral part of his story because they are each fragments of the same story of the inability to come of age in a world that never wanted them in the first place. In this context, sharing stories of their violent alienation from society is a means to create a momentary camaraderie which overcomes social estrangement, if only for the duration of the story-telling.

The coming of age of Fishboy is dramatised by his ability, or inability, to respond orally, or to respond in kind, to the stories that he is told. The importance of this is emphasised by the further account that Mr Watt gives of his life 'when I was about your age' (126). This tale is also one that dramatises Mr Watt's grotesque or monstrous appearance, in this case by making a clear allusion to Mary Shelley's *Frankenstein*: the farmer who provides a sanctuary for the outcast Mr Watt is blind and therefore he cannot be horrified by Mr Watt's appearance. Again oral deprivation is an important aspect of the story: 'The blind farmer had survived the winter eating his dead wife's shoes' (127). But, as in *Frankenstein*, society eventually catches up with Mr Watt, and he is forced to flee again after a mob senselessly murders the blind farmer. The story seems inconclusive; it is simply a tale about 'somebody doing something bad to somebody black', but it has an allegorical quality that Fishboy is expected to learn something from, a knowledge about the world from which he is temporarily absent aboard ship. But what is Fishboy to learn that will help him to grow up in such a world? In Mr Watt's story a father-figure is taken away and social relations are profoundly disrupted; the story illustrates the grotesque pointlessness of a society that is characterised by famine. The story's abrupt ending is puzzling to Fishboy, as it might be to the novel's readers:

> I wasn't sure what to say after Mr Watt finished his story. Was I supposed to beat his story like Lonny beat the cook's? Was I supposed to beat his story of somebody doing something bad to somebody black with my own story? (131)

There are two important images of reciprocity here, 'I finished covering him in his burned places with the lard', and Fishboy's final response to Mr Watt 'Thank you for the rich story' (131). Previously Fishboy had greeted story-telling with mute incomprehension and both of these gestures of reciprocity are indicative of his increasing maturity, of an increasing understanding of the adult world in which he finds himself. The story is also sufficiently evocative as to make Fishboy hungry, and his use of the word 'rich' is a complement to the linguistic richness of the story, even though it is a story about famine and starvation. This recognition and acknowledgement of Mr Watt's linguistic resourcefulness is an important feature of Fishboy's coming of age, especially in this environment where characters are defined by the credence and credibility of the stories that they tell.

The importance of linguistic resources to the ship's crew is also seen in the story of that crew member who is known exclusively as 'the weeping man who said *Fuck*'. This character is wholly defined by his single profane utterance, and the impoverishment of his identity is synonymous with his ludicrously attenuated vocabulary. This character does not even tell his own story, but Lonny and Mr Watt tell it for him. Like the personal histories of Mr Watt and Fishboy, this story is also characterised by a grotesquely problematic birth: when his mother was pregnant she was shocked by the sight of a steeplejack who fell from a spire onto the pavement beside her: 'the sight of the steeplejack pleading up to her from the pavement with his hips sprouting from his neck had caused her to faint and go into labor, and she gave birth alongside the burst man to an undersized infant' (66). Traumatic shock, gruesome death, and premature birth: the story of the man's origin defines him, and the violent personal history that is attendant upon such calamitous beginnings is inevitable and unavoidable because it is the necessary condition of being born in the first place: 'What he did had been decided before he was born, when his mother still carried him in her womb' (66). There is no place for free-will in a society so awry that the very circumstances of birth, or even pre-natal circumstances, will determine one's fate regardless. The weeping man who said '*Fuck*' subsequently discovers his wife's infidelity, he murders her, and then sews her together with one of her lovers:

> thousands of stitches, the bodies black with stitches and then black with flies as the stitching together took days. When he was through stitching them together he began to cry at what he had done and was only able to speak his one word. (125)

As if to mock the pain of these gruesome events, and to disable any emotional response to their suffering, Mr Watt observes laconically 'It made the papers' (125). The inability of the weeping man to say anything other than simply '*Fuck*' is indicative of his impoverishment, and also of the futility of human agency in the grotesque world that *Fishboy* depicts. As with the fiction of Nathanael West, emotional and physical pain is the subject of black humour, and the more painful the subject then the more humorous is the treatment. But the weeping man's relative speechlessness is also an important lesson for Fishboy, who has learned to recognise 'richness': orality has a rich redemptive potential, but it is important to be able to testify to one's own history and to be able to do so in a credible language that does justice to its allegorical possibilities. This is the aesthetic conviction from which Fishboy learns to compose his own story of coming of age.

These are the necessary conditions of existence in this microcosmic vision of American society aboard ship, and an awareness of these conditions is the terrifying realisation that Fishboy is initiated into as an integral part of being born. There is some faint possibility of redemption from these brutalising forces in acts of oral testimony because, in testifying to their terrible histories, the characters of *Fishboy* momentarily recapture that innocence that was originally denied them. The act of witnessing to lost innocence in a compelling yarn is a tacit plea for innocence to be restored, momentarily, in the confessional narrative. Oral testimony is thus a means to personal salvation in the individual's acknowledgement of sin and guilt; it is at the same time a vehicle for the potential salvation of others who might listen and then hasten to a reciprocal repentance. Further, an efficacious or compelling tale is one that aspires to an allegorical or mythical quality that encodes valuable forms of knowledge by which the crew members understand themselves and each other. Many of the stories of *Fishboy* are structured principally by repetition, by biblical rhetoric and extended Faulknerian sentences that contribute strongly to their portentous quality. The style suggests that these are stories that hold some truth for all men in this society, parables of experience that contain vitally important lessons for human conduct, especially for naive initiates like Fishboy. What is more, in the tales of how these characters became grotesque outcasts there are many vivid images of a profoundly disordered society. Beyond the apparently aberrant individual there is often a form of social critique that helps to account for monstrosity; there is a picture of a social world that has gone profoundly wrong and from which these ostracised crew members have been banished partly as a consequence of its unholy disorder. Widespread famine, social anarchy, family murder: these are common features of the crews' tales and they are symptomatic of an American society in a state of disintegration.

The emphasis placed on the value of the confessional story is seen in the particular relations that it creates between teller and auditor. In *Fishboy* the compulsion to tell a story is often followed immediately by the teller's desire to murder the auditor, because the auditor is now in possession of a vital personal secret that must be protected as a matter of life and death. Such stories are told against the teller's better judgement, a judgement which is suspended by the overwhelming compulsion to tell. Speaking, rather than writing, acquires great significance because of the authenticity of the personal knowledge that it conveys. For example, when Fishboy overhears the story of John's wife, he comments that he 'had heard what was breaking his heart and I wished I had never heard it' (82). The perils of this speaker-auditor relationship are characterised by the framing of the cook's tale:

> I knew he was going to tell me a story about a man with rubber arms, whether it was a true story or not. That did not matter. It only mattered that he wanted to tell it, and was going to tell, and I would listen whether I wanted to or not. (142)

Telling and listening create bonds that are expressive of a power and authority that is greater than either teller or auditor, and it is a power that cannot be resisted. The compulsion to tell is often matched by the rapture of the auditor in a relationship in which both are the passive agents of impulses that they do not understand and which they cannot control. During the cook's tale, for example, he recounts how the captain of the slave ship revealed to him the hidden daughter of the king whom he had secretly stowed away. Later, on a dogwatch at the rail, the captain sneaks up behind the cook and 'it was clear that he had intended to push [him] over' (147). The captain's paranoia is as unwarranted as his compulsion to reveal his secret in the first place: there is an abject terror in his actions that is expressive of a fear of unknown controlling forces. The cook's need to tell Fishboy this story is in turn an expression of the same neurotic anxiety. Similarly, at the end of the cook's story, he becomes confirmed in his own paranoid suspicions and attacks Fishboy for no reason: 'he was on me in a heartbeat with the rusty meat cleaver' (162). The cook is haunted by his own imaginings, having revealed the secret of his own psychological motivations, just as the captain in the cook's tale is terrorised by his. Again this is the particular territory of the grotesque, a mode in which its characters are painfully conscious of sinfulness and guilt in their own past for which contrition and confession lead not to an awareness of grace but to an even greater feeling of abjection, and one that only intensifies and perpetuates the novel's murderous cycle.

This scenario of violent paranoia in a world devoid of saving grace is further illustrated by the figure(s) of the men in prison blues. These men are really one man, divided in the classic doppelganger figure, a common characteristic of the grotesque, and one that can be seen at its most developed in the work of Samuel Beckett. The two men are not named but they are shackled together and identically dressed. Throughout the telling of their tale, as in Beckett's 'Watt', it is as if one person is speaking with two voices in a contrapuntal dialogue with himself. This divided self is a dramatisation of a schizophrenia which has its stylistic analogue in the conflicting impulses of horror and laughter that are characteristic of the grotesque. The men in prison blues exclaim ' "Save us! We'll confess!" ' when they are in peril of their lives, hanging from a rope over the side of the ship 'like a broken rosary' (108). This image of the failed devotional emblem is appropriate to their predicament: the rope by which they hang is held by the idiot and there can be no chance of salvation. Further, the tale that they tell is again one of murder and guilt in an anarchic world where values have been upturned. Thus their situation constitutes an absurd parody of the idea of confessional absolution which is germane to all of the oral narratives of the ship's crew. Where in Mr Watt's tale the land is afflicted by a famine that drives the mob to insanity and senseless murder, here we find 'the whole city burning' because 'the new king didn't want to be king' (111). Their identical weapons suggest that the mob that murders the blind farmer is perhaps the same mob that pursues the king with 'big long sticks with opened razors lashed to the ends' (115). The men in prison blues tell the story of a world that is anarchic and violent, where traditional social rituals and beliefs have collapsed, and where figures of authority such as kings and sheriffs can no longer be trusted. Consequently, it is a world in which survival is perilous because the proper rules of conduct are impossible to recognise. This disturbance is also indicative of a fallen world without hope of salvation. Moreover, although the men break out of prison, they are already guilty of an original crime that their story does not reveal. Although they save the king's life with the Heimlich manoeuvre, and although they might be guilty of his subsequent murder, their story never acknowledges their original sin, and therefore, as fallen men in a fallen world, they must always be the symbol of a violently self-divided conscience.

Again, the dramatic context of the tale has as much significance for Fishboy's education as the tale's narrative content. The men begin by furiously disputing who should best tell their story, and they end it by imputing guilt to each other in accusations of murder. The men's constantly antagonistic interpretation of their story culminates in a violent attack which results in the death of them both. This is partly a struggle for narrative control, for the authority of speech, and again it is one in which the story-tellers become wholly defined by the content of their story, as 'the ruby eater' and 'the king killer' (118). The story's focus on the activity of swallowing, as a form of oral consumption, is the narrative complement to the idea of story-telling as a form of oral production. This intense focus on orality is witnessed also in the men's final predicament, which combines the act of speaking with a terror of the all-consuming mouth: at the point of death, one man looks upward for salvation 'searching for a face to plead into' while the other looks downward in terror 'searching for a dark-form mouth to keep out of' (118–19). There is a complementarity in their final gestures that is suggestive of the divided conscience of the doppelganger and its conflicting impulses. The dramatic context of this ludicrous scene continues to emphasise orality; when the men in prison blues are 'delivered into the sea' their death is accompanied by the 'strangled speech' of the idiot who holds the rope that might have saved them. This sound is 'painful and fearful', but Fishboy admits 'I could not make out what the Idiot was trying to say' (119). Again the act of speech, and the recognition of the importance of speech acts, is a vital means to understanding and interpreting significant social experiences. In the grotesque world in which Fishboy struggles to come of age, orality is a signifying system on the verge of disintegration, and is frequently incomprehensible. The men survive briefly but die later on the verge of making 'some pronouncement' that is never properly heard (194).

The fact that Fishboy is a naive initiate puts enormous pressure on the value of these signifying practices and on his ability to recognise and interpret them as indexes of the social world in which he finds himself. If orality is a possible means to redemption and salvation then how might the novice learn its proper observances? For example, the men in prison blues are 'delivered' into the sea, and that word is significant because they make a symbolic return in a miraculous rebirth as innocent babies purged of sin and restored to a natural state. Their prison uniforms, a badge of guilt, are replaced by 'skins burned white', and they are delivered from the bowels of a shark 'like newborns' (166). It would seem that their contrition and repentance have earned them redemption before they die, and that the miraculous spectacle that they present to the crew is evidence of an alternative but mysterious means by which the ways of the world might be understood and innocence restored. The crew capture a giant shark; 'working his knife-like fingers over a large knot near the anus of the shark, John gave the carcass a good tearing pull' (166). The intensely visceral nature of this scene suggests a displaced representation of childbirth, or a macabre vision of childbirth in which the violently disrupted body evacuates its contents (literally, its viscera) and thus brings forth the miracle of newborn innocence: the men breathing for the first time 'goopy blood of hemorrhage from their noses' (166). If this is a miraculous vision of the moment of birth, a return to lost innocence that is suddenly granted to men steeped in guilt, then it is also a figurative return to the rebirth of Fishboy, who began his story in a swamp 'born again there, slithering out of the sack', and who acts as his own agent of oral self-determination by 'heaving up my own new creations of life in the mire' (2). Redemption might be possible if he too is prepared to speak of his fallen nature and to recognise, even in this grotesque world of enigmatic signifiers, the proper signs of divine providence. In this way, *Fishboy* becomes the story of its narrator's plea for a return to that original innocence that he was denied.

The narrative of *Fishboy* is crucially framed by his relation to the figure of Miss Magine, from whom he escapes at the beginning and to whom he is returned at the end. The novel's journey thus returns to the place where it began, and this is symbolic of a baulked coming of age, one in which the traditional teleological development is abruptly curtailed when the ship docks, for the only occasion in the novel, at the port where Fishboy joined it. This cyclical return is a representation of the impossibility of escape from the determining coordinates of this vision of the history of the United States. The expression of possession and ownership by which Big Miss Magine is characterised, '*You is mine, Fishboy, you is all mine*' (4), becomes literal at the end of the novel when Fishboy, rather than being evacuated as at childbirth, is taken back into the body of the woman, 'organs and all', literally consumed by the mother's mouth in a further image of orality and abjection. Fishboy becomes Miss Magine's flesh and sustenance, his body is swallowed by hers in a macabre inversion of childbirth, as a remedy for the injury that he did to her 'punctured gut' (226). Here the novel's focus on orality is supplemented by the faculty of vision as Fishboy becomes a haunting presence just beyond the range of sight and the limit of comprehension, a ghostly memory of lost innocence who reminds the reader that 'I, too, began as a boy' (227). This repetition of the novel's first line brings *Fishboy* to a close in a circular movement that is analogous to the ship's journey and to the restoration of Fishboy to the woman's body. The eyes of Fishboy and the eye of Miss Magine are each transfixed by the other, their mutual paralysis and passivity in the face of one another suggesting that they are each defined by the other's look:

> No matter how long or how often I looked away, I always turned my fish eye back to Big Miss Magine as she lay in her rotten cot, her big red-blue-purple egg of an eye staring straight back into my own. (225)

Miss Magine is a contemporary figure who is both black and unmarried, and the significance of her presence is partly elucidated by the reference to 'memories of ships with bellyfuls of tar-colored people, people linked ankle to ankle in perfect patterns' (27–8). The cook's tale is also a mysterious allegory of slavery, one in which he gives a confessional account of his refusal to save his (brown) brother Brune. In the cook's tale, familial and blood relations are violently disrupted, rituals of incest and recognition of racial difference are central to a society where pointless violence is socially sanctioned, and the idea of social disharmony has even infected the language: not only does the father demand the wages of the son in order to purchase the black woman whose childbearing will revitalise society, but he commands the cook to 'strike my brother if he become a bother' (152). The linguistic elision of 'brother' to 'bother' is suggestive of the ways in which the awareness of racial difference is integral to the very language of American society, such that blood relationships are awry and the father is defined not as the father but as 'our mother's husband' (152). The institution of slavery (aboard the slave ship, at the slave auction) underwrites an appalling disorientation of value throughout this American society, and the cook is haunted by the prospect of his murdered brother's resurrection. The cook is (d)riven by this fear, and his life of restless movement is an attempt to flee the spectre of history catching up with him. All movement is futile however because the cook's guilty anxiety can only be remedied by his own personal spiritual return to lost innocence: ' "Ye must be born again as I have been born again" ' (161). The cook is haunted by the possibility of the return of the repressed, which, like the black volcano of his story, is too naturally powerful to be fully contained. The cook's tale is in some ways an enigmatic and oblique analogue to the novel itself; Fishboy becomes the ghostly figure of a repressed history of slavery that haunts the contemporary American landscape, and the cook's tale becomes the suppressed story of Fishboy's pre-natal history, here returned in the narrative as an origin myth that can no longer be kept secret. The cook's tale ends when he mistakes Fishboy for his brown brother, a case of mistaken identity that Fishboy is only able to refute by the evidence of his blood: 'I still had the pins and needles so I was slow to raise it. The blood flowed back into my arm and I managed to make a fist I shook in his face' (162).

In this context, then, Miss Magine might be interpreted as a contemporary means to (i)magine the legacy of slavery, the imaginary body of the black mother who tells him 'you is mine', because she instantly recognises that he belongs to her racially. In this reading, Fishboy becomes the child of mixed parentage who was abandoned by the father whose shame the child embodied and who now haunts American society to remind it of its violent racial history. Fishboy is finally taken back into the body of the black mother whose child he is and who tried to possess him but from whom he fled in horror at her colour and what it signified. In *Fishboy* coming of age is a story of national significance, a tale of the United States' racial haunting and of the inability to come to terms with that specific history on which the nation's prosperity was founded.

The style of *Fishboy* is itself a dramatisation of the inability to speak directly and openly about this history, to acknowledge fully the racial conflicts that shaped the history of the United States. The novel's interpretation of the genre of the grotesque is its aesthetic response to this predicament; along with this, *Fishboy* historicises the grotesque by presenting it as having come about as a result of a monstrous American history. The coming-of-age genre is used here to articulate ideas about historical entrapment and paralysis, to address a history in which children are trapped by the sins of their fathers and cannot be released from this determining original American sinfulness. The novel dramatises a fear of the consequences of miscegenation that has a history in American literature at least as old as *The Last of The Mohicans* (1823), and which constitutes ' a dark and abiding presence that moves the hearts and texts of American literature with fear and longing' (Morrison 1992: 33). Fishboy begins in a vacuum, and he ends in a death without issue. This is why the novel concludes not with an ethereal image suitable to the tale of a ghost, but with the image of the blood: 'I am as close to you as the blood in your veins in your neck' (227). In this respect, Fishboy's beginning and ending, the pinched ends of his narrative, although abrupt and elusive, are as important in their symbolic value as the story itself.

Chapter 5

Lexicon of Love

Since its inception in Germany in the eighteenth century, the bildungsroman has traditionally been understood as a male genre. From *Huckleberry
Finn* (1885) to *The Catcher in the Rye* (1951), and Dale Peck's *What We
Lost* (2003), coming of age has been associated with the story of how boys
become men. As a result, Barbara White believes that critics 'have tended
to ignore female experience and universalise the experience of boys'
(White 1985: 15), and Elizabeth Abel argues that 'while male protagonists
struggle to find a hospitable context in which to realise their expectations,
female protagonists must frequently struggle to voice any aspirations
whatsoever' (Abel et al. 1983: 7). These two critical works, *Growing
up Female: Adolescent Girlhood in American Fiction*, and *The Voyage
In: Fictions of Female Development*, have been complemented by
other studies, such as E. K. Labovitz's *The Myth of the Heroine: The
Female Bildungsroman in the Twentieth Century* (1986) and Susan
Fraiman's *Unbecoming Women: British Women Writers and the Novel of
Development* (1993), which provide scholarly and theoretical support for
the idea that there is a tradition of women working in the coming-of-age
genre. The question is whether traditional conceptions of the genre are
fundamentally altered by women writers working in it (to the point where
an experimental novel such as Cisneros' *The House on Mango Street* is not
really a bildungsroman), or whether the genre, as it is conventionally
understood, simply does not permit women to express themselves properly. For example, one critic has outlined a counter-tradition of the bildungsroman that is written by 'disenfranchised Americans – women,
blacks, Mexican-Americans, native Americans, homosexuals' (Braendlin
1983: 75), while another believes that 'the authentic feminine bildungsroman remains to be written' (Baruch 1981: 356).

The two novels of this chapter dramatise young women struggling
with the stereotypes of domestic conformity, negotiating ideas about
social responsibility, and searching for a language of subjectivity that

evades the prescriptive determinations of patriarchal culture. Both novels are intensely literate in their understanding of how women have been represented, and of how cultural representations can have a formative influence on coming of age. There is a remarkably creative and erudite self-consciousness in these novels' depiction of female protagonists whose search for self-determination is conditioned by the knowledge that narratives of self-determination are traditionally male. Both novels are exceptional in the ways that they create unique textual voices from a synthesis of challenges that are both social and aesthetic; these are radical novels, both for the social politics that they espouse and for the aesthetic innovations by which they espouse them. That social politics is about gender, but also about a region of the United States: these novels address the historical legacies of the south and the west in ways that have consequences not only for gender identity, but also for national identity.

Marilynne Robinson, *Housekeeping*

Marilynne Robinson's *Housekeeping* (first published in 1980), is the coming of-age story of a girl called Ruth, whose mother commits suicide, and who is raised first by her grandmother and then by her aunt Sylvie. These women have a formative influence on Ruth's growing up; Ruth's other key relationship is with her sister, another young woman whose sense of female identity has an important bearing on Ruth's emergent adult identity. Although the novel is principally about relationships between women, and is notable for the absence of men, it begins with the story of Ruth's grandfather, Edmund, whose fate foreshadows a great deal that is important in the girls' development. Edmund 'took a train west' (Robinson 2004: 4) and got a job with the railroad company, but he was the victim of a spectacular derailment in which everyone on the train was killed, and he simply disappeared. Edmund's body is never recovered. The circumstances of this accident are almost completely unknown, except for the evidence of one boy who swam to the bottom of the lake into which the train plunged: 'This boy was an ingenious liar, a lonely boy with a boundless desire to ingratiate himself. His story was neither believed nor disbelieved' (8). This boy is almost the end of the novel's male presence, but *Housekeeping* returns often to the image of the grandfather at the bottom of the lake as a formative and determining moment in the lives of the women of this family – Edmund's wife and three daughters. Edmund's daughter, Helen, subsequently commits suicide by driving her car into this same lake, and Edmund's deracination and restlessness is reflected in the lives of his other daughters, Molly, who goes to China, and Sylvie, who departs for Spokane and is forever unable to settle decisively in any one place. The loss of their father is a traumatic event for the daughters, all of whom were teenagers at the time of his death; it is a loss that 'troubled the very medium of their lives' (15). Thereafter they become terminally restless, and their father's commitment to a quintessentially western mythology of mobility and rebirth contributes strongly to their shifting and unsettled lives.

At the same time, the loss of the father is coincident with the expression of important ideas about the nature, status, and origin of narrative that are also vitally central to the girls' coming of age. The grandfather's story is a point of origin, an account of how they came to be in the west in the first place, but it is a story hedged with doubt and uncertainty. The language of the quotation above, about the boy who confirms the presence of the train at the bottom of the lake, is also significantly concerned with credulity, and with the origins of narrative: does narrative necessarily originate in loneliness and social alienation, and, if so, should it ever be completely trusted as a historical record of the past? Further, Ruth's own narrative begins in language that alerts our attention to other stories: 'My name is Ruth'. This four-word opening sentence recalls the first sentence of Melville's *Moby Dick*, 'Call me Ishmael', and thereby sets up a relation that encourages readers to question the nature of intertextual origins. What will be the relationship between Ruth's story and those important antecedent stories from which its narrative paradigms are derived? Ruth's family lineage is expressed in a way that also calls attention to how family lineages are classically expressed in language:

> My name is Ruth. I grew up with my younger sister, Lucille, under the care of my grandmother, Mrs. Sylvia Foster, and when she died, of her sisters-in-law, Misses Lily and Nona Foster, and when they fled, of her daughter, Mrs. Sylvia Fisher. (1)

The style of Ruth's expression here clearly echoes the Bible, or, more precisely, offers 'a revision of biblical patrilinear genealogies' (Ravits 1989: 645). Each of these questions about narratives (Edmund's, the lonely boy's, Ishmael's, and the Bible), establish the uncertainty of narrative, and the question of narrative origins in particular, as a fundamental component of Ruth's coming-of-age story. The novel's opening chapter, in which family origins are elucidated, is as much about the idea of narrative as it is about those subjects that narrative expresses. There is a self-consciousness about the investments and procedures of story telling here that could be described as metafictional, and this self-consciousness remains a consistent feature of the whole novel. Further, it is an enquiry into the nature of narrative that has a distinctive gender politics. How does the story of a girl coming of age among women negotiate a textual relationship with a history of the genre that has been shaped by the stories of men, such as those of the Bible, classic nineteenth-century American literature, Ruth's grandfather Edmund (and his attendant male mythology of western adventuring), and the lonely boy whose ability to swim seems to give him the privilege to tell stories? Ruth's coming of age needs to come to terms with the male structures of society, but also with male structures of narrative: how else can a girl's account of coming of age avoid male stereotypes of domesticity (housekeeping), and how can Ruth tell her story without simply recapitulating the forms of male development that might well be inimical to her female identity? These are the serious and ambitious challenges that the novel sets itself, and they are essentially issues of the social politics of aesthetic forms. In what ways is story-telling informed by gender politics, and how can women writers create original stories that do justice to their difference from men when the whole language of the genre is historically male? *Housekeeping* is unusually self-conscious in the ways that it finds to address these questions.

Criticism has rightly paid significant attention to the feminist paradigms by which *Housekeeping* can be interpreted, and yet it is worth pausing briefly to consider the motivations of Ruth's grandfather. In a novel that is very much concerned with the importance of place, it was Edmund whose restlessness brought the family specifically to this place (the west, Idaho), and it is Edmund's restlessness which is his daughters' most singular characteristic. Edmund grew up in a sod house in the midwest, where his horizons were so severely circumscribed as to be deathly, and he therefore began to read accounts of mountains in travel literature that were so compelling that he took a train west to the margin, to the town called Fingerbone, to begin a new life in a new place, one characterised by 'a number of puzzling margins' (4). Edmund's classically western American desire to move on and to start over, is again fuelled by aesthetic consumption (he reads widely), and it is accompanied by aesthetic production (he begins to paint). Physical and geographical movement is closely associated with important personal investments in art. Edmund's three daughters are all teenagers when he dies, and each of them inherits from him a propensity to movement and a corresponding interest in creative arts; in this novel there is a particularly close association between mobility and creative energy, the energy of movement and creative energy that is quintessentially western and American. Simultaneously, Edmund's death precipitates a crisis for the women (his wife and three daughters, Molly, Helen, and Sylvie), in terms of their status and burgeoning identity, and this will crucially shape their relationships with men and with the structures of male society. Edmund's wife, for example, finds that 'with him gone they were cut free from the troublesome possibility of success, recognition, advancement' (13). Edmund's death radically alters the women's social relations. The two other widows from the train accident leave Fingerbone immediately, and within five years Edmund's widow is deserted by her three daughters, Molly for China and Sylvie and Helen further west to Seattle. Molly's departure for China is inspired by visual arts in the same way that her father's upheaval was, 'page 2 of a brochure of, it seemed, great and obvious significance. It was slick and heavy, like a page from *National Geographic*, and it was folded in thirds like a letter' (90–1). These family dislocations serve to confirm for Ruth's grandmother a loneliness that she has long felt: 'Old women she had known, first her grandmother and then her mother, rocked on their porches in the evenings and sang sad songs, and did not wish to be spoken to' (18). Alienation from social structures, social discourse, even from social life, is coincident with an aesthetic, sad songs that speak of that alienation. Ruth's grandmother articulates a belief in the origin of art not unlike that of Tennyson's 'The Lady of Shalott', or of the women of Toni Morrison's *The Bluest Eye*. In each case, the production of art is attendant upon an unwelcome or violent separation from society. Where the lonely boy who tells the story of grandfather is merely an ingenious liar who wishes to call attention to himself, the art of these women is a consequence of their material lives. This is the hallmark of a female aesthetic which begins to distinguish itself in its creative forms from a male history of narrative that has been more socially and artistically conventional. Moreover, Ruth's grandmother finds her life story completely re-written as the story of her husband's death; as E. A. Meese points out, when she dies, her obituary includes 'only her husband's photograph and none of her own funeral details' (Meese 1986: 59). *Housekeeping* writes the stories of women who are not defined by their subservient relationships to men, or by their function as wives and mothers, but principally in relation to each other.

The daughters also find relationships with men problematical. Sylvie marries Fisher, Helen marries Stone; both women abandon their husbands. Not only does Ruth never know her grandfather, but her father is only 'putative' (14), and, like Edmund, he has no corporeal presence: 'I have no memory of this man at all' (14). In many ways then, the novel's beginning interrogates the very idea of beginnings, both in terms of gender relations and of narrative conventions. *Housekeeping* begins by clearing a space in which it might write about women's lives independently of men, and also by establishing the terms on which such an aesthetic practice might be founded. The independence of the women of the Foster family is shared by the novel's other women, Nona and Lily and

Bernice, all of whom sustain themselves outside the reaches of male society, not unlike the female communities of Willa Cather's western novels (*My Antonia* in particular). By telling these stories, and by depicting women characters who themselves tell stories of separation and alienation, *Housekeeping* generates its own sense of a narrative community, one with distinctive and innovative aesthetic practices. To some extent, this is put forward for women as an alternative to the tradition of the Bible, *Moby Dick*, and, at a more local level, of lonely boys who invent stories about lost grandfathers.

Into this world of independent women comes Ruth's Aunt Sylvie, the most radically independent woman, and the one who will have most influence on the development of the child protagonist. It is vitally important to the novel that Sylvie is a transient, a drifter who has to be recalled from Billings, Montana (specifically from the Lost Hills Hotel of Big Sky Country), because no one can be sure of her exact whereabouts. Sylvie is thirty-five years old and married, but 'she had simply chosen not to act married, though she had a marriage of sufficient legal standing to have changed her name. No word had ever indicated who or what this Fisher might have been' (43). The politics of Sylvie's choice here is vital to the model of female behaviour that she presents to Ruth, and that 'word' is also an important signal, reminding the reader again of the legacy of narrative language, and of its vital association with the murky origins of identity. Moreover, Sylvie is not only a traveller but also a story teller, and again the creative energy of those twin activities is closely associated, because 'every story she told had to do with a train or a bus station' (68). Sylvie's stories are exclusively about women, and specifically about women who are at the margins of society, either by travelling or by institutionalisation: the stories of boxcar Edith, of Alma, and their mutual friend at the state institution who 'wept with anger' (89). Here again is the important presence of the aesthetic, in the form of the song 'Irene', which is overheard at the truckstop and which becomes the lament of all women who find themselves at the limit of conventional society. Sylvie's stories suggest to Ruth a whole world of ostracised women; they are outside conventional social conformity but they constitute a community in themselves, and especially a community of narrative. These narratives are sad songs of their difficult but necessary separation from (male) society, 'intricate and melancholy tales of people she had known slightly' (84). Sylvie's stories are part of a shared mythology of women on the road, of those encounters which constitute only a frail travelling coincidence, but which are not without significant social implications. This is true both for women who find themselves outside socially sanctioned domestic roles and for the orphaned Ruth: 'That was the first Lucille or

I had heard of the interest of the state in the well-being of children, and we were alarmed' (68). Ruth has lost her mother, she then loses her grandmother, and she is subsequently passed over by Nona and Lily: it becomes vital to her survival that aunt Sylvie stays in Fingerbone and keeps house if Ruth is not to be taken away by probate court to 'a farm or something' (68). But Sylvie is so desperately restless that she is drawn to the railroad by every passing train, and at one point Ruth watches her contemplating suicide from the bridge into the lake where Sylvie's father and sister both drowned. Sylvie is simply 'not a stable person' (82), and even in the house she retains 'the habits of a transient' (103), by sleeping fully clothed with her shoes under her pillow. One of the challenges of Ruth's childhood therefore, is to encourage Sylvie to stay, because, as she puts it, 'It seemed to me that if she could remain transient here, she would not have to leave' (103). This becomes a crucial issue to Ruth's coming of age.

How is this to be done, and how might its accomplishment impact upon Ruth's childhood? Part of the answer lies in opening the business of keeping house to the outside world, so that inner and outer, domesticity and mobility, might be broken down as mutually exclusive categories. More conceptually for this novel, Ruth learns from Sylvie that these category differences are best managed and negotiated by exposing them to dissolution: 'Sylvie in a house was more or less like a mermaid in a ship's cabin. She preferred it sunk in the very element it was meant to exclude. We had crickets in the pantry, squirrels in the eaves, sparrows in the attic' (99). Sylvie is the agent of a subversive social agenda in which the structures of home are opened to the forces of the open range: 'Sylvie believed in stern solvents, and most of all in air. It was for the sake of air that she opened doors and windows' (85). Ruth comes to understand that if the open air is allowed to permeate the house, then the free range of the western frontier might also be permitted to inhabit it. This recognition is vital to Sylvie's continued residence at the house, and it has immediate consequences for Ruth's engagement with those social structures that are represented by school teachers and town sheriffs. In one scene, for example, a curtain catches fire from the candles of a birthday cake: 'Sylvie had beaten out the flames with a back issue of *Good Housekeeping*, but she had never replaced the curtain' (101). Here again is the significant presence of the authoritative text, a reminder that there is a narrative of proper domestic conduct from which Sylvie radically departs. It is part of the politics of the novel to challenge those representations that sanction a particular narrative of female domesticity. The ironic use of *Good Housekeeping* by Sylvie, and its resonance with the novel's title, reminds us that Robinson is engaged in a process of revision and re-writing from a new perspective that is both social and aesthetic. The novel later satirises 'those magazines full of responsible opinion about discipline and balanced meals' (110), and those that are 'full of new hairstyles' (122), because they are regarded as the agents of a patriarchal authority that infantilise women and keep them in subordinate roles.

Ruth's coming of age is conducted principally under the auspices of her relationship with Sylvie, and in the context of the female aesthetic of narrative that Sylvie exemplifies, and which the novel both creates and self-consciously interrogates. This is a very sophisticated and self-reflexive process, one in which the material conditions of Ruth's life are lived out, even while simultaneously its narrative possibilities as an aesthetic artefact are explored and investigated. This is the particular imbrication of the social and artistic that distinguishes this novel from others in the coming-of-age genre that are less ambitious. For example, Ruth discovers that listening to Sylvie's stories stimulates her own imagination, and she begins to find that 'I was always reminded of pictures, images, in places where images never were' (90). This burgeoning imaginative capacity is an invitation to join an aesthetic community, and even to attempt to create a definitive expression of it, by writing the account of coming of age that becomes the novel *Housekeeping*. Inevitably Ruth's coming of age is bound up with 'the discomforts of female adolescence' (97), but it is also coterminous with the birth of the narrative and lyrical ability with which she is able to write *Housekeeping*. The awakening that the novel depicts is therefore both social and artistic, and these dual aspects are inextricable. Coming of age is simultaneously political and artistic, and the politics of Ruth's art is integral to its aesthetic value. The self-consciousness with which this is executed is remarkably subtle; it is reminiscent of the activities of hairdressing and quilting that take place in Alice Walker's *The Color Purple* (1982), activities that take place specifically between women in shared and reciprocal gestures of social and creative bonding. It is worth noting, too, that creative ability is integral to the changing female body: 'What twinges, what aches I felt, what gathering towards fecundity, what novel and inevitable rhythms, were the work of my strenuous imagining' (97). The physical differences between Ruth and her sister Lucille are important because they prefigure ideological differences between women that are fundamental to the novel's politics. Again there is a sense of the social differences between them having an origin in their respective physical development into adulthood, 'While she became a small woman, I became a towering child' (97).

These scenes of Ruth's emergence into adulthood are precipitated by another loss, that of her sister Lucille. The differences between the sisters, which results in their opposing choice of lifestyle, originate in different interpretations of their mother:

> Lucille's mother was orderly, vigorous, and sensible, a widow (more than I ever knew or she could prove) who was killed in an accident. *My* mother presided over a life so strictly simple and circumscribed that it could not have made any significant demands on her attention. (109)

The two sisters have different ideas of what constitutes authentic female identity, and those ideas originate with their memories of Helen, however imperfect those memories might be. Lucille's defection to 'the other world' (95) is partly a result of her impatience with Sylvie's behaviour. It is significant that Ruth's awakening in chapter 8 follows immediately her sister's departure for the house of Miss Royce, the school's home economics teacher:

> Miss Royce was a solitary woman, too high strung to be capable of friendships with children . . . And now here was Lucille, wandering through the dark to her house. Miss Royce gave her the spare room. In effect, she adopted her, and I had no sister after that night. (140)

Rosette Brown's mother also has become the barometer of social embarrassment for Lucille where, again, the social is closely associated with the aesthetic. Mrs Brown's sense of (aesthetic) propriety is offended by Sylvie's stories of women who had 'ridden the rods from south Dakota', and she asks with patrician indignation 'How could people of reasonableness and solidity respond to such tales?' (104). Lucille is sensitive to Mrs Brown's social criticism and decides that she can no longer live with Sylvie and Ruth.

Lucille's departure is a terrible loss to Ruth, who has not only shared her traumatic childhood with her sister but who thinks of the two of them 'almost as a single consciousness' (98). It is a loss that will haunt her right through to the novel's last page. It is a defection from that community of women who sustain each other by common ideological resistance; as the narrator of Christina Rossetti's *Goblin Market* claims: 'For there is no friend like a sister/In calm or stormy weather/To cheer one on the tedious way/To fetch one if one goes astray/To lift one if one totters down/To strengthen whilst one stands'. Lucille has learned to become sensitive to that project of fastidious self-improvement so particular to the United States, the socially-learned drive 'to make something of herself' (132), partly by writing a diary and reading novels. This is a project from which Ruth absents herself, and opts thereby to ally herself with the alternative American world of Sylvie. It is a programme of American self-fashioning that can be seen in many classic American texts, such as in *The Great*

Gatsby, where the adolescent James Gatz writes a schedule of 'General Resolves' on the fly-leaf of *Hopalong Cassidy* including 'read one improving book or magazine per week' (Fitzgerald 1974: 180), and in William Carlos Williams' poem 'Pastoral': 'When I was younger/it was plain to me/I must make something of myself.' It is not an easy choice for Ruth, to absent herself from this tradition of self-determination, but a deeply challenging one, as the encounter with the adult authority of Mr French demonstrates: ' "what *does* matter to you Ruth?" ' (135). This is a question about value that goes to the heart of Ruth's burgeoning self-determination, as does Mr French's injunction ' "You're going to have to learn to speak for yourself, and think for yourself" ' (135). Ruth does not speak the same cultural language as her sister, and the language that she is learning from Sylvie is not one that Mr French, Mrs Brown, or the town sheriff, would recognise the value of. It is, nevertheless, the language in which *Housekeeping* is written, and it is a strikingly original idiom because it has its roots in a radically different social politics from that of the novel's other characters.

As her surrogate mother, Sylvie is responsible for Ruth's symbolic birth into adulthood. This takes place in chapter eight, in which Sylvie takes Ruth across the lake and into the woods where she temporarily abandons Ruth to the elements. The sun rises on this October day 'like a long-legged insect bracing itself out of its chrysalis' (147), and images of birth abound as they cross the lake of 'my grandfather's last migration', the place that he brought his wife and daughters to, 'trailing us after him unborn' (149). It is here that Ruth comes to terms with the loss of her mother, and her future as an adult companion to Sylvie is decisively shaped. It is characteristic of the novel that coming of age takes place both in material terms and, simultaneously, in terms of a response to important antecedent narratives that readers are encouraged to reconsider. The glacial erosion of northern Idaho provides a symbolic landscape for Ruth's awakening, where the story of Lot's wife is revised:

> If there had been snow I would have made a statue, a woman to stand along the path, among the trees. The children would have come close, to look at her. Lot's wife was salt and barren, because she was full of loss and mourning, and looked back. But here rare flowers would gleam in her hair . . . and they would forgive her, eagerly and lavishly, for turning away, though she never asked to be forgiven. Though her hands were ice and did not touch them, she would be more than mother to them, she so calm, so still, and they such wild and orphan things. (153)

Lot's wife is the woman in the Bible who makes the mistake of looking back, and is turned into a pillar of salt, forever fixed in the static and agonising position of a retrospective that has come to define her utterly. But at this moment in Ruth's imagination, Lot's wife is transformed into an image of marvellous fecundity. The idea of forgiveness for 'turning away', and the use of the word 'orphan', link Lot's wife with Ruth's mother to dramatise a crucial emotional reconciliation with loss and bereavement; that reconciliation will enable Ruth to move forward into adulthood with this fundamental psychological issue resolved. This scene occurs during Sylvie's abandonment of Ruth (a reprise of the loss of the mother in a minor key), and it takes place at the derelict homestead which is clearly a symbol of ruined domestic history. Although this is a crucial moment in Ruth's rite of passage, it is important that it takes place through the medium of a biblical story because that specifically textual negotiation (a feminist revision) is a vital aspect of the novel's aesthetic politics. Here again the novel reveals itself as a narrative that is importantly engaged in productive and creative renegotiations with other authoritative narratives that it seeks to offer fresh interpretations of. This process of textual revision is integral to the novel's ambitious interpretation of the coming-of-age genre and shows how the genre can be renovated to a specifically feminist politics while simultaneously creating a uniquely compelling story. A similar process is at work in chapter eight's characterisation of Noah's wife, 'a nameless woman', whom Ruth imagines walking into the water of the flood until, like Ruth's mother Helen, she drowns. Ruth makes this connection because 'we knew the story from our childhood' (172), but here Noah's wife is given a consciousness, an identity, and a role, and she is thereby changed in the way that Lot's wife is changed, by an association with Ruth's mother.

Following this imaginative interpretation of the story of Lot's wife, Ruth begins to contemplate explicitly the memory of her mother:

> If I could see my mother, it would not have to be her eyes, her hair. I would not need to touch her sleeve. There was no more the stoop of her high shoulders. The lake had taken that, I knew. It was so very long since the dark had swum her hair, and there was nothing more to dream of, but often she almost slipped through any door I saw from the side of my eye, and it was she, and not changed, and not perished. She was a music I no longer heard, that rang in my mind, itself and nothing else, lost to all sense, but not perished, not perished. (159–60)

This moment of realisation is perhaps the heart of the novel, the point at which the painful history of Helen's apparent maternal indifference is accommodated by her daughter's maturing consciousness. It is here that Sylvie returns with a physical gesture, 'her hand on my back', and Ruth also recognises Sylvie's crucial role in facilitating her rite of passage:

'I was angry that she had left me for so long, and that she did not ask pardon or explain, and that by abandoning me she had assumed the power to bestow such a richness of grace' (161). The language of redemption and salvation is an indication of the kind of secular transcendental fulfilment that Ruth experiences here as she passes into another state of being. The remarkable scenes in chapter eight accomplish many things at once through the intensity of their lyrical language, and they define the terms in which Ruth's coming of age takes place. For Ruth, becoming adult is not a process of negotiation with fathers, but with mothers and mother-surrogates, and, at the same time, in the context of a tradition of male narratives of adolescent experience to which *Housekeeping* offers an alternative. These scenes show how an ambitious and original interpretation of the genre of the bildungsroman is possible, while still dramatising the importance of the coming-of-age narrative for American adulthood. As Martha Ravits argues:

> This female rite of passage is muted in comparison with male rituals, often typified by some form of competition, hunting, or violence in American fiction. The female hero's courage consists not of physical fortitude tested against external dangers but of courageous subjectivity in the face of isolation and neglect. (Ravits 1989: 659)

This 'fortitude' is dramatised by Ruth's emotional survival, and in the challenges of the life that she chooses with Sylvie, despite the social and cultural pressure of the kind to which her sister proves susceptible.

The difficulty of these challenges, and the serious cost of meeting them, is dramatised by the novel's enigmatic and oblique conclusion, in which Ruth laments the loss of her sister to another lifestyle, but in ways that reveal a robust acknowledgement of the different paths they have followed. In the novel's final chapter, the sheriff is on the brink of taking Ruth away to a 'custody hearing' (213), and so Sylvie and Ruth burn down the house and flee, 'and there was an end to housekeeping' (209). They cross the railroad bridge on foot, a rubicon that commits Ruth irrevocably to a life of drifting, and they are subsequently presumed dead in the lake beneath the bridge that claimed Ruth's grandfather and mother. The novel ends many years later with the continued contemplation of origins, in what Ruth terms 'some bleak alchemy' (215) by which she was conceived. The novel also ends with a return to Ruth's lost sister Lucille, who is imagined by Ruth to be in Boston pursuing a lifestyle utterly different from Ruth's life in Montana: 'No one watching this woman . . . could know how her thoughts were thronged by our absence, or know how she does not watch, does not listen, does not wait, does not hope, and always for me and Sylvie' (219). This profusion of

negatives in which the novel ends, recalls the annihilation of consciousness which concludes Wallace Stevens' 'The Snow Man': 'For the listener,
Who listens in the snow/And, nothing himself, beholds/Nothing that is
not there and the nothing that is.' The impossibility of a reconciliation
between Ruth and Lucille is augmented by an imaginative final flourish
in which even the imagination is extinguished, and yet the novel creates
something remarkable even from that loss.

Housekeeping is a novel that puts the coming-of-age genre to some
exceptionally sophisticated uses, and it has attracted a remarkable
amount of excellent academic criticism, especially for an author's first
novel (and Robinson's second novel, *Gilead*, was not published until
2005). This attention is partly due to the novel's undoubted artistic qualities, but also because of the wider cultural implications of Ruth's coming
of age. Martha Ravits has argued that the novel 'brings a new perspective to bear on the dominant American myth about the developing individual freed from social constraints' (Ravits 1989: 644); Maureen Ryan
designates Ruth 'the New American Eve', the feminist response to R. W.
B. Lewis's 'American Adam' of this book's Introduction (Ryan 1991: 79);
Nancy Walker argued that *Housekeeping* is revolutionary because
'Robinson challenges the authority of the Creation story by recasting its
central figures as women and giving Ruth the power to be its author'
(Walker 1995: 37); Susan Rosowski argues that *Housekeeping* is characterised principally by its serious 'engagement with epistemological and
political questions of the literary West' (Rosowski 1999: 177); Elizabeth
Meese argued that it is 'a work endowed with striking originality and
artistic force' (Meese 1986: 58), and Ann Romines called it 'one of the
best American novels of recent decades' (Romines 1992: 295). This is by
no means a complete account of the claims that have been made on
behalf of Robinson's first novel, but it gives a sense of the quality of attention the novel has received, and of the cultural terms on which it is
valued. It is testimony to the coming-of-age genre that *Housekeeping*
can deploy its conventions as a vehicle for such a major engagement with
fundamentally important aspects of United States' culture.

Josephine Humphreys, *Rich in Love*

Josephine Humphreys' *Rich in Love* (1987) begins with its seventeen-
year-old protagonist, Lucille Odom, returning home from school in a
suburb of Charleston to discover that her mother has absconded and left
her to take responsibility for the household. This is a dramatic and completely unexpected development in the Odom family. For Lucille, it is

inexplicable that her mother should suddenly abandon her in this way, and it precipitates an enquiry into the history of her mother's life, and of her parents' relationship, that situates Lucille's childhood in the contemporary south. This is the characteristic search for significant points of historical origin that is typical of the contemporary coming-of-age novel. Lucille's father is paralysed by his wife's departure, and this compounds Lucille's sense that she is called upon to take control of a very adult predicament. Lucille's elder sister, Rae, returns home from Washington DC, but only to announce that she is newly married and pregnant. To make matters worse, Lucille has a sexual relationship with her sister's new husband, and the domestic situation threatens to implode. These are the central moments of crisis in the novel, when Lucille's coming of age seems to have gone disastrously wrong as a consequence of her mother's sudden departure. However, the birth of sister Rae's baby brings about the surprise return of Lucille's mother, and it also effects a reconciliation between Rae and her husband. In many ways then, *Rich In Love* conforms to the enlightenment teleological structure of coming of age, in which the adolescent struggles with new challenges and thereby moves toward a more mature understanding of themself and of the world. It is a challenging but purposeful movement toward mature adult self-knowledge, and one that takes place (in the typical temporal compression of the coming-of-age novel) in one long summer vacation. This synopsis shows how there are many important ways in which *Rich in Love* subscribes to the coming-of-age genre: there is a new and urgent interest in origins; the adolescent struggles to find the appropriate language by which to articulate this new transitional phase, and this sense of sudden change is, typically, situated in a social context that is also transitional: the adolescent's coming of age is symptomatic of forms of important cultural change that the novel wishes to examine.

Rich in Love is only one of a number of novels of female development written recently by southern women about girls coming to terms with the changed circumstances of 'the new south'. Fred Hobson argues that there are 'any number of contemporary renderings of *Huckleberry Finn*, usually but not always with a different voice, often a different gender' (Hobson 1991: 77), and he cites Beverly Lowry's *Emma Blue* (1978), Jill McCorkle's *The Cheer Leader* (1984), and Kaye Gibbons' *Ellen Foster* (1987) as constituting a canon of such novels; they have an important antecedent not only in *Huckleberry Finn* but also in Carson McCullers' Mick Kelly in *The Heart is a Lonely Hunter*. What distinguishes *Rich in Love*, however, is its narrator's particular interest in language and subjectivity, an interest that gives the novel a remarkable sophistication and complexity for a story recounted by a teenager. This consistent conceptual focus on the forms of language that are available for female self-expression, recalls a different southern antecedent, the voice of Addie Bundren in Faulkner's 1930 novel *As I Lay Dying*. Addie's remarkable disquisition on the nature of the language that she has inherited from her southern (male) culture, and especially her feeling that 'words don't ever fit even what they are trying to say at' (Faulkner 1988: 136), provide a model for the female semiotic that Lucille's coming of age strives to articulate.

The immediate crisis in Lucille's life is brought about by the abrupt departure of her mother, who has left home 'to start a second life' (Humphreys 1992: 18), and so the novel begins with a dramatic crisis that throws the teenager into a suddenly new and challenging set of circumstances. Because this crisis occurs in the novel's first chapter it is the purpose of the structure of the narrative to work back to this point and to provide, eventually, some historical explication of it. One of the features of *Rich in Love* that makes it particularly notable is that although it is a first-person narrative account (and therefore necessarily limited by that perspective), a great deal of valuable information is provided concerning the departure of Lucille's mother. Helen Odom is forty-nine years old, and has begun to feel that 'she'd married too young and had not had time to get her fill of children's games' (23). Like some of Anne Tyler's southern heroines (for example, Maggie Moran in *Breathing Lessons*) Helen seeks to escape, suddenly and emphatically, from her marriage and from the suffocating social expectations of southern femininity that seem typical of her culture. Helen does not conform to the stereotype of 'the Charleston matron' (28), and she has become resentful of her social definition as simply 'somebody's wife, somebody's important wife' (25). Helen's marriage has changed radically from the circumstances in which it began; she married Lucille's father, Warren, because he represented for her 'the whole world of chance and risk' (192–3). But, because of his Depression-era mentality, Warren has gradually abandoned these qualities to slide 'back towards the safety of feet on the ground and money in the bank' (192). The social escape that Warren once offered to a woman 'marooned in old Charleston' (192) has now ossified into new structures of confinement that Helen could not have anticipated, and from which she now seeks to escape. More importantly for Lucille, seventeen years ago her mother had sought to terminate her pregnancy, at least according to the testimony of Lucille's sister Rae, and it was only an error in this termination that resulted in Lucille's surprise birth. This information is a key aspect of the new and shocking re-evaluation of the past from which Lucille's coming of age is created.

The departure of Lucille's mother has a catastrophic impact on her father, and his paralysis further intensifies the coming-of-age challenges of the teenage protagonist. Warren is first emasculated by the loss of his driver's license (which is the final straw for his marriage), and the image of him fleeing the house on a motor mower is evidence of a bathos from which he never fully recovers. As Lucille asks rhetorically, 'Can a man become effeminate as the result of the loss of his wife?' (55). In fact, Warren regresses into a form of adolescence in which he becomes increasingly solipsistic: he gains weight, sleeps too much, and sits by the telephone in the hope of calls from his absent wife. Warren's regression further forces Lucille into the role of a parent. Moreover, Lucille constantly characterises her father as 'innocent', and she complains that 'I felt his innocence trapping me' (36). Lucille becomes as constrained by her father's behaviour as her mother was, and his tendency to regard himself as the passive victim of circumstance forces his daughter to take control in ways that are clearly at the limit of her competence. It is significant that this predicament takes the form of a statement about the responsibilities not of the father but of women, with Lucille declaring: 'The time had come, because of my mother's abdication and my sister's carelessness, to take the reins of this family' (150). Mothers, sisters, and daughters are the agents here, because the father has become a child; even Lucille's father's new girlfriend Vera is regarded as behaving like 'a lovesick teenager' (122), and when Lucille catches them in bed together she quickly becomes the indignant parent, morally outraged that they could 'carry on like that under my roof' (124). The dilemma for the adolescent girl, then, is partly the result of the collapse of the authority of the father. Lucille's parents, meanwhile, are depicted as trying to recover some experience of their own adolescence that they feel it is important to retrieve. Warren's attitudes and aspirations stem from a depression-era anxiety about economic security, and a specifically southern antipathy to the north; in particular, he remembers the hardships of the year 1936 and the feeling that 'if we had money, we would be safe' (54). But Lucille is deeply sceptical of his romanticised version of the past, and she rejects specifically the 'poetic tone' of his sentimentalised memories of his childhood. It is important to recognise this as the daughter's repudiation of the style of her father's narrative language; it is a male way of understanding and articulating the past that is of little value to Lucille as a young woman growing up in the new south, and she emphatically rejects his version of history.

Lucille's father is integral to the new southern regeneration; he owned a very successful demolition company that helped to clear the way for the new look of the contemporary southern downtown, and he 'could claim partial credit for the new look of the cities he loved' (81). Warren, then, is centrally complicit in the destruction of southern history, and it is precisely in the construction of a new sense of history, and a new historical language, that his daughter Lucille is engaged. Lucille's narrative is one in which she questions and revises some received ideas of historical events, while simultaneously trying to discover and to articulate a new language of history. *Rich in Love* becomes a disquisition on historical narratives with a specifically southern inflection. Lucille rejects her father's language of a southern childhood in the depression because she is seeking to define her own aesthetic of history as a young woman in the new south. The coming-of-age genre is used by Humphreys to present the challenges that young southern women face in reconstructing a sense of their historical context, one that will help them to come to terms with the changed conditions of the new (postmodern) south that their parents helped to create.

It is significant that in a genre conventionally devoted to identifying the determining experiences of young adults in *Rich in Love* the adults themselves are still trying to discover their own personal narratives, and still in the process of coming of age. Lucille's mother leaves home because of an urgent wish for a new direction and a new future; she wants to be true again to a conception of herself that she has lost touch with. This crisis occasions her husband's enquiry into the origins of his personal history. Warren looks back on himself as a child in 1936 and comments 'I think that was the formative moment' (55). That moment for Warren is crucially defined by economics, and by a specifically male drive towards financial security; it is also one that has infantilised him: as Lucille comments, 'It disturbed me to hear him say the word "daddy", and I didn't like the poetic tone I detected in this account' (54). Lucille's attempt to situate herself in a historical context that can contribute to a fulfilling sense of identity, is coterminous with her parents' engagement with a history gone awry. This historical sense is characteristic of southern fiction and of the coming-of-age genre, and the conflation of the two genres helps to account for the profusion of recent southern bildungsroman.

Lucille has a remarkable and precocious interest in language, and *Rich in Love* is an exceptional novel partly for the ways in which the self-consciousness commonly associated with adolescence is put to some sophisticated conceptual uses. Lucille is characterised by her rigorous intellectual scrutiny of the language of historical representation, and by a shrewd curiosity about the social and political implications of that scrutiny. Lucille's teenaged self-consciousness becomes an awareness of how her language and her own personal narrative is bound up with the history of the south, with historiographical issues, and a matrix of power relations, especially gender politics. This permits claims to be made on behalf of this novel that cannot be made of other contemporary coming-of-age novels; its intellectual sophistication is very subtlely accommodated to its seventeen-year-old narrator's perspective. For example, Lucille's vocabulary includes words such as 'discombobulation' (32), 'patrician' (25), and 'odalisque' (55), and it is clear that her high school Latin class has given her a particular interest in etymology which she demonstrates by showing a knowledge of the origins of the words 'exercise' (128), 'permanent' (204), 'premonition', and the Latin 'simper parata' (33). Lucille is also particularly attentive to the word choice of people around her, and she is self-reflexive about her own decisions to use words like 'nonchalant' and 'vigilant'. Lucille's coming of age is partly an account of language acquisition, a text in which its author's self-consciousness about linguistic knowledge becomes integral to her development.

Even beyond this linguistic scholarship, Lucille is very sensitive to the ways in which semantic units are arranged into narratives of power. Lucille understands at an early age some complex theoretical issues of narrative organisation, and she is able to think tactfully and with fine discriminations about what is relevant, and about why and how to prioritorise. Lucille's first real coming-of-age moment in *Rich in Love* is an awakening into the possibilities of narrative organisation; she knows that the story she is about to tell is 'one in which events appear to have meaning' for the first time, and that her life has suddenly become 'a series of events worth telling' (1). This is a kind of fall from innocence in itself, an awakening to the consciousness of narrative potential, a burgeoning sense of narratology as a form of discourse, and a sudden matching of her life's events with a concept of narrative value. This is a fall from innocence because it is the moment at which Lucille becomes aware that she has a culturally-sanctioned story to tell, and that there are specific ways of telling it that involve important aesthetic and social decisions. This might be understood as a fall from innocence in terms of Lucille's recognition of the social ideology, and the gender politics, of learned narrative codes.

Lucille's self-consciousness about the shape of her own narrative comes partly from her scepticism about the nature and status of the received historical narratives of her region, including those of her father. This scepticism (which is always healthy and enquiring and not subject to the paralysing paranoia that is sometimes seen in American narratives about historical credulity), is demonstrated at two particular points in Lucille's story. The statues of John C. Calhoun and the Seminole Indian chief Osceola, in Charleston and Fort Moultrie respectively, are local

icons that arrest Lucille's attention and give her occasion to expound a
theory of history. The statues are markers of local recognition and veneration, but for Lucille they both have a secret history. For example,
Lucille is inclined to believe that Calhoun 'was the true father' of
Abraham Lincoln (47), and that the story of Osceola is not to be found
in history books, but in a special room at the library:

> You won't find the whole Osceola story in the history books, of course. I dis-
> covered these facts in the South Carolina room in the library, where I worked
> on Friday afternoons. The room was kept locked – they said, to keep out
> winos and children. But I made some discoveries in that room, and I think I
> know the real reason they locked it. There was a lot of history in there that
> they didn't want to let out. Similarly, in the contemporary world, something
> was going on behind the scenes. (71)

Lucille rejects the official historical record in favour of a suppressed
story, and one that is confirmed for her by visual evidence: 'all you have
to do is look at pictures' (47). In Osceola's case, Lucille claims, 'you can
tell from the portrait' (71). This specifically visual faculty is an alternative way of reading, one that encourages Lucille to believe in subversive
historical stories about the origin of the nation and how they are implicated in ethnicity and power. Young Americans are encouraged to invest
in these icons, and in the officially sanctioned versions of American historical origins that they stand for. Lucille's departure from these beliefs
represents a different way of reading history, of rejecting these 'fathers'
as she rejected her own father's sentimentalised version of the depression.
Osceola's statue is inhabited by bees, leading one critic to argue that,
'The honeyed center adds the feminine to the figure of Osceola and suggests that Humphreys uses him as a rich emblem for the synthesis of race
and gender' (Kreyling 1998: 120). These are new ways of reading southern history that facilitate a feminist historiography by which Lucille can
understand herself and her place in southern culture. Again, contemporary coming of age is principally a story in which the protagonist situates
herself in the present moment by offering a revision of history and of the
power relations that it inscribes. As a young woman, Lucille contests the
images of venerated men as part of her desire to create a southern history
that can do justice to her experience, and to the experiences of women
like her mother and her sister.

Lucille's coming of age concerns not only a new understanding of
history, but of fiction too, and her discussion of Virgil and Twain are
subtle but penetrating insights into how an individual's subjectivity is
informed by a knowledge of the possibilities of narrative forms. This
knowledge in turn reflects back upon Lucille's attempt to articulate an

authentic and original sense of herself in relation to antecedent texts that might actually be a threat to that attempt. How can Lucille be original and authentic, for example, when she knows herself to be writing in the shadow of Twain, yet is eager to represent her difference from it:

> What I felt for Wayne was what you feel towards Huck Finn. A kind of affection, because he is so good and American. But when you read that book, if you are a girl, you say to yourself *this kid has a long way to go*. He is so happy with his Jim, and his raft, and his old river. The light never dawns on him. Boys have that extended phase of innocence. I do not think girls have it at all. Imagine Becky Thatcher writing that book and you have an altogether different concept. You have something dark. (146)

This profoundly self-conscious observation encourages the belief that *Rich in Love* might usefully be understood as a feminist revision of that classic novel of nineteenth-century American fiction, which also happens to be a coming-of-age story. Lucille's account offers 'something dark', because her gender gives her an utterly different concept of innocence to begin with, and this is why she is so often irritated by her father's senti-mental innocence. This quotation encourages readers to see the cultural specificity of *Huckleberry Finn*, in terms of its period, its gender, and its racial politics. It is a cultural specificity that makes it inadequate as some form of cultural template for all narratives of coming of age. This is a crucial political point about Lucille's specifically 1980s' sensibility, a revision of humanist assumptions about eternal verities and their uni-versal application. Twain is a fatherly text that Lucille must dispute in order to establish her independence from it, and she does so by contest-ing the specifically male concept of innocence that she believes it depicts. Virgil's *Aeneid* is another canonical text that, under her interpretation, enables Lucille to understand how an individual's subjectivity is defined partly by the language that is available for self-expression:

> The story at this point was starting to drag . . . But the words still held me, the perfect sentences so much more precise than English. Latin tried to pin things down. English, I realized, didn't even have a subjunctive mood, for use "in matters of supposal, desire, possibility," according to the grammar note . . . My moods, the feelings that came upon me without warning and seemed to have no name – that's what they were. Subjunctive moods, somewhere between what's real and what's not. Maybe they were nameless in English, but in Latin they were well recognized and given grammatical status. (217)

It is interesting to note that this is an error of reading (English does have a subjunctive mood), in which Lucille, struggling to discover a lan-guage of female desire, finds it not in English but in Latin. This grammar of self-expression is a linguistic microcosm of the other grammars of discourse that shape, or even determine, Lucille's subjectivity. Lucille's misinterpretation is analogous to that scene at the end of Bobbie Ann Mason's *In Country*, in which Sam Hughes reads her name on the Vietnam Memorial and thereby suddenly understands her place in history. This too is dependent upon a misreading; but to what extent do such misinterpretations undermine the value of the epiphanies that they facilitate? For both Sam and Lucille, misreading might be said to result in a further alienation from that sense of self which coming-of-age narratives are dedicated to articulating, and, for both of them, this condition is integral to their predicament as contemporary, or postmodern, southern women.

Rich in Love is also attentive to the social consequences of language-knowledge, and language issues are very closely related to gender politics. For example, Lucille re-writes her mother's farewell note, changing its dispassionate and pragmatic tone for something more strongly emotional. This is not only about the language of subjectivity, but also about the nature of historical origins; as one critic points out, 'on some level she believes that if she can re-write the note, she can somehow re-write the story' (Jackson 1994: 279). This textual revision demonstrates Lucille's readiness to take responsibility, and it shows how social responsibility is bound up with a knowledge of the appropriate language. This is the novel's second coming-of-age moment in the area of narrative and linguistic awareness: what is the best language with which to bid farewell to a twenty-five-year marriage? Lucille's failure here is registered in her father's immediate recognition that the language of the note is not his wife's. However, when Lucille subsequently repeats that language to her mother, Helen confirms its language and its sentiments, right down to the repetition of Lucille's word 'adrift'; she remarks that 'you put it exactly the right way' (26). These struggles over language are complemented by many other comparable scenes in the novel, for example the game of scrabble between the Frobinesses: 'Once I saw the Frobinesses, when they were still intact, sit down to a cutthroat game of Scrabble played entirely in silence until the end, when violence erupted' (100). Lucille and Billy, meanwhile, play Scrabble cooperatively. Later, a struggle over the appropriate word for the 'genitals' precipitates an argument that ends in divorce.

The entrapment of women by men is still an urgent contemporary issue, and not one that is confined to the era of Lucille's parents. Billy traps Rae into marriage by systematically puncturing condoms until she becomes pregnant. The economics of this relationship is different from that of Lucille's parents; Rae has a good job with the government in

Washington, while Billy is a struggling graduate student who has not finished his dissertation and who looks destined to teach high school. Like
Lucille's father, Billy has the potential to be infantilised by his memory
of the past, and by the belief that 'high school is the only American institution that hasn't changed'; he even thinks that by working there 'I can
pretend I am back in tenth grade' (170). Billy's feelings of powerlessness
are assuaged by exercising control over Rae and committing her to a
future with him: 'I got her pregnant' (231). The novel is unflinching in
its portrayal of Rae's unwilling conscription to this role, and with her discomfort at being pregnant, and especially with the confinement that goes
with it. The scene at Fishbones, the juke joint, is very important in
dramatising the nature of the sacrifices that Rae must make, and in
showing Lucille's growing awareness of how adults are defined by these
kinds of choices and decisions. Rae's singing is a kind of aesthetic performance that is vitally important to her identity, and it is not only about
personal self-expression, but a creative quality that has a significant
social dimension too; it is one that returns her to an earlier version of
herself: 'Rae didn't look at all like a singer. She looked like a teenager'
(119). What Lucille sees in this scene is something of fundamental
importance as a young woman coming of age; she closes her eyes to listen
to her sister's singing voice, and she has a momentary vision:

> I closed my eyes all the way and tried to see back toward the retina, the optic
> nerve, and beyond. I saw people. There was a singing girl, but even more
> astounding, there were other sorts as well, a gang of them in there. I opened
> my eyes fast, out of fright. Maybe people with multiple personalities got
> started just this way, by looking inside. (120)

This is a glimpse of a female aesthetic that is rich, diverse, and mutable;
it is strongly reminiscent of the symbolic space of the juke joint in
Alice Walker's *The Color Purple* (1982), where Shug Avery expresses
her unique sense of self-confidence through aesthetic performance. In
Humphreys' novel, Lucille realises that 'every woman has a singing self'
(120), and her association of that creative potential with adolescence is
further evidence of the vital importance of coming of age to the culture
of the United States. Now that Rae is destined for domesticity, she
unknowingly concurs with her mother's frustration when she says, ' "It's
over, that's all there is to it. That life is over" ' (122). This belief in the
unequivocal end of innocence inevitably places a huge premium for
women on those moments before marriage and housekeeping.

Lucille's final expression of desire is for a language that is not so badly
contaminated by historical deterioration, for a time in the past 'when
words were new and had no connotations' (260). This is expressive of

Lucille's impatience and frustration with the idioms and discourses that she has inherited as a girl in South Carolina at the end of the twentieth century. *Rich in Love* is a search for a new language with fresh political inflections, one that can do justice to new social realities, an attempt to locate 'a language we can only imagine' (260). It is a search for the origin of an imaginary language, but that linguistic origin is not an abstract one, it is coterminous with the origin of her mother's story, and with Lucille's ability to fashion an aesthetic artefact from its telling: 'I didn't tell her that I knew the whole story' (251). The story of her mother's termination is an origin, and it could be argued that the arrival of Lucille's sister's baby, Phoebe, provides some form of resolution for that narrative strand; they become inseparable, as if to show the fulfilment of the mother's desire. Again, however, the story is bound up with scepticism about narratives: it is Rae who tells Lucille the story of the termination, not her mother, and there is some vestige of doubt about that story's veracity and the state of Rae's knowledge. The narrative is a form of power, and a power that Lucille takes control of when she speaks to her mother but without telling her the full extent of what she knows. Lucille has a new kind of power here, a power that comes from control over historical knowledge and narratives of origin. What is important is Lucille's belief in it, and the concomitant sense of authority that it confers. The one thing that Lucille can control with authority is the conduct of her own story's search for an authentic language.

There are numerous surface correspondences between *In Country* (1985) and *Rich in Love* (1987) that are worth noting briefly: both novels are the coming-of-age stories of seventeen-year-old girls who are abandoned by their mothers and have an unsatisfactory boyfriend and an important relationship with an older man (Uncle Emmett, brother-in-law Billy). Both girls have a special interest in history, textuality, and language, and in forms of knowledge and power, and they both inhabit a changing southern environment where domesticity and new forms of mobility are crucial issues. Sam is a jogger, Lucille is a cyclist. Both protagonists are in search of a new language by which to express themselves satisfactorily, while at the same time searching for the full and truthful interpretation of a moment before their birth that is crucial to their self-definition. Sam Hughes wonders, 'If she couldn't know a simple fact like the source of her name, what could she know for sure?' (Mason 1987: 53), and Lucille complains 'I had lived a full ten years of my life without crucial information about my own origin' (50–1). Both novels use the coming-of-age genre to interrogate (southern) historical origins, and thereby to situate their female protagonists in a contemporary or post-modern south. Simultaneously, they articulate a new language of history, and an aesthetic of subjectivity, that necessitates formal innovations in the coming-of-age genre. Mark Graybill is right to bring the two novels together, and in an excellent Lacanian reading, which capitalises on two papers on *Rich in Love* that were published in *Mississippi Quarterly* in 1994, he characterises Lucille's predicament in these terms:

> Caught between an imaginary realm that is inherently inarticulatable and a symbolic domain that demands differentiation and thus fragments identity, we move uncomfortably back and forth, journeying underground for a picture of the truth as the archetypal epic hero does, only to find when we return to the world that we cannot tell it. (Graybill 2002: 258)

Lucille's search is for a language of subjectivity that is authentically female, in a postmodern culture which does not make such a language available for her to speak; she can only appropriate a lexicon which is incapable of doing justice to the sense of identity she wishes to articulate. If postmodernity, rather than the south, is the paradigm by which *Rich in Love* should be interpreted, then the key female antecedent is not Addie Bundren but Oedipa Maas, from Thomas Pynchon's *The Crying of Lot 49*, first published in 1966. Oedipa is the first woman to come of age amid that proliferation of representations which is believed to have contributed to the collapse of metanarratives, and which is known as postmodernity. Oedipa's existence is made more meaningful by her pursuit of 'America', where previously her life was spent 'shuffling back through a fat deckful of days which seemed (wouldn't she be first to admit it?) more or less identical' (Pynchon 1979: 6). The fact that the quest is not definitively resolved does not make questing futile.

Memoirs and Memorials

The coming-of-age novel is traditionally a narrative in which its protagonist progresses from naive or callow youth towards a sense of a mature adult consciousness and fulfilling social integration. The narrator finds their self and their sense of a proper place in society, as a consequence of working through the challenges of adolescence. But what does a true and satisfactory achievement of adulthood consist of, and how can it be known or evaluated? In a piece of writing such as a novel, how does an author find a satisfactory language by which to articulate a sense of the authentic self and a fulfilling resolution of the vicissitudes of adolescence? What investments in a particular language of subjectivity does this involve, and how is it possible to know, or to evaluate, that concept of the self which the novelist's language hopes to bring to life?

The novels of this chapter are both first-person narratives of childhood and adolescence that are characterised principally by pain, violence, and other forms of physical and emotional anguish. Where *Prozac Nation* asks questions about the nature of illness and the concept of the 'real' person who is to be uncovered by the remedy for that illness, *Bastard out of Carolina* depicts a child in impossibly difficult circumstances whose coming of age is profoundly affected by physical abuse. Both texts depict children in positions of extreme powerlessness, and it is that very powerlessness which defines them, and which they attempt to overcome by writing these works of self-realisation. These experiences are not outgrown or resolved but become a permanent and lasting feature of their lives; they are fundamentally conditioned by the experiences of adolescence. Further, both texts are characterised by formal or generic complexities that contribute to the examination of the idea of the self. *Prozac Nation* calls itself 'a memoir' and purports to be a work of non-fiction; any attentive critical reading of the text quickly shows this not to be so straightforward. *Bastard out of Carolina* is a work of fiction, but its author has spoken and written at length about its closely autobiographical nature to the extent that it has often been understood as a work of non-fiction. In both cases, the issue of the text's formal status has consequences for that concept of the true and authentic self which they are striving to articulate.

Also, both of these works devote a great deal of close critical attention to the specific cultural and historical circumstances that had most influence on their protagonists as they were growing up. In retrospect, their authors see themselves as having been crucially affected by social factors beyond their control. That powerlessness stands in contrast to popular ideas about the sovereign self and American self-fashioning. One response to that powerlessness lies in the writing of the text: reading and writing is vitally important to both narrators, and it is part of an awareness of their own textual status; for each author the writing of their book was an invaluably redemptive act, a statement of identity which was not only cathartic but which gave them a public persona that was necessary to their emotional and economic survival.

Dorothy Allison, *Bastard out of Carolina*

Dorothy Allison's *Bastard out of Carolina* (1992) is an account of the childhood of Ruth Ann Boatwright in the town of Greenville, South Carolina, in the 1950s. The novel begins with the dramatic circumstances surrounding her birth following a car accident in which her pregnant mother is hurled through the windshield of Uncle Travis' Chevy. 'Mama' lies in a coma for three days, in which time Ruth Ann is born and named after her mother's sister; her mother's absence from proceedings at this crucial time is compounded by a lack of knowledge about her father, and as a result Ruth Ann is branded illegitimate. This inauspicious beginning is partly remedied by Mama's subsequent marriage to Lyle Parsons, a local boy who has a job pumping gas at his cousin's Texaco station. This marriage removes the stigma of illegitimacy only temporarily, because Lyle dies tragically young in a car accident, and once again, Mama finds herself alone, and now with two young children to care for. It is Mama's second marriage, to Glen Waddell, that introduces into the narrative the figure who is to have a catastrophic influence on Ruth Ann's childhood and adolescence, and her abusive relationship with him becomes the central subject of this harrowing coming-of-age novel. Classically, the act of naming is inherent to the beginning of a novel, and with it, unavoidably, ideas about identity and social status. Ruth Ann's mother is absent, even from the experience of birth: she is first presented as sleeping heavily at the time of the accident, and then 'she didn't wake up for three days' (Allison 1993: 2), by which time Ruth Ann has been named by her aunt. This naming is fraught with difficulty, however, because of the absence of the father. In a sense, Ruth Ann is born into her wider family and community rather than strictly into a direct relationship with her parents, and this is why she is 'out of' Carolina rather than simply 'from' Carolina, as if to emphasise the region's role in her origins; she is named, in writing, as 'Ann, Anne, and Anna', because neither her grandmother nor her aunt 'could write very clearly' (2). Even Ruth Ann's nickname, 'Bone', is the diminutive of 'knucklebone', a word uttered by family members Uncle Earl and Deedee at Ruth Ann's birth. This is not a culture that sets great store by the written word. Ruth Ann's father's name is not spoken of: 'as for the name of the father, Granny refused to speak it' (3). It is curious that Ruth Ann does not say 'my' father here; she has already erased him as a significant contributor to her origins.

All of these names (plus the designation 'bastard') are an important part of the struggle between speaking and writing that the novel dramatises. Mama is convinced that she might have refuted the accusation of illegitimacy merely by the force of speaking: if she '*said* she was married firmly enough that no one would have questioned her' (3). This act of speech stands in opposition to the authority of writing that governs institutional practice: 'It's only when you bring it to their attention that they write it down' (3). The absence of the name of the father results in the designation 'bastard' that takes the place of 'Ruth Ann' in the novel's title. This is especially important because the bildungsroman was conventionally named after its protagonist (*David Copperfield, Jane Eyre, Huckleberry Finn*). The word 'Bastard', rather than perhaps 'Bone' in the novel's title, directs the reader's attention toward social institutions and questions of social status that are integral to the novel's presentation of southern society. The word 'bastard' in this novel is also partly a mark of social inferiority, a mark that signifies a class position that carries with it many other words by which social inferiors are stigmatised: '*No-good, lazy, shiftless*' (3), and therefore Mama's story concerns her determination to erase this 'stamp' from her life and from her daughter's life. This is partly a struggle between the authority of writing and the authority of speaking, which, in the working-class culture of the south in the 1950s, is shown to have a crucial influence on every individual's fate.

The incident at the beginning of the novel, in which a fire at the courthouse destroys all of the official records, is a symbolic repudiation of the authority of writing and of its power to define and to subjugate individuals. When Mama hears of the fire she burns her daughter's birth certificate, with its stamp of the word 'illegitimate', in a miniature domestic conflagration in the kitchen sink which destroys the recorded history of her daughter's origins. This act is characteristic of the whole community's shared relief: 'It was almost as if everyone could hear each other all over Greenville, laughing as the courthouse burned to the ground' (16). This dramatisation of the defeat of the official discourse of writing should be understood as part of the novel's valorisation of the authority of oral history that is integral to this southern community. For example, Ruth Anne says of her grandmother: 'I never could be sure which of the things she told me were true and which she just wished were true, stories good enough to keep even if they were three-quarters false. All the Boatwrights told stories, it was one of the things we were known for, and what one cousin swore was gospel, another swore just as fiercely was an unqualified lie' (53). Although written discourse can be a punitive injustice in its uncompromising, fixed and officially-sanctioned status, Ruth Ann is sensitive at an early age to the potential duplicity of the spoken word. In this respect she recognises that both writing and speaking are forms of communication that occasionally test the auditor's credulity. Most important, in this family mythology of tale-telling, is that particular aesthetic quality that is alluded to here in the idea of 'stories good enough to keep', regardless, perhaps, of their veracity. Ruth Ann has inherited from her family and community a talent for fiction and narrative invention, and she is uniquely alert to its power. She shows a sensitivity to the authority and truthfulness of the spoken word that acquires a profoundly ethical dimension in her narrative when she finds later that she cannot speak (with confidence or authority) of her stepfather's abuse of her. Here suddenly the activity of 'telling tales' becomes a fundamental ethical concern, both for the novel (which establishes its individuality as fiction by writing uncompromisingly about a taboo subject) and for the teenaged protagonist who is growing up in a culture where speaking openly of family history is integral to her sense of identity. Here is the productive and dynamic tension between the protagonist's prohibition against speaking about her experience (the taboo) and the novel's need to write directly about it in order to constitute itself as a work of art that we take seriously. The sense of a true or authentic subjectivity lies somewhere in the matrix of this tension.

One of the valuable contributions that *Bastard out of Carolina* makes to the depiction of coming of age is in accommodating the story of Ruth Ann's mother. 'Mama' is only sixteen years old when she becomes a mother, and the novel is therefore as much a story of her coming of age as it is of her daughter's. This, too, is part of the novel's depiction of social issues that has broader significance for southern culture than simply the depiction of a solitary individual, as is common in the genre.

A substantial part of the novel is devoted to Mama's coming of age as a teenaged parent and to dramatising the consequences, for adulthood, of a childhood that is shaped in this way. Thus the reader is able to see how the experiences of Mama's adolescence have a crucial impact on her daughter's adolescence. Although Mama is in many respects a typical product of her time and her culture, she is also vitally different from it in her recognition of the power relationship between writing and speaking. In this southern culture of the 1950s, oral tales and the shared or communal activity of tale-telling are an important part of the family mythology that shapes an individual's sense of identity, as we saw with the naming of Ruth Ann as 'Bone'. In this culture, writing is emphatically relegated. But Mama at least recognises the power that writing can have, especially in respect of social class and the authority of formal institutions such as designate her daughter 'bastard'. This is a knowledge of the power of the written word that she passes to her daughter, who in turn becomes the author of the written text known as *Bastard out of Carolina*. The daughter, Ruth Ann, repays her mother's gift of knowledge by writing a compelling account of her mother's struggles as a teenaged parent.

Bastard out of Carolina is written from the first-person perspective of Ruth Ann, and because of the limitations of this point of view there are some things about her mother that we cannot know. Most importantly, Ruth Ann cannot tell the reader exactly what it is that made her mother different, but she can offer a statement of the limits of her knowledge:

> It wasn't even that I was so insistent on knowing anything about my missing father. I wouldn't have minded a lie. I just wanted the story Mama would have told. What was the thing she wouldn't tell me, the first thing, the place where she had made herself different from all her brothers and sisters and shut her mouth on her life? (31)

The terms of this question are significant because they express a desire for a knowledge of origins that has less to do with wanting to know her father's name than with showing recognition of her mother's cultural difference. That difference is associated with 'the place' and with a refusal to participate in her family's oral culture, to 'shut her mouth'. These questions about origins cannot be answered because they lie beyond the limit of the narrator's knowledge, but they do nevertheless crucially inform the narrator's sense of identity as regards the centrality of the novel's geographical location and the importance of a struggle between speaking and writing which informs the sense of self that her book is trying to dramatise.

Yet despite the first-person perspective, the mother's narrative is included in some detail and it is a significant coming-of-age story in itself. As a teenaged mother, Mama has the attributes of both the young and the old: at the courthouse she can write 'in a fine schoolgirl's hand', but at the same time she 'drew breath like an old woman with pleurisy' (4). Mama returns to the courthouse annually, and because she has a child she is forced to grow up quickly: 'At seventeen she was a lot older than she had been at sixteen.' Mama is characterised in terms of adult challenges and responsibilities, and by the determination with which she confronts the written authority that stigmatises her and her daughter. Her marriage to Lyle to some extent ameliorates this family stigma, but he too is only a boy, in fact, 'a too-pretty boy tired of being his mama's baby' (6). Lyle is a boy who regards taking on adult responsibilities as a way of proving himself a man, but even his wife privately calls him 'manchild' (6). Lyle's sudden death only serves to accelerate Mama's growing up, and she becomes a widow with two children by the age of nineteen. This duality of youth and age is nicely caught in her sister's language at Lyle's funeral: 'You're as old as you're ever gonna get, girl' (8). Where Lyle's early death ensures that he is remembered forever as a boy with 'not a mark on him', Mama too is frozen in time by the events of her childhood and can grow up no more. Thus a knowledge of Mama's coming-of-age story is crucial to the form and circumstances of the young protagonist's narrative. In fact, there is a deeply reciprocal relationship between mother and daughter, one in which Ruth Anne presents her life as closely analogous to her mother's. The novel devotes a great deal of attention (unusual in this genre) to the circumstances of Mama's hardship and entrapment, and to showing the pressure of social conditions in shaping the individual woman's predicament. Ruth Ann lists these pressures and comments: 'all combined to grow my mama up fast and painfully' (10). Ruth Ann also grows up fast, and she learns to be attuned to adult situations ahead of her years. Despite the fact that adults are often portrayed as behaving like children (the men especially), the real children of this community learn quickly to be alert to adult experiences in order to survive.

The novel's representation of the loss of innocence is augmented by its depiction of Greenville, South Carolina, as a version of Eden. In particular, the summer of 1955 is remembered as a prelapsarian moment that is characterised by family unity and natural fecundity, with a strong sense of loving and creative nurture, and as a time of harmony, generosity, and sympathy. These epithets are, of course, the very stuff of nostalgia, of a particularly fond remembrance of time passed. But, most of all, 1955 is remembered as a time of security: 'When I think of that summer . . . I always feel safe again. No place has ever seemed so sweet and quiet, no place ever felt so much like home' (22). There is no place like the nostalgic memory of home, and it is this place from which Bone is to be banished. But although this place recalls 'the place' in which Mama made herself unique it is also a history, and 1955 is remembered as a time out of history, suspended forever by the unwelcome and violent advances that make this moment, in retrospect, seem inviolable. The novel needs to establish this period as Edenic in order that Bone's exile from it can have the full impact of a tragic fall from innocence to experience.

To what extent does this nostalgia for the summer of 1955 colour everything that is remembered there? In this place at this time the imagery of childhood is pervasive; the men of Bone's extended family are remembered as 'overgrown boys' whose pranks are indulged like those of harmless children or 'rambunctious teenagers' (23) and whose authority consists entirely of violent outbursts but who, like all juvenile delinquents, have not themselves properly grown up. Among these men, Bone's favourite is Uncle Earle, characterised by Aunt Ruth as 'a hurt little boy' (25), one who women find especially attractive because of his apparent vulnerability and because maternity and domesticity are so central to their identities as southern women. Earle has some resemblance to Elvis Presley; this was in 1955 when Elvis himself was twenty years old. But even the young narrator is able to see that Earle 'had none of Elvis Presley's baby-faced innocence' (24), because there is a crucial difference between maturity and the appearance of maturity, between innocence and duplicity. So when Aunt Ruth characterises 'youngsters playing at being something' (24) she identifies a central problem with this whole culture and community: that there is something arrested or even infantile about it that is corrupting and paralysing. In this cultural context Bone's real father was also 'a boy', one who left Mama to marry 'another little girl' (26). Bone's stepfather, Glen, is a man who has to buy his shoes in the boy's department of the Sears, Roebuck store (34). Glen's courtship of Mama helps her to recover a vestige of her own lost childhood, turning her into a 'giggling, hopeful girl' (35). It is possible, of course, to read these 'boys' and 'girls' as affectionate colloquial terms that were particular to the south in the 1950s, but the novel's adult voices suggests there is more to it: Granny observes something odd about Glen in these terms: 'That boy's got something wrong with him' (37), and the novel makes it clear that Glen has indeed been infantilised by his own family relationships; he is treated with disdain by his overbearing father and regarded as a foolishly diminutive sibling by his brothers. Glen's idea of masculinity, like most of the men here, finds its principal expression in outbursts of violence, sometimes murderous and uncontrollable, and when he discovers that Mama is pregnant we are told that 'Glen was like a boy about the baby' (44). It is the failure of his wife's pregnancy and the collapse of the myths of fatherhood that are paramount to Glen's own coming of age that lead directly to the abuse of Bone. Emasculated by the loss of fatherhood and by the illusions of instant maturity that accompanies it, Glen seeks to assert his authority in another direction. It is thus important to recognise that Glen's abuse of Bone is caused partly by the failure of his own coming of age, and by the immature conception of masculinity that is endemic to this culture. That failure of masculinity is visited upon Bone, and her story dramatises the suffocating claustrophobia of this culture in which both Glen's life and Mama's are thwarted from the outset. The full cultural circumstances of Bone's parents' predicament are important to take into consideration: Bone is not simply an isolated and tragic individual but the victim of a whole culture which is unable able to grow up. Bone's Aunt Ruth recognises Glen's failure immediately: ' "There's a way he's just a little boy himself, wanting more of your mama than you, wanting to be her baby more than her husband. And that an't so rare, I'll tell you" ' (123).

This analysis has devoted a great deal of attention to the circumstances of Bone's beginnings, partly because of the importance of beginnings to the genre, and partly because in this southern culture of the 1950s it is in the representation of beginnings that patterns are set and conditions defined that govern the subsequent action almost wholly. When, in chapter five, Mama addresses her husband with 'Glen, Baby' (64), the reader knows that it is more than simply a term of endearment. At the same point, Bone is forced by these circumstances into behaviour that is at odds with her age: 'I wasn't a baby anymore. I was eight' (66). The novel also devotes great attention to beginnings because this is a classically southern way of dramatising the importance of history, of family lineage, and of showing how individuals are often crucially informed by a history to which they are heir. In this respect, the autonomy of the individual to live a different life is severely circumscribed, and the freedom of self-determination that is a common theme of the bildungsroman is here strictly curtailed. Here, social class is a defining cultural discourse and institution, one from which there is little possibility of escape. This is partly why Ruth Ann's first-person singular 'I' emerges only very tentatively from the narrative of Mama in the novel's early chapters. *Bastard out of Carolina* is at pains to delineate the social factors that condition its protagonist's life, and this is relatively uncommon in the bildungsroman, where the sovereign self often fills the page to the exclusion of all else, and where this sense of self-absorption is itself often presented as characteristic of adolescence.

An important aspect of the novel's depiction of social class is seen in the status of Glen Waddell's family. Glen's father runs a dairy, and this economic position gives his whole family a sense of their social superiority to the working-class community that Bone is born into:

> It was not only Daddy Glen's brothers being lawyers and dentists instead of mechanics and roofers that made them so different from Boatwrights. In Daddy Glen's family the women stayed at home. His own mama had never held a job in her life, and Daryl and James both spoke badly of women who would leave their children to 'work outside the home'. (98)

This socially-aspiring family culture creates pressures for the young Glen that he finds difficult to keep up with (and from which his relationship with Mama Boatwright is to some extent a defensive retreat), and the class tension between the Waddell and Boatwright families underwrites the power relations between individuals that becomes a significant part of the social critique in which Bone's coming of age is embroiled. Unlike those of the Waddell women, Mama's life is shaped by the necessity of work outside the home and by the exigencies of economic hardship. The hierarchies of social difference seem to sanction Glen's abuse of Bone: she is disempowered in terms of her age but also by her gender and class. Bone's narrative of her self is thus characterised by a powerful sense of her worthlessness, by the absence of self-esteem that is caused by her awareness of social class. Bone's culture tells her that she is poor white trash and her expectations of her life are consequently diminished:

> Stupid or smart, there's wasn't much choice about what was going to happen to me, or to Grey and Garvey, or to any of us. Growing up was like falling into a hole . . . No wonder people got crazy as they grew up. (178)

Bone has a strong sense of the futility of becoming adult because she is trapped in a working-class culture that makes her feel that she has no future worth aspiring to. There is a crushing inevitability about this class position that makes growing up seem pointless, and that pointlessness is reflected back to her in the lives of the adults in her community.

Bone occasionally expresses her frustration with family members, like Grey and Garvey, who conform to a stereotype of southern fecklessness, and who seem unaware of the debilitating effect that it has on the whole community and on individuals who are growing up in that community. Bone's frustration sometimes turns to anger, as in the scene when she sees the school bus:

> a bus from Bushy Creek Baptist with flat-faced children pressed against the windows staring at me hatefully. I glared back at them. Anger was like a steady

drip of poison into my soul, teaching me to hate the ones that hated me. Who do they think they are? I whispered to myself. (262)

Here Bone's anger is self-corroding; her awareness of social class acts principally as a poison that feeds a futile antagonism that does not have a creative or social outlet. Nevertheless, anger can be power, and this scene is a significant development from Bone's earlier sense that her social standing was principally to do with her family rather than part of a wider class hierarchy:

We moved so often our mail never caught up with us, moved sometimes before we'd even gotten properly unpacked or I'd learned the names of all the teachers at my new school. Moving gave me a sense of time passing and everything sliding, as if nothing could be held on to anyway. It made me feel ghostly, unreal and unimportant, like a box that goes missing and then turns up but you realize you never needed anything in it anyway. (65)

Bone's transient lifestyle contributes strongly to her feelings of lack, to the absence of a properly grounded social identity; her subjectivity here is an empty box, one which haunts her with a sense of identity that is not sufficiently stable or secure but always contingent or 'unreal'.

This emptiness is filled by writing. It is important to note that in the quotation above about the school bus, Bone's Aunt Raylene admonishes her in a particular way:

You're making up stories about those people. Make up a story where you have to live in their house, be one of their family, and pass by this road. Look at it from the other side for a while. Maybe you won't be glaring at people so much. (262)

This injunction to use the imagination, to empathise with a different perspective and to fictionalise, is not so much a palliative as a form of empowerment. Aunt Raylene's imperative to 'make up a story' is invaluable advice for Bone because she has her family's native talent for mythologising, and she has learned early that writing is a form of institutionally and socially sanctioned discourse that has enormous cultural authority. The single word 'bastard' is sufficiently illustrative of that.

One day at school, for example, Bone learns how empowering it can be to make up a story about who she is:

It scared me that it was so easy . . . that people thought I could be a Roseanne Carter from Atlanta, a city I had never visited. Everyone believed me, and I enjoyed a brief popularity as someone from a big city who could tell big-city stories. (67)

This creative expedient is a direct product of that anger Bone feels about her social position, 'anger hit me like a baseball coming hard and fast off a new bat', and it might be interpreted as a creative response to the punitive social class hierarchies of her life, from which the entire text of the novel is created. There is no doubt that the novel's narrator is conscious of the world of representations that her text necessarily participates in and seeks to be taken seriously as a part of. Bone acquires a reputation as a captivating story-teller and she learns the authority of fiction as 'everyone was quiet and well-behaved while I told stories' (119). This inventiveness is supplemented by Bone's voracious reading:

> The librarian gave me *Black Beauty, Robinson Crusoe*, and *Tom Sawyer*. On my own I found copies of *Not as a Stranger, The Naked and the Dead, This Gun for Hire*, and *Marjorie Morningstar*. I climbed up a tree to read the sexy parts over, drank water out of the creek, and only went home at dark. (119)

It is tempting to make more of the passing reference to *Tom Sawyer* here, because it is a southern story of coming of age from which the narrator might have learned the conventions of the genre, but all of these library books contribute to the narrator's literacy and to her sense of the importance and value of writing. The cultural power and authority of books is given a major statement by the narrator's political engagement with the southern classic by Margaret Mitchell:

> Aunt Alma had given me a big paperback edition of *Gone with the Wind*, with tinted pictures from the movie, and told me I'd love it. I had at first, but one evening I looked up from Vivien Leigh's pink cheeks to see Mama coming in from work with her hair darkened from sweat and her uniform stained. A sharp flash went through me. Emma Slattery, I thought. That's who I'd be, that's who we were. Not Scarlett with her baking powder cheeks. I was part of the trash down in the mud-stained cabins, fighting with the darkies and stealing ungratefully from our betters, stupid, coarse, born to shame and death. I shook with fear and indignation. (206)

Reading *Gone With The Wind* is an important experience in Bone's coming of age; her critical understanding of the novel is based on her recognition of the discrepancy between the social standing of its heroine and her own class position. This sudden recognition is itself a vital moment in her growing awareness of social politics, one in which she sees past the seductive aesthetic appeal of the work's surfaces and becomes painfully conscious of the ways that it identifies her social inferiority. But this moment of class consciousness is simultaneously a recognition of the power of novels and films to present compelling artistic images that are deeply persuasive and authoritative. This consciousness becomes, in turn, an integral part of the political aesthetic of the novel, which then offers its own compelling and authoritative images of the class politics of the south.

This textual alertness and critical acumen is also brought to bear on Bone's local newspaper. For many years Aunt Alma has kept a scrapbook of newspaper clippings about the Boatwright family. Here, the Boatwrights are reduced to hapless buffoons whose births, marriages, and deaths, are vehicles for satirical tabloid captions and comic one-liners that complement their ridiculous pictures:

> In those pictures, Uncle Earle looks scary, like a thief or a murderer, the kind of gaunt, poorly shaven face sketched on a post office wall. In that washed-out gray print, he looks like a figure from a horror show, an animated corpse. Granny, my mama, uncles, aunts, cousins – all of us look dead on the black and white page. (293)

There is a flavour of mortality about a working-class family in this culture because they have no prospect of social mobility and the rigid class system therefore simply subjects them to reification. This deathliness is a further expression of that paralysis, entrapment and futility that is characteristic of Bone's life. As with Bone's interpretation of *Gone with The Wind*, Alma's scrapbook is not simply about the politics of social class but about the politics of representations. *Bastard out of Carolina* is a work that understands the power of images and wants to participate in that power by writing back against the southern class system that objectifies people like Bone. Bone's coming of age, then, is as much about learning the value of writing as it is about presenting a particular critique of social class.

Allison's novel is not the first to depict the sexual abuse of a young girl by a man in her family; Maya Angelou's *I Know Why the Caged Bird Sings* (1969), Toni Morrison's *The Bluest Eye* (1970), and Alice Walker's *The Color Purple* (1982) all depict the rape of a child. The suffocating confinement of the patriarchal cultures that these novels portray is succinctly expressed by Bone when Sheriff Cole comes to investigate her injuries following her assault: 'His voice was calm, careful, friendly. He was Daddy Glen in a uniform. The world was full of Daddy Glens, and I didn't want to be in the world anymore' (296). In fact, it might be argued that the most powerful dramatisation of Bone's entrapment is not in the scenes of violence, which are certainly visceral and uncompromising, but in the novel's conclusion. Following Glen's final attack, Bone is hospitalised; Mama has deserted her, and, unable to take properly adult responsibility for what has happened to her daughter, leaves Bone in the care of Aunt Raylene. Bone is traumatised and consumed with self-loathing: 'I had looked at myself in the mirror and known I was a different person. Older, meaner, rawboned, crazy and hateful . . . I was who I was going to be, and she was a terrible person' (301). These nihilistic feelings are compounded by Mama's absence, but she makes one final appearance in the novel, to say goodbye and to leave Bone's birth certificate (a copy of the one she burned in the sink). The novel thus ends with an emphatically circular return to the point of its own beginnings. The final depiction of the ways in which both Mama's story and Bone's are characterised by historical inevitability is in some sense a repudiation of the traditional telos of the coming-of-age genre. Bone's story goes forward by returning to the precedence of her mother's story: Mama had been told at Lyle's funeral that she would always look the same now, and Bone finally discovers that 'in all the years since, that prophecy had held true' (305). This fatalistic determinism has profound consequences for Bone's future: 'The child I had been was gone with the child she had been' (307). At the end, Bone is still striving to dis-cover and to articulate a sense of that crucial origin that remains beyond the limits of her knowledge and which nevertheless defines her: 'How could I begin? Where would I begin?' (296). The novel also returns to the importance of that formal written document which designates Bone as 'bastard', a document that Bone has never seen but which her mother now bequeaths her as a parting gift. These final narrative returns attempt to compensate for the final absence of the mother and the emotional anguish caused by Mama's departure with the man who has been abusing Bone.

Bastard out of Carolina constitutes itself as a coming-of-age novel partly by writing about representations and by dramatising its protago-nist's negotiation with the dominant images of the culture that she sets out to examine. Of course, it is also a coming-of-age novel in the way that it depicts a young girl struggling to survive and to achieve some degree of autonomy as a young adult in brutally difficult circumstances. The violent attacks of Bone's step-father Glen, and the emotional cir-cumstances of Mama's attachment to Glen, are a serious impediment to Bone's self-fulfilment as an adult. The novel approaches a denoument with the depiction of Glen's most vicious assault in chapter twenty. Bone is not even thirteen years old, but she has finally reached the point where she can begin to defy Glen; up until now 'I had always felt like it was my fault'. In this final, cathartic scene Bone overcomes her earlier terror and tries to resist him: 'I wouldn't hold still anymore' (282). This whole scene is characterised by a claustrophobic intensity in which Bone's new deter-mination not to 'hold still' is accompanied by a powerful and desperate desire for movement away from the conditions of her entrapment. Mama's sudden arrival during the rape seems to hold out the promise of escape, but when she carries Bone's body to her car she is once again stalled. Glen's self-abasement stops Mama in her tracks, and Bone with her: 'The air had become thick as jelly' (289). This is the moment in which Bone's historical determinism is forged, when the intensity of the violence causes the future and the past to be suddenly conflated: 'I stared at his face like it was a road map, a route to be memorised, a way to get back to who I really was' (288). Glen's face is an inscrutable avenue of escape, not a way forward but a way back to the circumstances of the life before his arrival, a means to recover her lost future. As we have seen, the circumstances of this paralysis are as much to do with southern culture as with the individual's predicament, and this is partly what gives the novel its value.

Making a useful comparison between Allison's novel and Jim Grimsley's *Dream Boy* (1995), Matthew Guinn argues that the relocation of the self outside the south is impossible for Bone:

> The result is a new conception of a tragic south, illumined from beneath by the story of a southerner expendable to the region's established cultural narrative, a young woman whose native means of negotiating identity call the validity of the entire culture into question. (Guinn 2000: 30)

The novel also returns significantly to an idea of story, specifically to the veracity and the gender politics of Aunt Raylene's narrative of emotional pain. Raylene is also an isolated woman with a history of unhappiness caused by a difficult and ultimately intractable love relationship. Like Mama and Bone, Raylene is defined by this history, but it is one that she is reluctant to speak about, and this reluctance itself has consequences for her and for her community. Bone learns from Raylene the dangers of not speaking out, and Bone's story becomes partly a warning about how damage can be compounded by secrecy. This too is a key part of the novel's politics of representation.

The language of the novel's penultimate paragraph is especially revealing:

> Who had Mama been, what had she wanted to be or do before I was born? Once I was born, her hopes had turned, and I had climbed up her life like a flower reaching for the sun. Fourteen and terrified, fifteen and a mother, just past twenty one when she married Glen. Her life had folded into mine. (309)

The final conflation of Bone's story with her mother's has the effect of circumscribing severely the very idea of coming of age at the novel's end. As one critic points out, 'this is a daughter's autobiography with her mother's biography at its core' (Malin 2000: 64). The emphatic return to the circumstances of Mama's life is the novel's most powerful expression of its anger at the southern class system that delimited Bone's development. She can never get beyond the historical conditions of her mother's life. Bone ends the novel abandoned by her mother, and this is closely reminiscent of the novel's beginning, from which her mother is also crucially absent. This is characteristic of the novel's final circularity. Contemporary southern fiction is often preoccupied with forms of historical entrapment and with the ways in which the future is informed by the pressure of a southern past; Allison's use of the coming-of-age genre to address the stultifying effect of that pressure gives this historicism a unique power, one that is expressed by the very form of the novel. The social indictment that *Bastard out of Carolina* articulates derives a great deal of its force from its expression in this particular genre. In the novel's last paragraph, Bone comments, 'I would be thirteen in a few weeks. I was already who I was going to be' (309). Twelve years old is an age at which we might expect a coming-of-age novel to begin, and Bone's has already ended.

Elizabeth Wurtzel, *Prozac Nation*

Peter Kramer's *Listening to Prozac* was published in 1993 and it quickly became a national bestseller. The book is a series of case studies, mostly of women, in which Kramer examines the effect of the anti-depressant fluoxetine (brand name Prozac) on a variety of clinical conditions. Kramer's book scrutinises the benefits that Prozac seemed to offer, not only for the alleviation of genuinely depressive symptoms among his patients, but for the fundamental alteration of personality, or what he termed 'cosmetic psychopharmacology' (Kramer 1994: xvi). Kramer was concerned that contemporary psychology had begun to believe that 'if it responds to an anti-depressant, it's depression' (Kramer 1994: 15) and that Prozac was therefore being widely prescribed by doctors in order to change patients' sense of their own personality, rather than to treat genuinely clinical depressive conditions. But from where, Kramer asks, do we retrieve an understanding of a patient's 'real' self to begin with? How can we know, definitively, who the 'real' person is, and how can we evaluate precisely the extent to which symptoms of depression are hindering that person from being 'really themselves'? These are questions about the ontology of being that the manufacture of Prozac brought to the attention of the public in dramatic new ways: what constitutes the 'real' person from which the depressed person is an unhappy departure, and if Prozac can be used to make people more content with themselves even when they are not suffering from depression then what concept of the authentic self is being invoked in the first place? Kramer's *Listening to Prozac* is partly an examination of these questions, and the book quickly brings to the reader's attention the issue of the ways in which personal subjectivity is socially and culturally constructed. In many ways Kramer's book tacitly asks what the self is, how can we know it, and how we can assess or evaluate departures from what are deemed to be its authentic characteristics. In short, from where does one recover a concept of authentic being?

Although Kramer has no particular interest in teenagers in *Listening to Prozac*, the case study of the patient he calls 'Lucy' is particularly notable because she is an undergraduate student with a pathological craving for attention which Kramer terms 'rejection sensitivity'. Prozac can mitigate the ill-effects of this condition. There is a problem, however, because, as Kramer explains, 'late adolescence is a time in which it is normal for rapidly changing moods to accompany an unstable sense of self. Identity, which includes sensitivity to approval and rejection, is a central developmental issue' (Kramer 1994: 100). This must lead us to query whether adolescents should be medicated for 'symptoms' that are in fact merely forms of behaviour that are integral to the challenges of (normal or healthy) growing up. Again the question arises: how can we know this? How can we measure departures from a concept of 'normal' that is not quantifiable and which is clearly socially contingent, and to what extent is medical intervention for such 'conditions' really appropriate, or even ethical?

Elizabeth Wurtzel's *Prozac Nation* was published a year after Kramer's book in 1994, and it is a very candid and uncompromising account of a profoundly unhappy childhood and adolescence. The book gives a very detailed depiction of many painful experiences, and it is often compelling and harrowing in its delineation of personal anguish and suicidal despair. The representation of depression in *Prozac Nation* often seems deeply personal and heartfelt, and there is a genuine and authentic sense of Wurtzel's suffering that is at times irrefutably individual. Wurtzel's drug overdoses, suicide attempts, and miscarriage are testimony to an adolescence that is fraught with painful experience; she is dominated by the presence of depression in a way that overwhelms many years of her life and it becomes the principal emotional experience of her teenage years. Many of the scenes of *Prozac Nation* are vivid and visceral in their attempts to convey to readers the true awfulness of depression and its seriously debilitating consequences. *Prozac Nation* is a remarkably direct depiction of a very unhappy adolescence at the end of the twentieth century, and the only reason that it might be excluded from the present study of American innocence is that it announces itself as a 'memoir' and is therefore, technically, what is termed 'non-fiction'. This is a generic distinction which is not as straightforward as it might appear at face value, and it is one that the text of *Prozac Nation* sets out at many points to interrogate and to dissolve. There are several important respects in which *Prozac Nation* displays a canny artfulness in the ways that, as a piece of narrative writing, it chooses to construct and to represent the experiences of its protagonist.

For example, there is clearly some artfulness in the narrative structure of *Prozac Nation* in terms of the aspects of Wurtzel's life that it selects and prioritises. Chapter five, 'Black Wave', finds Wurtzel a student at Harvard University. But in the previous chapters leading up to this, there is no mention of her application to college, nor of her aspiration to attend one of the United States' most prestigious institutions, nor to any particular form of study leading to her application and admission. Wurtzel's arrival at Harvard comes to the reader as no small narrative surprise. She is suddenly transformed in the book, by this temporal sleight-of-hand, into a young woman who is not only very bright and precocious, but also ambitious and successful. Similarly, the reader is informed at the beginning of chapter seven that Wurtzel won the *Rolling Stone* college journalism award 'somewhere down the road' (Wurtzel 1995: 132). There is no account of how she does this, but the reader must assume that, like her application to Harvard, it was during one of the previous chapters when she purports to have been completely debilitated by depression. The significantly coming-of-age event of losing her virginity is also part of the artful structure of Wurtzel's text. This experience is depicted in the form of a double retrospective, as something that happened during the temporal frame of a previous chapter, but which was not mentioned at the time. This structure permits a particular kind of control over the presentation of experience, but it is also a significant part of the calculated narrative technique of the text; Wurtzel suddenly confesses: 'It hadn't even been a year since I lost my virginity' (140). This 'retrospective within a retrospective', a calculated disruption of the linear temporal structure of the text, is a clever temporal shift that enables the protagonist of *Prozac Nation* to manage the depiction of experience and to marshal and manipulate the reader's perception of her subjectivity by means of its narrative organisation. Some readers might find these structural elisions strategic and ingenious (or disingenuous, or even duplicitous in a text that claims to be a memoir), but it should be recognised as a technique that is integral to any written narrative's desire to offer a particular version of the self in writing, and as a story that is organised in ways that engage the reader's curiosity and attention. Although the text of *Prozac Nation* adheres to a linear temporal structure that is integral to its claims to verisimilitude as a memoir, the strategic suppression of certain pieces of information, or what we might call narrative details, is clear textual evidence of the author's artful control of the reader's knowledge and understanding. Discerning readers can see immediately the ways in which our perception of Wurtzel's life story is subject to forms of narrative contrivance that make it less innocent as a strictly factual record than the designation 'memoir' might imply. The depiction of the teenaged protagonist in *Prozac Nation* is deeply informed by its author's desire to create a compelling piece of writing, and there are many points in her story at which that artistic aspiration takes precedence.

It is also worth noting that the protagonist of *Prozac Nation* shows herself to be a very erudite writer, one who has a wide-ranging critical knowledge of fiction and poetry, and one who expresses a strong desire to transform the anguish and unhappiness of her adolescence into art. *Prozac Nation* is a text that aspires explicitly and self-consciously to the achievements of fiction. For example, chapter ten, 'Blank Girl', begins with an epigraph from the American confessional poet Robert Lowell's most anthologised poem, 'Skunk Hour': 'I myself am hell'. This is especially interesting because it is not only a poem about the excruciating self-consciousness of mental illness but also because at the moment when it seems to express this awareness in its most agonised personal moment, 'my mind's not right . . . I myself am hell', the poem does so by quoting Mephistopheles in Marlowe's *Faustus*, and Satan in Milton's *Paradise Lost*, both of whom claim 'I myself am hell'. Thus the most personal is simultaneously the most literary, a recognition which makes some difference to the apparent spontaneity of the confessional moment. Wurtzel's confession is also artfully composed of many such intertextual moments, where even the most compellingly authentic or visceral expressions of a uniquely suffering subjectivity are an affect of language.

Wurtzel subsequently describes herself as 'an artist manqué' (201), and one who is unhappy principally because she has not yet discovered her artistic metier; she complains that she is possessed of 'a definite energy that can't find its medium' (202). At this point Wurtzel appears to find, albeit retrospectively, her proper genre, and here she makes a salutary confession of her own: 'And here I am, years later, when it is supposed to be clear that I am a writer, that it is through words that I will escape this sense of having no art form' (202). Here as elsewhere, *Prozac Nation* exhibits a specific determination to create something artful, something accomplished in the discipline of good writing; it is a text that 'discovers' the redemptive potential of artistic creation as a way to make meaningful the unhappiness of a painful adolescence. This discovery is not innocent of the techniques of fiction. The narrative eloquence of *Prozac*

Nation should not seduce readers into a credulous acceptance of its depiction of a profoundly unhappy adolescence. Wurtzel's writer-protagonist is consumed at many points by a creative anxiety about her ability to construct something artistically valuable from her depression: 'What do you do with pain so bad it has no redeeming value? It cannot even be alchemized into art, into words . . . there is no way to objectify it or push it outside or find its beauty within' (220). This romantic desire to create something artistically worthwhile from the most debilitating of experiences is at the heart of *Prozac Nation*, and it helps to account for some of its inevitable creative contrivance. Wurtzel composes an enduring account of an especially difficult adolescence as a way to write herself out of the overwhelmingly negative experience of depression, and she resorts to the challenge of narrative and of language 'hoping it might afford me the same sense of release that it once had' (220). Again there is a temporal control at work here, because that time when 'it once had' is never given an account of or elucidated in the text. The protagonist of *Prozac Nation* has clearly considered the implications of this strategy as a theory of artistic creativity, and she is careful to distinguish her depression from anything more glamorous: '*I have studiously tried to avoid ever using the word madness to describe my condition*' (259). Madness is closely associated with creativity, but depression is paralysis and inertia. However, the author also recognises that some of the symptoms of depression could at times make her seem '*melodramatic and entertaining*' as a person and that, on occasion, depression had '*all the selling points of madness, all the aspects of performance art*' (290). These are not quotations that the reader can pass over easily, especially the implications of the 'selling points' of performance art that are bound up with the publication, and the marketing, of the book *Prozac Nation* in an American culture that is saturated by the cult of celebrity.

In fact, the text of *Prozac Nation* has a particular aesthetic quality that most memoirs or autobiographies do not possess; it is foremost a piece of creative writing, and a principal reason that many readers find it compelling is the engaging and effective nature of its figurative language, regardless of the truthfulness or otherwise of what that language conveys. This language might at times be particularly indebted to Sylvia Plath, or a synthesis of the numerous textual influences that the book reveals, but it can be uniquely arresting. The paragraph at the beginning of chapter five, for example, brilliantly parodies the kind of college life that she might have had as a student:

reading Foucault and Faulkner at my rolltop desk in my garret room with hardwood floors, full of whimsical plants and chimes hanging from the ceiling and posters of movie stars from the forties and bands from the sixties on the slightly paint-chipped ivory walls. There were going to be lots of herb tea and a beautiful Mediterranean hookah and paisley cushions and oriental rugs on the floor so that I could run my own bohemian salon from my guileless little love pad. (95)

This is a witty and perceptive caricature of student life at Harvard, and its sardonic humour is one quality that makes *Prozac Nation* more than simply a work of narcissistic non-fiction. Elsewhere the protagonist shows her linguistic ingenuity by describing how her childhood depression was allowed to kindle slowly into a 'nightmarish psychic bonfire' (306); when she is about to be separated from her boyfriend she writes, 'I was like a farm covered in locusts, being destroyed' (192), and when she looks back on the legacy of her parents she observes 'all they gave me was an empty foundation that split down the middle of my empty, anguished self' (25). This concerted dedication to the craft of artful language, the consistent determination to write something accomplished that does full justice to her adolescent depression but which is simultaneously valuable as creative writing, is seen throughout *Prozac Nation*. The verbal wit and ingenuity of Wurtzel's presentation of her illness is part of her attempt to turn it into art. This aesthetic quality is only one of the features that make *Prozac Nation* more than simply a 'memoir', and turn it into such a compelling and engaging portrayal of adolescence.

Many of these pieces of writing, although they have a heightened emotional intensity because of the author's illness, are nevertheless characteristic of the high drama of adolescence, and the significance of adolescence is a consistent focus of attention in *Prozac Nation*. Wurtzel felt that she did not have a childhood, and especially that the innocence of childhood was something that she was forced to forgo. For example, when she becomes a student at Harvard she complains to her mother, ' "I never got to be a little kid" ', and she blames this partly on the role-reversal that characterised her relationship with her mother: ' "I hated the way you were so dependent on me" ' (114). Wurtzel notes that when she was a twelve-year-old she and her mother 'had switched roles so often [that] I was afraid to abandon the parental responsibility I felt for her' (48–9). Typically in the depiction of difficult and unhappy childhoods attention turns quickly to the parents' responsibility; in this case Wurtzel presents her parents as victims of their own *'unexamined emotional immaturity'* (68), and she argues that the consequences of this adult immaturity for their children are catastrophic and debilitating: *'It is no surprise that a generation of children of divorce have grown into a world of extended adolescence'* (68). Wurtzel is careful not simply to blame her parents' divorce exclusively for her depression, but her parents' inability to conduct a mature and responsible relationship with each other, or with their daughter, contributed significantly to the young girl's sense of neglect, and to her need for care and attention. Wurtzel consistently characterises her parents as not having fully grown up themselves: her mother cannot cope, and her father is feckless and distant. Wurtzel presents herself as having been used by both of them as part of their marital power struggle, and she exclaims at one point, in a classically adolescent voice, 'who died and left *me* in charge?' (93). Wurtzel's feels that her childhood was uncommonly adult, and her adolescence only occurred much later in her life, during her twenties. The writing and publication of *Prozac Nation* is an intensely adolescent activity, and its production might be interpreted as a demand for the kind of attention she did not receive as a child; the diary-like quality of the text contributes significantly to that adolescent fervour with which she writes about her inability to grow up – 'this is *so* high school . . . But then, how would I know? I never did stuff like this in high school' (252)– or her reluctance to grow up: 'Why be mature? Why accept adversity? Why surrender with grace the follies of youth?' (7). It is only at the very end of *Prozac Nation*, when the narrative of the text is an accomplished piece of work, that coming of age can properly begin: 'At age twenty six, I feel like I am finally going through adolescence' (307). It is worth asking how culturally or socially widespread this phenomenon might be. Is American adolescence extended into the twenties by a social prosperity which might in an earlier period have seen young people at work?

The writing of *Prozac Nation* becomes a form of work in itself, the means by which its protagonist establishes her own distinctive voice and her independence; writing this book puts her parents at a critical distance and enables her to assert her autonomy for the first time. Wurtzel's parents were incapable of facilitating this transition because they were not sufficiently mature themselves: 'I needed a good therapist to help me learn to be a grown-up' (307). There are interesting cultural consequences for adolescents at the end of the twentieth century in this respect: 'One of the striking elements of this depression breakout is the extent to which it has gotten such a strong hold on so many young people' (298). If this is true (that Prozac is most commonly prescribed to young people, or that young people are more commonly diagnosed with depression than other age groups), then what does this tell us about the attitude to adolescence of the United States' Medical profession at the end of the twentieth century? Perhaps that medication is a quick-fix remedy for conditions that are simply not pathological? Or perhaps it is the case that more young Americans are suffering from depression as a consequence of cultural conditions of the end of the century? The issue here is that the desire for a drug like Prozac, or a sense of a need for it, is clearly created by the drug company that produces it, because consumer desire is the product of a capitalist economy that perpetuates itself by creating needs which it can subsequently satisfy with a variety of products, such as Prozac. Bradley Lewis, in a paper entitled 'Prozac and the Post-human Politics of Cyborgs', which investigates a cultural studies of science, argues that 'neither medical science nor medical ethics even scratch the surface of articulating the social, cultural, and political dimensions of a medical technomedicine like Prozac' because of the newly contingent nature of questions of identity. Instead, 'clinicians are in danger of becoming glorified distributors of the new technologies for the giant transnational biotech corporations' (Lewis 2003: 52). Abigail Cheever is also concerned with those questions of the contingency of identity that Prozac raises:

> Wurtzel implies that there are people on Prozac, and there are people on Prozac who are *really* depressed – the others are phoneys, posers, wannabes, with no business claiming to be depressed at all. The category of the authentic, so crucial to the existentialist construction of the *individual* self, becomes a criterion of *group* identity, with real Jews and phoney Jews, real depressives and phoney depressives, debating standards of belonging.

The contingency of identity (in the contemporary United States) is thus demonstrated by the fact that 'it is easier for an upper-middle-class, well-educated woman to lay claim to the benefits of depressive identity (book contracts and the like) than a taxi driver' (Cheever 2000: 361–2). Prozac becomes an issue of identity politics as much as depression, because neither depression nor authenticity can be defined but only contested by rival or competing social groups.

Although *Prozac Nation* is partly a search for the genesis of depression, an attempt to understand how and why Wurtzel came to suffer from it, this search for an authentic point of origin is often characteristic of the American coming-of-age genre. Fictional protagonists often use narrative to try to identify an elusive but determining single moment in childhood that accounts for the circumstances of adulthood. As Wurtzel expresses it, 'I'm always trying to get back to some imaginary somewhere' (71). This 'imaginary somewhere' is a succinct expression of the desire to discover a sense of happiness that many fictional adolescents are chasing. That origin is the definitive point in history that offers an explanation for the circumstances of the protagonist's life. Wurtzel is a very confident historian of her own past in this respect; as an eleven-year-old girl, she had a powerful consciousness of death which prompts her to take an overdose of antihistamines and thereby attract the concern of a counsellor: 'since I wasn't even twelve yet, she couldn't blame this on adolescent angst' (13). Wurtzel's mother attributes these feelings to the onset of menarche, but this putative point of origin is superseded by another possibility: that she suffers from the hereditary condition Graves disease, which is (apparently) present in her family. The artful structure of the prologue of *Prozac Nation* dramatises this kind of search very well: it begins with a crisis at a party when Wurtzel is twenty-five, then goes back to a portrait of Wurtzel at the age of eleven, and then to a point before she was born when her genetic structure determined her future. This structural organisation is part of the attempt to historicise Wurtzel's problems, and contributes to its value as a piece of writing about ado-lescence. William Styron, in his own account of a struggle with depres-sion, is unequivocal about the pointlessness of a search for a beginning: 'I shall never learn what caused my depression, as no one will ever learn about their own' (Styron 1991: 38). This statement was made by an adult who was struggling to accept the trials of depression, whereas *Prozac Nation* dramatises an adolescent struggling to battle depression by seeking out its origin. That process inevitably involves composing a number of possible narrative explanations, stories of where it might have originated that compete for credence at various stages in her life. This search helps to give *Prozac Nation* its historical interest and its cultural currency, because the book becomes a forensic critical interrogation of late-twentieth-century American culture. Styron does make a connection between creativity and illness: 'When one thinks of these doomed and splendidly creative men and woman, one is drawn to contemplate their childhoods, where, to the best of anyone's knowledge, the seeds of the illness take strong root' (Styron 1991: 36). It is its interrogation of the cultural and historical circumstances of her childhood and adolescence that makes Wurtzel's book more than simply a Freudian personal narra-tive because her aetiological investigation acquires a broad cultural cur-rency that challenges received ideas about subjectivity. These are also characteristics which align Wurtzel's book closely with the fictional genre of coming of age as it is interpreted in the contemporary period.

The literary references of *Prozac Nation* are numerous and wide-ranging, the product of the twenty-six-year-old author's education and part of the attempt to understand herself by interpreting texts of all kinds that seem relevant to her self-definition. A catalogue of these references would be exhausting, but Wurtzel clearly has a special affinity for the poetry of Sylvia Plath and Anne Sexton, and the narrative of Plath's *The Bell Jar* (which is itself a form of coming-of-age novel) is in some ways closely akin to her own. Wurtzel also understands herself to be writing within a specific genre, one that includes Carrie Fisher's *Postcards From the Edge* and Susanna Kaysen's *Girl, Interrupted*, both of which were popular publishing successes before *Prozac Nation* appeared and both of which characterise young American women in crisis (the latter partly in a diary-memoir format). Fisher's novel depicts a fictional young woman called Suzanne Vale who, like Wurtzel, has aspirations to be a serious writer: 'So, my script. My script about my experiences in the rehab and my insights into that whole world. Maybe it could be the story of somebody who is accidentally put into a clinic, like *Cuckoo's Nest*' (Fisher 1987: 60). Suzanna Kaysen's *Girl, Interrupted* is an 'autobiography', which the *L.A.Times Book Review* described as 'a minimalist relative of *One Flew Over the Cuckoo's Nest*'. This book takes its title from Kaysen's sense of her correspondence with the image of a girl in a painting by Vermeer who is 'interrupted in the music of being seventeen, as her life had been, snatched and fixed on a canvas: one moment made to stand still and to stand for all the other moments, whatever they would be or might have been' (Kaysen 1995: 167). Both Fisher and Kaysen acknowledge self-consciously an awareness of their narratives' viability as a commercial enterprise; this has serious implications for *Prozac Nation*, which has to work much harder to intervene successfully in this particular marketplace.

Wurtzel also knows that there exists a critical tradition of the study of women in literature which had an important focus in Gilbert and Gubar's *The Madwoman in the Attic*: 'I wasn't just the madwoman in the attic – I was the attic itself' (121). It is evident that Wurtzel has learned how to present the protagonist of *Prozac Nation* from her understanding of antecedent texts (which might include, in this allusion alone, Gilbert and Gubar, Charlotte Brontë's *Jane Eyre*, and Jean Rhys's *Wide Sargasso Sea*), and especially from her interpretation of the concepts of the self that these works dramatise. When Wurtzel gives an account of the history of her family for example, she observes: 'all this information is no more outstanding than the plot of an Ann Beattie novel. Or maybe it's not even that interesting' (29). This quotation (and there are many others like it), shows an awareness of the demands of the fiction-reading public, demands for a narrative that is dramatic and original; it shows a recognition that her form of narrative has been written before and that *Prozac Nation* therefore needs to be a new and striking contribution to the genre, sometimes known as the genre of the abuse memoir. *Prozac Nation* exhibits a constant anxiety that the vicissitudes of a troubled adolescence have already been copiously documented elsewhere, and that her story of unhappiness and illness is neither new nor newsworthy. This anxiety is part of the acute self-consciousness of her malady but also a serious concern for any writer who seeks to have their work published in the first place. A conflation of depression and author-anxiety precipitates the phrase 'meta-depression', which Wurtzel visualises in terms of an audience at a horror movie:

> As usual, my problem seems to be that I am one step removed from my problems, more a nervous audience member at a horror movie than the movie itself. "So you think I'm suffering from meta-depression?" I ask Dr Sterling in a moment of humor. (204)

There is a close conflation of illness and creative anxiety here in which the illness itself is expressed as the symptom of a pathological self-surveillance and self-scrutiny, a morbid self-consciousness that is the real malady, and which has its origin not in depression but in the desire to write outrageously (well) about the suffering self.

The range, variety, and sheer number of cultural references is also symptomatic of the fragmentation of her sense of self. The text's intense critical interest in art of all kinds (but principally film, music, and writing) is expressive partly of an adolescent need for a satisfying form of cultural identification that helps to make sense of the self in crisis. What the cultural references do, in part, is to dramatise a frantic and desperate desire to find the self fully reflected, in a satisfying emotional and intellectual way, in the culture that surrounds her. It is a search for identification and recognition, an expression of the adolescent need for a significant and useful identification with its surrounding adult culture: 'being Ali MacGraw in *Love Story* or Ali MacGraw in *Goodbye, Columbus*, or anybody else in anything else. My God, where on earth do I have to go to get away from me?' (95). This is a desperate desire to identify with images in her surrounding culture, a crisis not only of the self but of the culture which conditions the self to respond in terms of these kinds of search. In some ways this might be interpreted as a search for the language of the father, for the right adult cultural language by which to understand and to articulate the burgeoning sense of the self's autonomy. This activity and this desire are in a state of crisis in *Prozac Nation* partly because of the parents' inability to provide adult models worth aspiring to but also because of a lack in the culture. These forms of cultural critique also contribute strongly to the value of *Prozac Nation* in which coming of age is a process of cultivating an appreciation of the proper art form, of reading one's culture, and of matching it to an image of the self that is intellectually and emotionally fulfilling.

Wurtzel characterises Nirvana's 'Smells like Teen Spirit' and Beck's 'Loser' in terms of what she calls 'a call to apathy' (309). By the end of *Prozac Nation*, Wurtzel confidently claims that Douglas Coupland's *Generation X*, Richard Linklater's *Slacker,* and Nirvana's *Nevermind* have a unique cultural resonance (for American adolescents) and that their particular aesthetic qualities distinguish them unequivocally from earlier expressions of disaffected youth. These three texts are all from the year 1991. In future years, it is possible that literary historians might prefer a different text from 1991, Brett Easton Ellis' *American Psycho*, whose protagonist is the same age as Wurtzel and whose text ends with the words 'THIS IS NOT AN EXIT' (Ellis 1991: 399). These comments about popular culture are part of the book's useful attempt to characterise the unique emotional tenor of the end of the American century, in which the children of the 'summer of love' of the late 1960s were born into a bankrupt American culture that taught them suicidal despair at a very early age. This, Wurtzel believes, is the unique cultural legacy that American adolescents were heir to at the end of the century.

To some extent it could be argued that *Prozac Nation* characterises a late-twentieth-century cultural tendency to treat adolescence as a newly medical condition. Where previously adolescence was interpreted sociologically (rebellion, anomie, disaffection, or violent aggression) in the 1980s and 1990s it began to be regarded as a 'condition' that was suddenly amenable to forms of medical treatment, as a result of changes in prescription drugs or medication. For the first time the difficult or socially disruptive aspects of adolescence could be ameliorated by prescription medication, and it was the advent of drugs like Prozac that made this possible. In this way Prozac was mysteriously 'discovered' as a possible remedy for what was previously understood as a relatively harmless period of adolescent social adjustment. Adolescence, like some adult social behaviour, thus becomes newly subject to forms of medical discourse that had not been deemed necessary before the discovery of the effects of Prozac. The sudden and dramatic alleviation of Wurtzel's depressive symptoms brings her text to an abrupt end, but still it could be argued that the manufacturers of Prozac, Eli Lilley, and the culture of the late-twentieth-century United States more generally, exploited a business opportunity to sell a product, and that American doctors were seduced by its expeditious panacea potential. In this case, *Prozac Nation* dramatises an American medicalisation of the self during adolescence, a psychopharmacological remedy for biological and emotional changes that would be interpreted by other cultures as entirely natural and healthy. The dramatisation of this development at a particular historical moment gives *Prozac Nation* a uniquely personal insight into this crucial historical shift in American cultural attitudes to the self, in medical understandings of what the self really is, and in knowledge of what impact that has on understandings of adolescence. *Prozac Nation*, like *Listening to Prozac*, is an important late-twentieth-century document about how American society understands personal subjectivity and how it believes that difficulties with individual identity can be remedied not by self-knowledge but by the intervention of medicine. Medicine, as the advent of Prozac amply demonstrates, is a form of discourse about the self that is socially constructed, and both of these books expose the cultural terms in which that social construction takes place.

Following the success of *Prozac Nation*, Elizabeth Wurtzel published *Bitch: In Praise of Difficult Women* (1998) and *More, Now, Again: A Memoir* (2002). This latter book is principally an account of how she produced the earlier book, *Bitch*, as if, having nothing more to confess, Wurtzel can only make a confession of how difficult it is to write a book when there is nothing valuable left to say. This predicament is partly a function of the celebrity culture in which Wurtzel is trapped, but it is also symptomatic of an inability to move beyond the defining moment of the publication of *Prozac Nation* and its depiction of adolescence. At the beginning of *Bitch*, Wurtzel claims that

> in the pageantry of public life, in the places where women invent personae, the one statement a girl can make to declare her strength, her surefootedness, her autonomy – her self as a *self* – is to somehow be bad, somehow do something that is surely going to make her parents weep. (1998: 3)

Even in this second book, and at that late age, Wurtzel must continue to define herself in terms of a parent-child paradigm that situates her as a perpetual adolescent for the market. This is evidence, not of Wurtzel's failure to grow up, but of the United States' huge cultural investment in a concept of innocence, which adolescence is believed to exemplify.

Conclusion

The popularity of the coming-of-age genre in the United States is partly a symptom of Americans' abiding fascination with the idea of innocence. This innocence is conceptually biblical in origin and is therefore further evidence of the nation's fundamentally religious character. At the same time, the narrative of coming of age permits writers to interrogate the historical circumstances that have separated their protagonists from an original innocence which is mythical, imaginary, or nostalgic. The novelist's representation of that history thereby facilitates a close critical scrutiny of the specific cultural pressures of American socialisation, or, as Cleo Birdwell expressed it in her memoir, *Amazons*, 'Only childhood is ours. The rest belongs to strangers' (Birdwell 1980: 1). The coming-of-age genre taps into a rich legacy of American representations of innocence, and it also engages with the politics of historiography in ways that can always be given a contemporary inflection; the genre is thus anchored by a sense that there are antecedent voices that give it a historical provenance that is uniquely American.

For example, both Philip Roth's *American Pastoral* (1997) and John Updike's *Memories of the Ford Administration* (1992) give broad currency to these ideas, beyond the parameters of the genre of coming of age. Roth's novel has an absolutely forensic interest in ideas about innocence and origins, and it is structured in terms of sections entitled 'Paradise Remembered' and 'The Fall'. The story tries to discover the source of Merry Levov's aberration, the reason that she became the Rimrock Bomber. Does it lie in the history of her parents (Catholic and Jewish), or in other cultural factors such as witnessing the immolation of a monk on television? To what extent is the story of her origin a means to discover the origin of American social upheaval in the 1960s? The novel also interrogates the source of the writer Zuckerman's interest in Merry's father, Levov: where did it begin and why? How can such originatory points be known definitively, or are they always merely a consoling fiction? The willfulness of Levov's faith in his daughter's innocence is shared by Roth's narrator, because it is an expression of the idea of a tragic departure from a state of grace that cannot be relinquished: 'No one in his family was going to fall into doubt about Merry's absolute innocence, not so long as he was alive' (Roth, 365). Updike's *Memories of the Ford Administration* is similarly obsessed with origins; it interrogates its narrator's interest in the American President James Buchanan while also creating a history of the narrator's life during the years of Gerald Ford's presidency. Updike also dramatises the role of textual duplicity in these searches for origins and original American innocence: 'the air had been let out of our parade balloon, and still we bumped on, as we had in 1865, with wandering steps and slow, as out of Eden we took our solitary way' (Updike, 247–8). The Garden of Eden is a specific point of reference for many recent American coming-of-age novels, not only for the American Adam, but increasingly, since the 1970s, for the American Eve whose coming of age consists partly of disputing the gender politics of the ideology of the Fall.

Many good examples of the coming-of-age story appeared in the early twenty-first century: Eden Robinson's *Monkey Beach*, 2000; Brian Roley's *American Son*, 2001; Lee Durkee's *Rides of the Midway*, 2001; Pete Fromm's *As Cool As I Am*, 2003; Curtis Sittenfeld's *Prep*, 2005; and Jim Lynch's *The Highest Tide*, 2005. It might be assumed that these novels constitute something of a resurgence in the coming-of-age novel, but the genre has never really gone away, and it is especially disappointing to have to omit, only through pressures of space, such exemplary treatments of innocence as Barry Hannah's 'Get Some Young', Kevin Canty's *Into The Great Wide Open*, and Mark Poirier's *Goats*. The coming-of-age genre will always be employed by American writers who are looking for a narrative voice that can be used as a vehicle to express social disaffection, and to offer a critique of forms of American socialisation. These narrative functions make the genre amenable to a variety of social and political interpretations while still preserving a space for an individual voice that is unique and compelling.

Bibliography

Abel, E. Hirsch, M. Langland, E. (eds) (1983), *The Voyage In: Fictions of Female Development*, Hanover, NH: University Press of New England.

Alexie, S. (1997), *The Lone Ranger and Tonto Fistfight in Heaven*, London: Vintage.

Allison, D. [1992] (1993), *Bastard out of Carolina*, New York: Penguin.

Banks, R. [1995] (1996), *Rule of the Bone*, London: Minerva.

Barth, J. (1967), 'The literature of exhaustion', *Atlantic Monthly*, 220, 2 August, 1967.

Baruch, E. H. (1981), 'The feminine bildungsroman: education through marriage', *Massachusetts Review*, 22: 335–57.

Baudrillard, J. (1988), *America*, London: Verso.

Beaver, H. (1987), *Huckleberry Finn*, London: Allen & Unwin.

Birdwell, C. (1980), *Amazons*, New York: Holt, Rinehart and Wilson.

Bradfield, S. (1989), *The History of Luminous Motion*, New York: Vintage.

Bradfield, S. (1993), *Dreaming Revolution: Transgression in the Development of American Romance*, Iowa City: University of Iowa Press.

Braendlin, B. H. (1983), 'Bildung in Ethnic Women Writers', *Denver Quarterly*, 17: 75–87.

Buckley, J. H. (1974), *Season of Youth: The Bildungsroman from Dickens to Golding*, Cambridge, MA: Harvard University Press.

Burner, D. (1996), *Making Peace with the 60s*, Princeton, NJ: Princeton University Press.

Campbell, N. (ed.) (2000), *The Radiant Hour: Versions of Youth in American Culture*, Exeter: University of Exeter Press.

Cheever, A. (2000), 'Prozac Americans: depression, identity, and selfhood', *Twentieth Century Literature*, 46(3): 346–68.

Chu, P. P. (2000), *Assimilating Asians: Gendered Strategies of Authorship in Asian America*, Durham: Duke University Press.

Culler, J. (1975), *Structuralist Poetics: Structuralism, Linguistics, and the Study of Literature*, Ithaca: Cornell University Press.

Curnutt, K. (2001), 'Teenage wasteland: coming-of-age novels in the 1980s and 1990s', *Critique: Studies in Contemporary Fiction* 43(1): 93–111.

Currie, M. (1995), *Metafiction*, London: Longman.

De Man, P. (1979), 'Autobiography as de-facement', *Modern Language Notes*, 94: 919–30.

Doctorow, E. L. [1975] (1985), *Ragtime*, London: Picador.

Egan, M. (1977), *Mark Twain's Huck Finn: Race, Class and Society*, London: Sussex University Press.

Ellis, B. E. (1991), *American Psycho*, London: Picador.

Eugenides, J. [1993] (1994), *The Virgin Suicides*, London: Abacus.

Eugenides, J. (2003), *Middlesex*, London: Bloomsbury.

Faulkner, W. [1930] (1988), *As I Lay Dying*, London: Penguin.

Fiedler, L. (1955), *An End to Innocence: Essays on Culture and Politics*, Boston, MA: Beacon Press.

Fiedler, L. (1966), *Love and Death in the American Novel*, New York: Stein & Day.

Finnegan. W. (1999), *Cold New World: Growing Up in a Harder Country*, London: Picador.

Fisher, C. (1987), *Postcards From the Edge*, London: Picador.

Fitzgerald, F. S. [1925] (1974), *The Great Gatsby*, London: Penguin.

Fracassa, M. (1999), 'Medicating the self: the roles of science and culture in the construction of prozac', *Journal of Popular Culture*, 32(4): 23–8.

Fraiman, S. (1993), *Unbecoming Women: British Women Writers and The Novel of Development*, New York: Columbia University Press.

Furman, A. (2000), 'Immigrant dreams and civic promises: contesting identity in early Jewish American literature and Gish Jen's *Mona in the Promised Land*', *MELUS*, 25(1): 210–26.

Gilmore, L. (2001), *The Limits of Autobiography: Trauma and Testimony*, Ithaca: Cornell University Press.

Giroux, H. A. (1997), *Channel Surfing: Race Talk and the Destruction of Today's Youth*, Basingstoke: Macmillan.

Gonzalez, B. S. (2001), 'The (re)birth of Mona Changowitz: rituals and ceremonies of cultural conversion and self-making in *Mona in the Promised Land*', *MELUS*, 26(2): 225–42.

Graybill, M. (2002), 'Reconstructing/deconstructing genre and gender: postmodern identity in Bobbie Ann Mason's *In Country* and Josephine Humphreys' *Rich in Love. Critique: Studies in Contemporary Fiction*', 43(3): 239–59.

Grice, H. (2002), *Negotiating Identities: An Introduction to Asian American Women's Writing*, Manchester: Manchester University Press.

Grossberg, L. (1992), *We Gotta Get Out of This Place*, London: Routledge.

Guinn, M. (2000), *After Southern Modernism: Fiction of the Contemporary South*, Jackson, MI: University Press of Mississippi.

Hardin, J. (ed.) (1991), *Reflection and Action: Essays on the Bildungsroman*, Columbia: University of South Carolina Press.

Hassan, I. (1961), *Radical Innocence: Studies in the Contemporary American Novel*, Princeton, NJ: Princeton University Press.

Hemingway, E. (1936), *Green Hills of Africa*, London: Jonathan Cape.

Hobson, F. (1991), *The Southern Writer in the Postmodern World*, Athens, GA: The University of Georgia Press.

Hume, K. (2000), *American Dream, American Nightmare: Fiction Since 1970*, Urbana, IL: University of Illinois Press.

Humphreys, J. [1987] (1992), *Rich in Love*, London: Penguin.

Hutcheon, L. (1980), *Narcissistic Narrative: The Metafictional Paradox*, London: Methuen.

Jackson, S. M. (1994), 'Josephine Humphreys and the politics of postmodern desire', *Mississippi Quarterly*, 47: 275–85.

James, H. [1903] (1979), *The Ambassadors*, London: Penguin.

Jameson, F. (1991), *Postmodernism, or, The Cultural Logic of Late Capitalism*, London: Verso.

Jay, P. (1984), *Being in the Text: Self-Representation from Wordsworth to Roland Barthes*, Ithaca: Cornell University Press.

Jen, G. [1996] (1997), *Mona in the Promised Land*, New York: Vintage.

Kayser, W. (1981), *The Grotesque in Art and Literature*, New York: Columbia University Press.

Kaysen, S. (1995), *Girl, Interrupted*, London: Virago.

Kilgour, M. (1995), *The Rise of the Gothic Novel*, London: Routledge.

Kramer, P. [1993] (1994), *Listening to Prozac*, London: Fourth Estate.

Kreyling, M. (1998), *Inventing Southern Literature*, Jackson, MI: University Press of Mississippi.

Kristeva, J. (1982), *Powers of Horror: An Essay on Abjection*, New York: Columbia University Press.

Kristeva, J. (1984), *Revolution in Poetic Language*, New York: Columbia University Press.

Lewis, B. (2003), 'Prozac and the Post-human politics of cyborgs', *Journal of Medical Humanities*, 24(1–2): 49–63.

Lewis, R. W. B. (1955), *The American Adam: Innocence, Tragedy and Tradition in the Nineteenth Century*, Chicago: University of Chicago Press.

Lin, E. T. (2003), 'Mona on the phone: the performative body and racial identity in *Mona in the Promised Land*', *MELUS*, 28(2): 47–57.

Lowe, L. (1996), *Immigrant Acts: On Asian American Cultural Politics*, Durham: Duke University Press.

Lynn, K. S. (1959), *Mark Twain and Southwestern Humor*, Boston, MA: Little, Brown.

Malin, J. (2000), *The Voice of the Mother: Embedded Maternal Narratives in Twentieth-Century Women's Autobiographies*, Carbondale: Southern Illinois University Press.

Martin, R. K. and Savoy E. (eds) (1998), *American Gothic: New Interventions in a National Narrative*, Iowa City: University of Iowa Press.

Marx, L. (1964), *The Machine in the Garden: Technology and the Pastoral Ideal in America*, New York: Oxford University Press.

Mason, B. A. (1987), *In Country*, London: Flamingo.

McElroy, B. (1989), *Fiction of the Modern Grotesque*, Basingstoke: Macmillan.

Meese, E. A. (1986), *Crossing the Double Cross: The Practice of Feminist Criticism*, Chapel Hill: University of North Carolina Press.

Meindl, D. (1996), *American Fiction and the Metaphysics of the Grotesque*, Columbia: University of Missouri Press.

Messent, P. (1997), *Mark Twain*, Basingstoke: Macmillan.

Moody, R. [1997] (1999), *Purple America*, London: Flamingo.

Moretti, F. (1987), *The Way of the World: The Bildungsroman in European Culture*, London: Verso.

Morrison, T. (1992), *Playing in the Dark: Whiteness and the Literary Imagination*, Cambridge, MA: Harvard University Press.

Myers, B. R. (2001), 'A Reader's Manifesto', *The Atlantic Monthly*: 104–22.

O'Connor, F. (1972), *Mystery and Manners: Occasional Prose*, edited by S. Fitzgerald and R. Fitzgerald, London: Faber.

O'Connor, W. V. (1962), *The Grotesque: An American Genre and Other Essays*, Carbondale: Southern Illinois University Press.

Oster, J. (2003), *Crossing Cultures: Creating Identity in Chinese and Jewish American Literature*, Columbia: University of Missouri Press.

Peck, D. (2002), 'Moody Blues', *The New Republic*, (1 July): 33–9.

Poe, E. A. [1838] (2006), *The Narrative of Arthur Gordon Pym of Nantucket*, London: Penguin.

Pinsker, S. (1993), *The Catcher in the Rye: Innocence Under Pressure*, New York: Twayne.

Pynchon, T. [1996] (1979), *The Crying of Lot 49*, London: Picador.

Ravits, M. (1989), 'Extending the American Range: Marilynne Robinson's *Housekeeping*', *American Literature*, 61: 644–66.

Richard, M. (1993), *Fishboy*, New York: Anchor Books.

Robinson, M. [1980] (2004), *Housekeeping*, London: Faber.

Romines, A. (1992), *The Home Plot: Women, Writing and Domestic Ritual*, Amherst, MA: The University of Massachusetts Press.

Rosowski, S. J. (1999), *Birthing A Nation: Gender, Creativity, and the West in American Literature*, Lincoln: University of Nebraska Press.

Ryan, M. (1991), 'Marilynne Robinson's *Housekeeping*: the subversive narrative and the new American Eve', *South Atlantic Review*, 56: 79–86.

Said, E. (1975), *Beginnings: Intention and Method*, New York: Basic Books.

Salzberg, J. (ed.) (1990), *Critical Essays on Salinger's The Catcher in the Rye*, Boston, MA: G. K. Hall.

Salzman, J. (ed.) (1991), *New Essays on The Catcher in the Rye*, Cambridge: Cambridge University Press.

Smith, H. N. (1950), *Virgin Land: The American West as Symbol and Myth*, Cambridge, MA: Harvard University Press.

Spacks, P. (1981), *The Adolescent Idea: Myths of Youth and the Adult Imagination*, New York: Basic Books.

Steig, M. (1970), 'Defining the grotesque: an attempt at synthesis', *Journal of Aesthetics and Art Criticism*', 2: 253–60.

Steinle, P. H. (2000), *In Cold Fear: The Catcher in the Rye, Censorship Controversies, and Postwar American Character*, Columbus: Ohio State University Press.

Stone, A. E. (1961), *The Innocent Eye: Childhood in Mark Twain's Imagination*, New Haven: Yale University Press.

Styron, W. (1991), *Darkness Visible: A Memoir of Madness*, London: Jonathan Cape.

Twain, M. [1885] (1994), *Adventures of Huckleberry Finn*, London: Penguin.

Udall, B. (2001), *The Miracle Life of Edgar Mint*, London: Jonathan Cape.

Walker, A. [1982] (1985), *The Color Purple*, New York: Pocket Books.

Walker, E. A. (1994), 'Josephine Humphreys's *Rich in Love*: redefining southern fiction', *Mississippi Quarterly*, 47: 301–15.

Walker, N. (1995), *The Disobedient Writer*, Austin: University of Texas Press.

West, P. (1987), 'In defense of purple prose', *Sheer Fiction*, London: McPherson and Co.

Wheeler, K. M. (1999), 'Constructions of identity in post-1970s fiction', in Rod Mengham (ed.) *An Introduction to Contemporary Fiction*, Cambridge: Polity Press.

White, B. (1985), *Growing up Female: Adolescent Girlhood in American Fiction*, Westport, CT: Greenwood Press.

Williams, A. (1995), *Art of Darkness: A Poetics of Gothic*, London: University of Chicago Press.

Wolff, G. [1995] (1996), *The Age of Consent*, New York: Picador.

Wurtzel, E. [1994] (1995), *Prozac Nation: Young and Depressed in America*, London: Quartet.

Wurtzel, E. (1998), *Bitch: In praise of Difficult Women*, London: Quartet.

Yanarella, E. J. and Sigelman L. (eds) (1988), *Political Mythology and Popular Fiction*, Westport, CT: Greenwood Press.

Index